The Mature Traveler's Guide™

To

Walt Disney World®

And Other Orlando Attractions

BY KERRY SMITH

Mercurial Press
Oviedo, Florida

The Mature Traveler's Guide™ To Walt Disney World® and Other Orlando Attractions is an independent and objective guide. Contents are neither reviewed nor approved by the Walt Disney Company or any other Central Florida attraction. Certain names — including but not limited to Adventureland, AudioAnimatronic, Disneyland, Epcot, Fantasyland, Magic Kingdom, Space Mountain, Walt Disney, and Walt Disney World — are registered trademarks of the Walt Disney Company.

The author and publisher have done exhaustive research to ensure the accuracy of this book. However, we assume no responsibility for errors, omissions, or any other inconsistency within the Guide.

Back cover photo courtesy of Cypress Gardens (© 1996 Florida Cypress Gardens, Inc. All rights reserved.) Front cover photo courtesy of Church Street Station and the Orlando/Orange County Convention & Visitor's Bureau, Inc. (© Church Street Station. All rights reserved.)

Attention Senior Organizations and Retirement Communities:
Quantity discounts are available on bulk purchases of this book. For more information, contact:

Mercurial Press
P.O. Box 622616, Oviedo, FL 32762
Fax (407) 359-3959
e-mail: Mcurial@epochworks.com.

To Walt Disney. This book has no affiliation with his company or park — but I think Walt would enjoy it anyway.

And to my wife, Kelly, who believes this to be the best guidebook ever written.

TABLE OF CONTENTS

PREFACE

Chapter 1
FIRST THINGS FIRST   **1**

Planning Suggestions • Visiting With Children

Chapter 2
WALT DISNEY WORLD: AN OVERVIEW   **7**

Chapter 3
BEFORE YOU LEAVE HOME   **11**

What Time of Year Should You Visit? • Weather • Where
to Stay — Off Property or at a Disney Resort? • Disney
Transportation System • Advance Reservations — More
Than Just Hotel Rooms • Crime • Is It Better to Book a
Package Plan? • Pets • Don't Forget…

Chapter 4
WALT DISNEY WORLD ON-SITE HOTELS   **26**

Shades Of Green • Magic Kingdom Resorts • Epcot
Center Resorts • Moderately Priced Resorts • Budget
Hotels • Fort Wilderness • Other On-Site Resorts

Chapter 5
OFF-SITE HOTELS   **62**

Major Hotel Areas "Outside the World" • Elderhostels
• Questions to Ask When Booking an Off-Site Hotel

Chapter 6
MONEY QUESTIONS   **70**

Allocating Vacation Dollars: What Do You Want to See?
• Walt Disney World Tickets: Options, Costs • Tickets:
Where to Buy • Discounted Tickets • Discounted
Coupons to Other Area Attractions

Chapter 7
HANDICAPPED TRAVELERS   **83**

General Information • Hearing Impaired Guests
• Sight Impaired Guests

Chapter 8
PARK TOURING TIPS   91
Always Go Left • Disney Style of Queuing • Get to
the Park Early • Park Early-Entry Days • Which Day
of the Week Is Best? • Theme Park Dining

Chapter 9
THE MAGIC KINGDOM   98
Getting to the Magic Kingdom • First Things First
• Touring Tips • Guidelines For Those Who Don't Mind
a Lot of Walking • Lands and Rides • Parades and
Shows • Magic Kingdom Restaurants • Shopping
• Don't Miss…

Chapter 10
EPCOT CENTER   143
Getting to Epcot • First Things First • Touring Tips
• Guidelines For Those Who Don't Mind a Lot of
Walking • Lands and Rides • Shows • Restaurants
• Shopping • Don't Miss…

Chapter 11
DISNEY-MGM STUDIOS   184
Should You Visit Universal Studios or Disney-MGM
Studios? • Getting to Disney-MGM Studios • First
Things First • Touring Tips • Guidelines For Those
Who Don't Mind a Lot of Walking • Attractions
Parades and Shows • Restaurants • Shopping • Don't Miss…

Chapter 12
OTHER DISNEY ATTRACTIONS   209
• Water Parks • The Disney Institute • Discovery Island
•Disney's Boardwalk Resort • Downtown Disney

Chapter 13
OTHER DISNEY DINING AND SHOWS   225
Dinner Shows • Resort Restaurants

Chapter 14
THE SPORTING LIFE: DISNEY STYLE   **236**
Golf • Tennis • Boating • Fishing • Skis, Horses, and Bikes

Chapter 15
AND ALSO AT DISNEY...   **245**
Disney Weddings • Walt Disney World Sports Complex • Indy 200 • Character Warehouse • Celebration • Disney Cruise Line • Disney's Animal Kingdom

Chapter 16
OTHER BIG TOURIST DRAWS   **253**
Cypress Gardens • Sea World of Orlando • Splendid China • Universal Studios Florida • Busch Gardens, Tampa Bay • Church Street Station • Kennedy Space Center's Visitor's Center • Dinner Shows, Gators, and Other Orlando Stuff

Chapter 17
UN-TOURIST THINGS WORTH YOUR TIME   **279**
Wekiwa Springs State Park • The Rivership Romance on The St. Johns River • Harry P. Leu Gardens • Lake Kissimmee State Park • Bok Tower Gardens • Blue Spring State Park

Chapter 18   **286**
TRAVEL TIPS FOR FIRST-TIMERS
Flying • Trains • Car Rentals • Hotel Rooms

WALT DISNEY WORLD MAP   **296**

INDEX   **298**

PREFACE

Most Walt Disney World (WDW) guide books orient themselves to three types of people: a) trivia fanatics that want to know absolutely everything about WDW, b) those who don't visit often and want to make each second count even if it means running from ride to ride, or c) parents who hope for nothing more than to come out of the experience alive, with a few good family videos to show how much fun they had.

This guide book is for you if:
- You believe a vacation should be relaxing.
- You want to minimize walking and explore Walt Disney World at your own pace.
- You understand that in one week, you can't see absolutely everything.
- You need guidance on resorts, restaurants, and parks.

Realistically, you will see more of the WDW parks if you arrive at the crack of dawn, run from land to land, and plan each minute like a military commando. But that's not a vacation. By following these guidelines, you might see a little less, but you will leave the park feeling less exhausted and infinitely superior to visitors who base their day on a stopwatch and a good pair of running shoes. Simple touring plans move you from land to land. Out-of-the-way spots are described. You receive just enough information about an attraction to determine if you want to ride— how much it moves, the age group it attracts, and any problems with boarding — but without taking away the magic.

Each land in the Magic Kingdom has its own flavor, from the music to the sights, smells, and even food. The same is true of the themed hotels, Epcot, and the Disney-MGM Studios. A successful

Disney World vacation removes you from the real world and suspends reality. For a brief moment, you can believe in pixie dust and singing bears and haunted houses.

Recognizing the mature traveler, Disney World has, for the first time, actively advertised to the adults-without-kids generation. The recently opened Boardwalk Resort was designed to attract "mature guests the way Pleasure Island attracts twenty-somethings," according to a Disney publicist. Included in the hotel is a 1940's, seaside-style dance hall featuring the music of the Big Bands, playing tunes from World War II to the present, as well as a two-baby-grand piano bar and ESPN Sports Club.

Disney also has special senior programs for those 55 and over, most often run during slower times. In the off-season, WDW offers savings at selected resorts, recognizing the power of a market segment that has been historically ignored.

Finally, this guide describes other Central Florida attractions, from Disney competitors such as Universal Studios and Sea World, to the sights and sounds of the "real" Florida, the parts of the state unseen by most Orlando vacationers.

It's easy to dismiss Walt Disney World as "too commercial" or "too expensive," but Disney Imagineers (a Disney term combining "engineers" and "imagination") created an enclave where bad things happen outside. They've done it the way they create movies, using tricks, special effects, and psychology. They manipulate your senses until you believe the impossible.

Relax and enjoy the fantasy. That was Walt Disney's goal when he created the first park 40 years ago in California and, despite takeovers, multi-million dollar salaries, and controversial films, Walt Disney World still ranks as the top tourist destination in the world.

This guide is "unofficial," meaning the Walt Disney Company does not officially approve or disapprove of anything said. It is, however, pro-Disney. It's assumed that you want to visit Walt Disney World or you would not plan a trip. Here, you will be warned of potential problems, but problems are the exception, not the rule.

Today, more than ever, Walt Disney World is not just for kids.

FIRST THINGS FIRST

4   Planning Suggestions

6   Visiting with Children

Chapter One

FIRST THINGS FIRST

Visit Walt Disney World during the off-season. More than any other piece of inside information, that advice can make or break your vacation. I'll say it again:

Visit during the off-season.

During the park's busiest times, the Disney crowds are more visible than the attractions. In Adventureland, for example, tropical bamboo frames the walkway while the rustic Swiss Family Treehouse towers overhead. From hidden speakers, African music gives the land a 3-dimensional, safari-like feel. But during high season, it's difficult to hear the music when, beside you, a harried mother yells at her kids to "keep together." And it's difficult to appreciate the sights of the jungle when you spend half your time protecting your side from wayward elbows and your shins from strollers as other visitors fight their way to the Pirates of the Caribbean.

Other advantages to off-season travel:

• Lines for theme park attractions are short or non-existent. On a good day, visitors wait from zero to twenty minutes, with much of the wait not due to the length of the line but to the duration of the show. Even then, many of the most popular WDW rides that form longer lines later in the day — Splash Mountain and Space Mountain, for example — are not must-sees for many mature travelers.

• Reservations are either unnecessary at the better restaurants (with some exceptions) or, at the least, still available for dinner if made first thing in the morning. Since guests may make dinner reservations a year in advance, the best restaurants and seating times book early during busy season. You can, of course, reserve dining times well in advance of your trip, but you run the risk of having a vacation that tells you what to do rather than the other way around. While an 8:00 p.m. dinner reservation at a World Showcase restaurant may sound perfect before departure, it may prove inconvenient later.

• Price competition. In general, Disney charges less for hotel rooms during the off-season, as do off-site hotels — if you know how to find the bargains. Over the course of a seven-day stay, the savings can be substantial.

More important, however — Walt Disney World works the way it should during the off-season. The Disney cast members (the Disney name for employees) go to great lengths to "theme" the resorts and parks. At Wilderness Lodge, for example, everything feeds into the central theme of great National Park hotels built around World War I. The swimming pool appears to be a pond formed by a mountain stream that originated as a hot spring — even though it's not really a spring, a stream, nor does it actually empty into the pool. Massive chandeliers recreate Indian tents. Everything from the Artist's Point restaurant to the Whispering Canyon Cafe has the stamp of the Old West.

But it's not what Disney includes that makes themed areas special. It's what they don't include. At Wilderness Lodge, you see no palm trees as you drive through the entrance gates, only long-needled pines, native to Central Florida but reminiscent of the West. Palm trees would ruin the illusion. Quilts cover all beds, not generic comforters. If the illusion of the American West is to hold, then the viewer cannot see anything out of place, such as a palm tree, a waitress dressed in traditional white, nor even a rest room that lacks the wood decor and rustic artwork of the old West.

But Disney cannot control the crowds. When the hotel is full — or the lands of the Magic Kingdom or the countries of World Showcase — much of the illusion goes, stolen by jumbling crowds and yelling children. In other words, the people overshadow the event. A reader enjoys *Gone With the Wind* by momentarily believing that the Civil War still exists; that hoop skirts are the fashion standard; and that war is honorable. When visiting Wilderness Lodge, everyone over the age of six knows they're still in Florida. They know it's an illusion. But they *allow* themselves to believe the illusion for the same reasons that *Gone With the Wind* readers relive the Civil War. Namely, it's fun.

Disney crowds break the illusion. You might capture it for a few minutes in Frontierland as the riverboat glides by and banjo-picking music plays from a hidden speaker. But you lose it when a large, bearded man spills a soft drink on your shoe. Or when someone says, "S'cuse me," and slides by. Or when a stroller rams you in the ankle.

I'll say it one more time: Visit during the off-season.

PLANNING SUGGESTIONS

Specific touring plans are outlined in the Magic Kingdom, Epcot, and Disney-MGM Studio chapters. For now, however, you should pre-plan your vacation. What do you expect to happen? Why are you going? How do you hope to feel when the vacation ends?

Disney World stands as an icon of the modern world. At Christmas, televisions nationwide show Santa flying high over Main Street. At Easter, giant Disney bunnies walk the same route. For years, Walt's *Wonderful World of Color* focused on Disneyland's style, the attractions, and the technology. Walt Disney World — Disneyland's younger yet bigger brother — showcases the past, the present, and future.

Disney World is, of course, real. The special effects are created by computers and hydraulic pumps and motion simulators — not by magic. But once you arrive, it's easy to get caught up in the illusion. Even laden with high expectations, Disney does not disappoint. State-of-the-art special effects combine with cleanliness, courteous employees, and copyrighted characters that highlight the best America has to offer. But while you should allow yourself the fun — after all, that's why you came in the first place — prepare for the exhaustion.

Even following simple touring plans, visiting in the off-season, and taking time off in the afternoon for a nap or swim, you will be exercising. A lot. There is more to see and do at Disney World and Orlando than anyone can absorb in a one-week vacation. Every decision of "what to see" involves a trade-off. You can't visit one attraction without, simultaneously, deciding to skip another. If you spend a

4

day at Disney-MGM Studios, you may not have time for a round of golf. If golf is important and you choose to play, you may give up an afternoon of shopping or a trip to Cypress Gardens or high tea at The Grand Floridian. Acknowledge that you will face physical challenges. Understand that temptation drives even the best men and women to "the chef's famous Key Lime pie" or the "giant 50% off sale on Mickey T-shirts." Decide what you expect from the vacation — how you want the days to unfold, and how you hope to feel when you leave — then build in the components that will make it happen.

As you discuss the vacation, plan some non-theme park days for the middle of the week. It sounds simple, but Disney World is a smorgasbord and most people leave the buffet line with too much on their plate. If you spend an entire day at a park, you will be exhausted at 8:00 p.m., whether you're eighty-one or twenty-one.

Golf, tennis, boating, horseback riding, swimming, and a host of other activities can be enjoyed on an "off-day," not to mention a plethora of non-Disney attractions in the Orlando area. Sleep late if that's a special pleasure, then read the newspaper. Go for a swim. Shop. Have a leisurely lunch. While activities such as golf must be reserved ahead of time, many activities — at least in the off-season — do not.

A second suggestion to avoid Disney burn-out: Take an afternoon nap. This works well if you're staying on Disney property or if your car is conveniently parked in the parking lot, but it may not be practical if you're staying off-site or if the park is only open for nine hours. Decide for yourself. The human body has a natural rhythm that, for many, means a bout of tiredness in mid- to late-afternoon. Add seven hours of waiting in lines to that natural rhythm, and the benefits of a nap are immeasurable.

If a nap is not feasible, consider a late lunch at one of the resorts. If visiting the Magic Kingdom, you can take the monorail to the Grand Floridian, the Polynesian, or the Contemporary. After lunch, relax in a lounge chair on the white sand beaches of the Seven Seas Lagoon or find an out-of-the-way spot to prop your feet up.

It's easy to fall into the I-paid-$40-for-my-ticket trap and try to see too much. A successful theme park day is not judged by how much you did, but by how much you enjoyed yourself.

VISITING WITH CHILDREN

Don't do it.

No, seriously, visiting with children adds a whole new perspective to the adventure. But it's also a completely different experience than vacationing with only adults. At the risk of over-generalizing, those under twenty-one tend to be less impressed with atmosphere, cleanliness, technology, and service, than they are with "riding absolutely everything the first three hours we're there." In other words, adults and children want to take separate vacations at the same place.

Ideally, the kids you travel with are old enough to wear a watch, tell time, and meet you at the Brown Derby for lunch. If so, you may want to balance your time together. If visiting the Disney-MGM Studios, you can stay together for the Backlot Tour and the Art of Animation, then allow them to take off for Star Tours while you enjoy Voyage of the Little Mermaid.

If too young to tour apart from you, you're stuck. Hopefully, you love them. Young children, unable to separate the real from the illusion, want to take in whatever they see. Even the most well behaved child can be reduced to tears when denied a quick spin on the Grand Prix Raceway, even when the line is an hour long. Decide how you want the day to unfold, how influential you allow a child to be, then hope for the best. If up to it physically, follow the tour advice for those who don't mind a lot of walking.

Ideally, you should not visit Disney World with children your first time. Not only will you enjoy it on your own terms, but when you return with children, you'll see it through new eyes. By taking them on a second or third trip, you'll also have a working knowledge of the park's lay-out and, with hindsight, an idea which attractions you can skip.

Even with children, the number one rule still applies: visit during the off-season. This may be difficult and involve pulling children from school, but it's worth the effort, assuming they are good students. If trying to coordinate a time with a student's scheduled vacation, choose times when only the local school district does not schedule classes. Avoid national holidays. Even over President's Day, the parks experience a substantial rise in theme park crowds during the week before and after the holiday.

WALT DISNEY WORLD: AN OVERVIEW

2

Chapter Two

WALT DISNEY WORLD: AN OVERVIEW

In size, in scope, and in financial dollars, Walt Disney World is huge. Bigger than huge. It's gigantic.

Opened 25 years ago, it started humbly enough with 43-square miles of Central Florida wilderness, one theme park, and a couple hotels. Disneyland, Walt Disney's original park in California, was already a huge success but, due to limited funding, the company had purchased too little land for future growth. While they still wanted to enlarge Disneyland and have floated several ideas over the past few decades, their space is limited. In Florida, the company did not make that mistake.

Note that at Disney World, the word "resort" is used on both a macro and micro level. The entire complex is often called the Walt Disney World Resort, but on property, you also find The Caribbean Beach Resort and The Contemporary Resort. In other words, there are "resorts" within the "resort." To avoid confusion, you may wish to shun the word altogether.

To add to the confusion, the name "Walt Disney World" refers to the entire Florida complex — hotels, parks, golf courses, etc. — all 43-square miles. In California, "Disneyland" refers only to the theme park. It sounds as if "Walt Disney World" should be the Florida equivalent of "Disneyland," but the Magic Kingdom alone is roughly equal to all of Disneyland. Adding Epcot Center and the Disney-MGM Studios to the mix virtually triples the Disney offerings in Florida.

But there's more. Add in two major water parks, both with enough slides, rides, and rivers to encompass a whole day's entertainment. Add a third water park, smaller, but no less fun. Throw in a modest, certified zoological park. Then add a nighttime entertainment complex of themed bars — a Magic Kingdom for drinkers if you will — and a fair-sized shopping center. Include a state-of-the-art sports complex, an Indy-500 race track, a learning center, and over 22,000 hotel rooms and you get some idea of the size of Walt Disney World. It's gigantic. And that list still doesn't include Celebration, Disney's version of the perfect American town.

Memorizing the location of every resort and park goes beyond the basics for planning a vacation. It is, however, helpful to visualize the general lay-out before you arrive. On the south side of Disney property, Route 192 runs east to west. The closest town to Disney World, Kissimmee, lies to the east. (Not counting Celebration.) Twenty-five years ago, this was the only entrance to Disney World and today is still called the "maingate." In the beginning, most visitors not staying on property chose an off-site hotel close to this main entrance.

Turning into the maingate off 192, you travel north on World Drive and, since the Magic Kingdom is the northernmost theme park, you pass the other parks and selected hotels along the way. Compared to the Magic Kingdom, Epcot and Disney-MGM Studios sit fairly close together on your right. The Epcot center resorts — The Yacht and Beach Club, Dolphin, Swan, and Boardwalk Resort — sit between Epcot and Disney-MGM Studios, and are visible.

On your left, unseen beyond the trees but near Epcot and Disney-MGM Studios, sits the newest area under development, home to Blizzard Beach and Disney's newest resort complex, the All-Star Resorts. Animal Kingdom, a fourth theme park premiering 1998, is also under construction here.

After passing Disney-MGM Studios and Epcot, you pass through the Magic Kingdom Toll Plaza where day guests pay for parking at the Magic Kingdom's main lot. The road bears left into the parking lot. A single road to the right connects with Magic Kingdom hotels, Fort Wilderness Campground, Discovery Island, and River Country.

If you visualize two large, connected lakes — one straight ahead and one to your right — you can understand the general lay-out for the Magic Kingdom hotels. The lake straight ahead, Seven Seas Lagoon, is a Disney creation. Circled by the monorail, the Magic

Kingdom sits to the far north, across from the parking lot. Three hotels — the Contemporary, the Polynesian, and the Grand Floridian — are all lakefront and connected by the monorail. A recent addition — The Disney Wedding Pavilion — sits on a small island between the Grand Floridian and the Polynesian. Slightly farther to the west of the Polynesian and unseen from the lake is Shades of Green, an on-site hotel owned by the U.S. military for the exclusive use of men and women on active duty, veterans, and their families. The Magnolia Golf Course and Palm Golf Course surround Shades of Green.

The lake to the right, Bay Lake, fronts Wilderness Lodge followed by the Fort Wilderness campground. Discovery Island, a zoological park closing soon, sits in the middle of Bay Lake. River Country, Disney's smallest water park, is part of Fort Wilderness. The Osprey Ridge Golf Course and Eagle Pines Golf Course sit to the far right.

So far so good. But the rest gets tricky. Other resorts — Caribbean Beach, Dixie Landings, Port Orleans, Old Key West Resort, and the Village resorts — take up a large area roughly east of Epcot and unseen from World Drive. In this section, Typhoon Lagoon and Downtown Disney — a renamed section that includes Pleasure Island, the Village Marketplace, and Disney's West Side — front Buena Vista Drive, which runs roughly parallel to I-4. The area also has the Lake Buena Vista Golf Course and the Disney Institute. Many of the Disney executive offices — the Casting Center (job applications), SunTrust Bank Building (Disney weddings, Press & Publicity, etc.) and Team Mickey are also found here.

If driving on Disney property, take a map. You may be able to bluff your way to a destination using these simple guidelines, but pay careful attention to road signs and don't be afraid to ask directions. If you find yourself approaching a parking lot toll booth you never planned to use, tell your problem to the attendant. They'll give directions and allow you to turn around without charge.

To request a copy of the official property map, call Guest Information at (407) 824-4321 and ask for the Walt Disney World Resort Map.

BEFORE YOU LEAVE HOME

12 What Time of Year Should You Visit?

14 Weather

15 Where to Stay — Off Property or at a
     Disney Resort?

18 The Disney Transportation System

20 Advance Reservations — More Than Just
     Hotel Rooms

21 Crime

22 Is It Better to Book a Package Plan?

24 Pets

25 Don't Forget...

Chapter Three

BEFORE YOU LEAVE HOME

WHAT TIME OF YEAR SHOULD YOU VISIT?

First rule: Never visit when kids are out of school. This includes Thanksgiving, Christmas, President's Day, Easter, and the entire summer. Families with school-age children have little flexibility when planning a vacation and many travel when the kids have a scheduled holiday. During Easter, for example, Disney World fills up for two full weeks, from the weekend before Easter Sunday through the weekend after. Over Christmas — historically the busiest time of the year — the Magic Kingdom gets so full that it actually stops admitting guests on peak days. Disney World extends park operating hours to handle the herds, but longer lines and elbow-to-elbow crowds make a vacation less enjoyable.

During the off-season, parks may close as early as 6:00 p.m., but guests enjoy as many rides and shows in a nine-hour day as they can in fourteen hours during extended operating hours. And, at 6:00 p.m., guests still have enough energy to walk to their car or hotel.

There are two problems with traveling off-season, however: Certain events — notably the Magic Kingdom's SpectroMagic Parade and the Fantasy In the Sky Fireworks — are not always scheduled during the off-season. From a theatrical stand-point, both require darkness to work correctly and can't be performed in a park that closes before sunset. From a pragmatic stand-point, they cost a lot to operate. Guests who wish to see these attractions may want to plan a vacation that covers both busy and slow times, such as a Saturday to

Saturday vacation that starts on Labor Day weekend. You can see SpectroMagic the first weekend and enjoy thinner crowds later in the week. At Epcot, IllumiNations is presented year-round, regardless of the crowds.

The second problem in vacationing off-season: rides may be shut down for refurbishing. WDW is open 365 days a year and regular ride maintenance must be done during normal operating hours. While refurbishing behind the scenes is a Disney art-form, you may be disappointed to find "Pirates of the Caribbean" closed during your stay. Major refurbishing may occur during a busy season, but most routine maintenance is scheduled for the off-season.

Second rule: Avoid December, January, and February if you plan to swim, and possibly November and March. Avoid June through October if you're unnaturally afraid of hurricanes. (Chances are slight that the area will get hit by a hurricane and almost negligible that it will get hit while you're visiting.)

So what's left? To miss the crowds, the best times to visit Disney World are January, late spring, the fall, and the two weeks after Thanksgiving. In January, weather is cool but crowds thin, an ideal time for those unconcerned with swimming. In late spring, winter tourists have returned to the North. Many hotels offer specials; the parks are not crowded; the weather is pleasant. While temperatures sometimes reach the upper 80's, evenings are cool. In May, the final month of the school year, parents do not pull children out of school. Days can get hot but evenings remain comfortable.

The entire fall is also a good choice if you avoid Thanksgiving. Like in May, parents do not vacation in September because children need time to get established in their new classes, though Central Florida's steamy tropical weather hangs on into the fall. In October and November, crowds remain reasonable and the weather changes from humid, mid-90°, thunder-storm-in-the-afternoon norms, to low humidity, rainless, low-80° days.

One of the best times to visit is just after Thanksgiving. Christmas and Disney World go hand-in-hand and the two complement each other. In addition, crowds are rare. Few people have the time — or money or energy — to travel before the holidays and businesses rarely schedule December conventions. Unfortunately, word has spread that crowds are thin before Christmas and many travelers now plan their visit during this time. In addition, Disney gives all their employees an extra theme park admission over Christmas with dis-counted meals. If planning to enjoy Christmas at WDW — and everyone should do this at least once — try for early December. Expect cool weather and remember that regular parades and shows may be replaced by ones with a holiday theme.

Visiting from January through Easter can be pleasant if you avoid President's Day. Crowds are moderate, though thicker than in the fall. Like a Bell-shaped curve, crowds are thin in early January, slowly build until Easter, then thin out again through May.

WEATHER

Many first-time visitors from the North expect balmy summer temperatures year-round. They pack nothing but T-shirts and suntan lotion; the only winter garments they bring are the ones they wore to the airport. They then wear the same outfit the entire week, rising each morning with the unfulfilled hope that temperatures will reach 70°, the required base line to catch a few rays by the heated pool. They desperately need a tan to prove to people back home that they've "been to Florida."

From the end of May through September, weather is relatively constant. The temperature peaks around 93° and sinks as low as 72°. It is hot. It is humid. Almost every afternoon, a thunderstorm blasts its way through, sending human beings scurrying for cover until it blows over. Non-Floridians on vacation complain about the heat and the humidity, but air conditioning is usually easy to find. And, while it rains daily, downpours are short. Visitors rarely wake to an entire day of foul weather.

The rest of the year is not so predictable. In other months, Orlando weather varies just as it does in the rest of the country. Every few years, for example, the temperature falls below freezing at night, with daytime highs in the low 50's. It's rare, but Michigan guests visiting in mid-February feel slighted if they can't take off their down jacket. On the flip side, of course, a February heat wave could send temperatures into the low 80's.

When traveling October through May, hope for the best and plan for the worst.

For more detailed information, consult the following chart:

Month	Average High	Average Low	Average Rainfall (in inches)
January	75°	57°	4.9
February	71°	50°	1.5
March	75°	54°	6.3
April	79°	57°	1.8
May	85°	65°	2.3
June	91°	72°	4.5
July	94°	74°	6.5
August	92°	74°	6.0
September	90°	72°	5.4
October	84°	66°	4.6
November	77°	59°	0.2
December	70°	48°	0.8

Source: 1994 Florida Statistical Abstract

WHERE TO STAY — OFF-PROPERTY OR AT A DISNEY RESORT?

In years gone by, this decision was simple. If you wanted the total Disney experience, convenient access to parks and entertainment, and all resort amenities, you stayed at a Disney hotel. If you wanted to save money — a lot of it — you stayed somewhere else.

In the past ten years, things changed. With the opening of Disney's All-Star Resort in 1994, Disney added a budget hotel option. With on-site rates starting at $69 before tax, Disney's lowest nightly rate still exceeds those available off-property, but not by much. In addition, the resort amenities afforded all on-site guests — a major perk — are still part of the All-Star Resort's package. In other words, the choice of accommodation is more than a simple comparison of costs.

Decide first how much time you plan to spend at Disney. If visiting Orlando for the fourth time and, in the course of a week, you plan to spend a day at the beach, a day golfing, and a day at Cypress Gardens, you might prefer to stay off-site. No matter how great Disney's on-site amenities are, you don't want to pay for something you won't use. If, on the other hand, you plan to spend every minute within Walt Disney World, an on-site stay could save both time and money.

All Disney hotels have clean rooms and courteous employees, but keep in mind that "you get what you pay for." At the Yacht and Beach Club, a top-of-the-line resort, guests receive everything from Mickey toothbrushes to concierge service. The hotel lobby is decorated with detailed rugs, hardwood floors, nautical paintings, and brass ornaments. At the entrance to the hotel, a Disney cast member greets new arrivals, his only job to say "hello" or "good-bye" and make sure everyone is happy.

At the All-Star resort, rooms have two double beds, one dresser, and a small table. The hotel lobby is basic, the floor plain tile, and the decor based more on colorful line drawings than interesting architecture. But a room at the All-Star Resort costs about $150 less, per night, than a room at the Yacht and Beach Club.

You get what you pay for.

Look over the following advantages and disadvantages of staying on Disney property. Determine what you plan to do. Analyze your budget, then decide.

Staying within Walt Disney World advantages:
• **Atmosphere.** The nicest off-site hotels still feel like hotels. On-site hotels are themed, which gives the vacation a fantasy atmosphere.
• **Transportation.** On-site guests enjoy unlimited use of the Disney transportation system, meaning buses, boats, and monorails. It's possible to stay an entire week without ever driving a car or hailing a cab.
• **Parking.** Those who choose to drive their car from resort to theme park do not have to pay the parking fee, up to a $6 daily savings.
• **Preferred golf tee times.**
• **Convenience.** As a resort guest, every purchase — except for a few fast food locations — can be charged to one master account. In addition, merchandise bought within the theme parks will be shipped, free of charge, directly to your hotel room.

• **Guaranteed Park Admission.** Even on days when a park is so full that they cut off admission, resort guests will be allowed to enter. (However, if the park is that full, you don't want to go anyway.)
• **Early park admission.** On selected days, each park opens one hour early for on-site guests only.
• **Safety.** While crime knows no boundaries, Disney has its own security force. The lack of on-site crime is also a simple matter of logistics — it can take a thief a full half hour to run to a car and drive off property, with ample opportunities for capture. Thousands of off-site hotel rooms are more accessible.

Staying off-site advantages:
• **Finances.** Off-site hotels always have discounted hotel rooms, most notably in the slow season. It's possible to find decent accommodations as low as $30 per night if you know where to look and what to ask.
• **Food.** In general, food costs less off-site. While Disney-owned establishments offer a range of prices and products, McDonalds still serves a cheaper hamburger.
• **Accessibility**. Staying off-site is less convenient for touring the Disney theme parks, but decidedly better if you want to tour elsewhere.
• **Style.** Some people love a majestic hotel, such as the Hyatt Grand Cypress. While Disney's Grand Floridian is a majestic hotel — it tied the Hyatt in Zagat's latest survey of top 100 U.S. resorts and inns — the Grand Floridian cannot shake its roots: its view of Cinderella's Castle and the "outsiders" that wander in by way of the Disney transportation system. Those people oblivious to the Disney magic may prefer to stay elsewhere.

Some nearby hotels, such as the Grenelefe Golf and Tennis Resort, offer great rooms, top-flight golf, fine dining, and a number of other resort amenities. They're also located in the country, removed from virtually all tourist activities, yet only twenty minutes from the hub-bub of Disney. Some people love the recreation-theme park balance. Others find it inconvenient.

A final point to consider when deciding whether to stay off-site or on-site: Disney's Village Resort Area hotels now exist in a gray area between on-site and off-site properties. Twenty-five years ago, these hotels, located near Downtown Disney, were privately owned and they leased the land. Guests staying on-site, regardless whether the hotel was Disney owned or not, were accorded the same benefits. Disney augmented its number of hotel rooms with little investment and the hotels could advertise that they were "on property."

Today, things have changed. While the village hotels still sit on Disney property, the Disney transportation system no longer services many of them and typical on-site amenities vary from hotel to hotel. In addition, guests cannot enjoy early entry to the parks nor free parking. If considering a stay in one of these hotels, confirm which amenities they do — and do not — offer.

THE DISNEY TRANSPORTATION SYSTEM

In a nutshell, the Disney transportation system is complete. No matter where you stay on property, you can get to any other place without driving. While buses form the backbone of the system, it includes unique elements such as boats and monorails that, to quote an old advertisement, make "getting there half the fun."

Of course, sometimes you want to get to your destination fast and don't care if you have fun along the way. While Disney's mass transit system runs seamlessly, compared to driving yourself, it falls short. That is not a critique or complaint, merely an observation of problems faced by all mass transit systems. People used to instant gratification may prefer to take their own car.

The following types of transportation whisk guests around the Walt Disney World Resort:

• **Monorail.** The most famous monorail is the oldest — the one that circles the Seven Seas Lagoon with stops at the Transportation and Ticket Center (TTC), the Grand Floridian, the Polynesian, and the Contemporary (which it goes right through). Running parallel to this monorail is a second monorail used to transport day guests to the Magic Kingdom. While this one also passes through the Contemporary, it stops only at the TTC and the Magic Kingdom. A third monorail runs from the TTC to Epcot Center, circling Future World upon arrival, and giving first-time guests a preview of the park.

For guests staying in hotels serviced by the monorail, there is rarely a waiting line except in the busiest seasons and most crowded times (like at park closing). To get to Epcot, these hotel guests must disembark at the TTC and transfer to the Epcot monorail.

• **Boats.** Not counting those inside the theme parks, transportation boats connect selected resorts to the different theme parks and/or other resorts. Since Bay Lake connects to the Seven Seas Lagoon, both Wilderness Lodge and Fort Wilderness Campground guests can cruise to the Magic Kingdom. Day guests, finding themselves parked across the water from the Magic Kingdom, may travel on a replica of the Staten Island Ferry. Commuting to the Magic Kingdom by water takes only a few more minutes than traveling by monorail.

In the Epcot Center resort area, boats connect some hotels to Disney-MGM Studios and/or Epcot Center. Again, these can be congested during peak times and seasons. In addition, the Epcot boats deposit passengers by World Showcase rather than at the front entrance. It's convenient, but dampens Epcot's dramatic first impression for novice guests. From Epcot's main entrance, Spaceship Earth, futuristic water fountains, and well-manicured gardens form a grand entranceway. Starting your tour in World Showcase is like sliding through the back door — it gets you in, but you feel as if you missed something.

A pontoon boat connects Dixie Landings and Port Orleans to Downtown Disney. Both the ride (on a canal, but called the Sassagoula River) and the resorts have a fictionalized history which the "river captain" is happy to relate.

• **Tram.** All theme park lots are connected to the main entrance by trams. While trams usually cut down on the amount of walking required, they do not always save time, notably in the Epcot and Disney-MGM Studios' parking lots.

• **Buses.** In short, every connection not mentioned thus far is serviced by bus. All resorts have direct access to all theme parks and Downtown Disney. Note that "direct access" does not mean nonstop. The bus may pick up passengers at multiple locations. Since the buses allow standing and Disney can add service during peak hours, the system runs efficiently.

If planning to visit sites other than the three parks or Downtown Disney, however, the system can be tricky. For example, if you wish to visit Wilderness Lodge from your room in Dixie Landings, you have to change buses midway. You could take the Sassagoula River Boat, disembark in the Village Marketplace, cross through the shops to Pleasure Island, and catch a Wilderness Lodge bus there. Or you could take a bus to one of the parks, disembark, and wait for another bus (or a boat). Either way, the process takes time. With Disney's rapid expansion, getting-from-here-to-there has become so detailed that all on-site guests now receive a "Disney Transportation Guide." A large graph cross references destinations and walks guests through the transfer process. (Example: U+H+K in the chart translates to "board a boat to the Magic Kingdom, then board the monorail, then disembark at the TTC, and then transfer to the Epcot monorail.") Easy, really. But not simple.

No resort has a perfect location because of the size of WDW, but you should try to reserve a hotel close to the areas you plan to visit. As a rule-of-thumb, mature adults prefer Epcot and the Disney-MGM Studios over the Magic Kingdom. If true for you, staying at one of the Epcot area resorts affords a boat trip or short walk to Epcot and either a short bus trip or water transfer to MGM.

Off-site guests have fewer choices. Many (but not all — be sure to ask) hotels offer complimentary shuttle service to the three major parks. When offered, hotels usually (but not always) coordinate trips with other nearby hotels and the bus makes multiple stops along the way. This has the same advantages (no parking fee and convenient drop-offs) as the Disney transportation system along with the same problems (waiting for your bus and crowded conditions at opening and closing).

Decide what type of person you are. When it's time to go somewhere, are you impatient? Do you stare at your watch every 30 seconds when waiting for a bus? If so, drive. Is relying on others to take care of you part of a total vacation package? Does driving in unknown places pump your adrenaline level into the danger zones? Then use the transportation system.

ADVANCE RESERVATIONS — MORE THAN JUST HOTEL ROOMS

All visitors can now make dinner reservations 60 days in advance for most full-service restaurants and one-year in advance for dinner shows by calling (407) WDW-DINE.

Currently, Walt Disney World has two dinners shows, The Polynesian Review and the Hoop-De-Doo Musical Review. Both cost about $37.00 plus tax and both usually sell-out early. If you're a free spirit who refuses to be pinned down to a restaurant before arrival, call each morning of your stay and check for cancellations. You may get lucky. On the day of a show, call directly to (407) 824-3803 for the Hoop-De-Doo Review and (407) 824-1593 for the Polynesian Review. While it doesn't pay to be too optimistic, many people who reserved space nine months earlier are forced to cancel, freeing spaces for last minute diners.

CRIME

Florida received a ton of unfavorable publicity in the early 1990's, most of it undeserved. While criminals operate in Florida as elsewhere, there is little chance you will be affected. Most of the negative news reports centered on Miami where, like New York City and L.A., a small section of any city's population resorts to violence. In general, that is not found in Orlando.

That's not to say you can be complacent because tourists are easy targets. They have cash and they don't stick around to prosecute; criminals like that. While you must take intelligent precautions, don't let a fear of crime interfere with your vacation.

If concerned about crime, stay on Disney property. Thanks to a private security force and increased chances of capture, very few crimes occur within WDW. Most resorts have guard-gated entrances. When visiting parks, you're also fairly safe. Few thieves will cough up $40 to spend a day robbing guests when they can do it for free elsewhere.

If staying off-site, find a hotel with plastic card locks, the industry standard. Also, a high rise building is safer than a one- or two-story motel surrounded by a parking lot. Thieves are slower to hit twelfth floor rooms because they have to run down stairs and through a lobby to get to their car. Ground-floor rooms with parking right outside are most vulnerable. For more information, see Chapter 5.

IS IT BETTER TO BOOK A PACKAGE PLAN?

That depends. What do you want to do?

With every package booking, expect convenience. Most packages include Disney tickets along with a hotel, rental car or airport transfers, and all taxes. Many include gratuities. Some include airfare. Most include perks, such as a tote bag, guidebook, or other "extra."

It's easy to look at the ease of booking a package, assume it's a better deal, and reserve a space. But before signing on to a package, study the elements you won't be using. Some portion of every package must pay for those elements, even if they're advertised as "free" or a "bonus for booking." For example, assume a travel package gives you unlimited admission to all Disney parks during your stay. Being your third visit to Orlando, you plan to visit Cypress Gardens, Sea World, and spend at least two days golfing and relaxing by the hotel pool. That leaves only three days for theme parks. While the "go anytime" option is attractive for those who hate to plan, it also wastes money. Since park admissions can make a sizable dent in the vacation kitty, try pricing each component separately and compare costs. Many times, you can do better.

If traveling in the off-season — and if you're reading this book you should be — the deals on hotels, cars, and airfare might be lower if booked separately. Tour companies negotiate a rate with each supplier, tack on their profit margin, and resell it to you, the consumer. The price may compete favorably with high-season rates when few vendors discount, but in the off-season, it's possible to find great deals if you're willing to make some calls. A hotel, for example, might give a tour operator a 40% discount year-round, to which the tour operator adds his 20% profit. But in the off-season, that 40% discount might be the standard room rate, the higher, "discounted" rate charged only in high season. In addition, many hotels offer discounts to seniors, AAA members, and others — factors not available through tour operators. (The Delta Orlando Resort-Maingate at Universal Studios Florida and the Sheraton Orlando North both offer a 50% discount to those over 55, for example. The Peabody Orlando has a flat $89 per night rate.)

Consider the pros and cons of the following travel arrangements:

• **Charter flights.** A charter flight is usually the cheapest vacation package, many times with nonstop flights to Orlando. (This may change, however, as more low-fare carriers serve new markets.) In any travel deal, the general rule is: The cheaper the price, the more restrictive the arrangements.

In a charter flight, a company rents an entire plane for a contracted fee. The company has a financial break-even point, say when 75% of the plane is filled with passengers. After that, they turn a profit. Knowing that a Disney vacation is usually booked ahead of time and they would have trouble selling seats in the month prior to departure, the cancellation penalties can be expensive, many times 100% in the last month or two — a cheap deal but very restrictive.

Consider travel insurance but be careful of a pre-existing medical condition. Travel insurance generally covers new medical emergencies, but not a reoccurrence. If, for example, bone cancer is in remission yet resurfaces, it will probably not be covered. If cancer is discovered in a new area — even though you already had it elsewhere — it might be covered. Ask your travel agent for more details.

One more disadvantage: since you're flying in a rented plane with tickets issued privately, your ticket is invalid on any other carrier. That means if Aunt Charlene takes ill in the middle of your vacation, you cannot expect an airline to honor your ticket and fly you back early, even by paying a penalty. Again, consider insurance. Most is overpriced but if something happens, you'll wish you had it.

• **Go-Any-Day Packages.** These are similar to charter flight packages, but with flexibility since you fly on regularly scheduled airlines. On the plus side, your airline ticket is now worth something should Aunt Charlene get sick. On the down side, the package will probably be more expensive than a charter arrangement. In addition, the seats an airline gives up to tour customers roughly equate to the seats they give up for those cheap airfares. In other words, very few. If you plan to leave on a Saturday morning, you may find all available space booked even if the planes are not yet full.

For tour arrangements other than those with heavy restrictions, travel insurance is usually a waste of money and a big profit-maker for both insurance company and tour company. But consider it anyway. Remember that no one ever plans on emergencies. Compare the cost of insurance coverage to the package's cancellation penalties.

(Some may allow a full refund up to three days before departure.) Decide how much you're willing to gamble, and then make a decision.

• **Land-Only Packages.** The Walt Disney Travel Company offers its own packages, as does the Magic Kingdom Club, a subsidiary. Most other vendors also offer land-only arrangements. If you love spontaneity and have money to burn, book everything they offer. (Some even include all meals and a camcorder.) Otherwise, a small amount of preplanning can save a lot of money down the road.

The final consideration when considering a package tour is personal. Do you hate worrying about money, preferring to pay ahead of time for everything? Does the idea of making twenty Orlando phone calls and then comparing prices leave you cold? Package tours from reputable suppliers, even in the off-season, should not cost a lot more than booking components separately. For many, the ease of vacation planning makes a package tour worth any extra cost.

PETS

Pluto is the only dog allowed in the Disney parks unless servicing a handicapped person. (And maybe Goofy — Is he a dog?)

Only service animals may stay in Disney hotels, but guests staying on site can board their pet in one of the Disney owned Pet Care Centers. As a rule, the more exotic the pet, the less Disney cast members will help with its care. Bears and cougars have been accepted, as well as smaller, more domestic species such as hamsters, turtles, and snakes. Bring your own cage if you need to board an animal that does not fit easily into standard dog and cat cages. Overnight accommodations cost about $11 per day. Daily accommodations about $9.

Guests staying off-site cannot leave their pets overnight but can board them during the day while they tour theme parks. Florida law prohibits pet owners from leaving their pets in unattended vehicles. Not only against the law, it is also inhumane.

If you wish to keep your pet with you, a few off-site hotels accept them. The AAA Florida TourBook, available free to AAA members, includes information on pets in the hotel descriptions. For more information, contact the Orlando/Orange County Convention and Visitors Bureau at (800) 551-0181 or the Kissimmee/St. Cloud Convention and Visitor's Bureau at (800) 831-1844. A book, *The Florida Dog Lover's*

Companion: The Inside Scoop on Where to Take Your Dog, by Sally Deneen and Robert McLure, is published by Foghorn Press, retails for $19.95, and covers pet acceptance in all parts of the state.

DON'T FORGET...

• **Good walking shoes.** Buy them at least one month before departure and wear them every day. Walk outdoors. (If you're out of shape, keep it up after you get back home.) You'll enjoy the vacation more if not massaging aching muscles.

• **Sunscreen.** By absorbing Florida sun in twenty minute doses between attractions, it's easy to pretend it doesn't count. But it does. Use sunscreen liberally. Consider wearing a hat.

• **Rain gear.** Light ponchos are convenient and available in all the Disney parks for a reasonable rate. If you prefer a fold-up umbrella, pack one.

• **Prescription drugs.** A Goodings supermarket across from Disney property near the Village Resorts can fill many prescriptions, but to avoid trouble, bring enough for your entire vacation.

• **Fanny pack.** Sold in tourist shops throughout the U.S., these replace bulky handbags.

• **Comfortable clothes.** When touring the parks, never give up comfort for style.

• **Sense of Humor.** You should carry this one in a purse or wallet at all times. It comes in handy for emergencies.

WALT DISNEY WORLD ON-SITE HOTELS

31   Shades of Green

33   Magic Kingdom Resorts

39   Epcot Center Resorts

45   Moderately Priced Resorts

50   Budget Hotels

51   Fort Wilderness

55   Other On-Site Resorts

Chapter Four

WALT DISNEY WORLD ON-SITE HOTELS

When Disney opened their All-Star Resorts in 1994, the company broke from tradition in two ways. First, they themed a resort to an idea rather than a geographic location, and second, they built a budget resort, shooting for a market segment historically ignored. There are currently two Disney All-Star Resorts, Sports and Music, that celebrate their central themes in a bigger-than-life way. All other Disney resorts focus on a specific place. The Polynesian, for example, recreates islands in the Pacific; Wilderness Lodge imitates great hotels of the Northwest; even the Contemporary pretends to be somewhere it's not — the future.

Money and personal taste dictate which Disney resort to stay in with an emphasis on the former. The Grand Floridian and the Yacht and Beach Club, for example, enjoy similar amenities, but the Grand Floridian feels more formal. Some folks love that formality. Others would pay to avoid it.

The following hotel descriptions attempt to paint a picture of the atmosphere, prices, and convenience of each resort. Be wary of pricing. While Disney does not discount as rapidly as its off-site competition, it offers occasional specials. Sometimes, a specific resort that does not fill as expected will be discounted, usually in the last month or two before arrival. In the past, when Disney had fewer rooms to fill, they rarely had vacancies. Things have changed.

When reserving a room, expect different prices based on the view. Generally, a room with a parking lot view costs least, followed by a garden view room, followed by a lake view room. Some grander hotels have more than six different categories based not only on view but also on room size. It can get confusing. Before calling central reservations, decide how much time you'll spend in the room and how much you value the Disney panorama viewed from a private balcony. Many people pay extra for scenery then don't have the time or energy to enjoy it. Others love the way a room overlooking Cinderella's Castle threads the Disney magic through everything.

To add more confusion to the which-resort-should-I-book soup, certain hotels are located on Disney property but not owned by Disney, sort-of second class citizens. Even trickier, there are two classes of these second-class citizens: the almost-Disney resorts and the barely-Disney resorts. All but one (Shades of Green) can be booked through Disney's central reservations, but you will probably talk your way into a better priced room by calling individual hotels directly.

The Swan and the Dolphin, both Epcot Center resorts, are managed by Westin and Sheraton hotels respectively, and are almost-Disney resorts. Swan and Dolphin guests enjoy most — but not all — standard on-site amenities. They cannot, for example, charge restaurant meals eaten in other WDW areas to their master account. Other restrictions may apply. Shades of Green, a military owned hotel, is also almost-Disney but not open to the general public.

The Disney Village Hotel Plaza Resorts (seven hotels between I-4, U.S. 535, and Downtown Disney) are privately owned and barely-Disney, even though they're located on property. Twenty-five years ago, these hotels shared the same perks as any on-site resort and they accommodated overflow guests that couldn't find room at the more convenient Disney-owned properties. Through the years, contracts expired and Disney built more hotels. As a result, these seven properties have grown independent. Today, they share a bit of the perks, such as in-house ticket sales to Disney parks and early park admission, but not other important services such as guaranteed access to the transportation system. Since each hotel contracts individually with WDW, none offer identical packages. Ask questions when booking to avoid later disappointment.

Note that Disney resorts now have guarded entrances and you will be stopped upon arrival if you drive. The intent is not to keep people out — locals are encouraged to eat at Disney restaurants — but rather, to make crime more trouble than it's worth.

All Disney resorts except Shades of Green can be booked through Central Reservations at (407) W-DISNEY (which translates to 407-934-7639).

When booking, ask about the following discounts:

• **Florida resident.** This can work in the off-season, but be prepared to show a driver's license or other proof of residency on check-in.

• **Magic Kingdom Club member.** Offering 10% - 30% savings on off-season hotel stays (limited availability), MKC members also receive discounts at selected Disney World restaurants, Disney Stores, Pleasure Island, Downtown Disney shops, and partner companies such as National Car Rental. Membership is free to employees of selected companies or $65 for a two-year membership ($50 for adults over age 55). Price also includes subscription to *The Disney Magazine*. Applications are available at any Disney Store or by calling (800) 893-4763.

• **Senior citizens.** Disney just started marketing to older adults but special pricing is sporadic. Discounts may be offered in selected hotels that the company is trying to fill, notably at the last minute or in the off season.

• **Auto Club member.** At times, Disney works with auto clubs, notably AAA (American Automobile Association), and offers limited-time specials. AAA members currently enjoy priority parking at the theme parks.

• **Ocala Information Center**. Located off I-75 in Ocala, Florida, the information center sometimes offers substantial hotel discounts. The downside to this: the reservation must be made at the last minute en route to Walt Disney World. It's a good booking system for Disney because they fill a room that, left unsold, nets the company nothing. They make a slight profit; you get a great room. Disney has enough hotel rooms that something is almost always available in the off-season but it's still a gamble. For more information, call the Ocala Information Center at (904) 854-0770.

• **Cast Member friends or relatives.** If you know someone who works at Walt Disney World, have him or her make the reservation call. Disney offers a substantial discount to friends and relatives of workers, though you must book in the off-season or at the last minute. Unlike other discounts, this one also applies to lodging at the All-Star resorts, dropping the price to levels equal to the cheapest off-site hotels.

Off-season dates — like everything else at Walt Disney World — change from year-to-year. However, every resort offers some kind of discount during slow periods, though the actual amount runs 10% or less. Since a value season coincides with expected slow times, the savings on a hotel room coupled with the benefit of fewer crowds makes a winning combination.

Expect the following price structure:

Regular Season. At the Caribbean Beach, Dixie Landings, Port Orleans, and the All-Star Resorts, regular season begins in early February and ends before Labor Day. At all other resorts, regular season begins in early February and ends around Labor Day, except for a six-week period after Easter and before schools break for summer vacation.

Value Season. At the All-Star Resort, Caribbean Beach, Dixie Landings, and Port Orleans, value season runs from approximately Labor Day to 10 days before Christmas and the entire month of January. For all other resorts, value season covers the same periods, plus six weeks after Easter.

Holiday Season. All on-site Disney rooms cost approximately 5% more over the two week Christmas holiday.

In addition to the seasonal room rate, all Central Florida hotel guests pay 11% in hotel taxes. When tacked on to the room's weekly cost, this additional outlay can make a substantial dent in the vacation coffers if not penciled into the budget. For the mathematically challenged, you can figure your total room bill before leaving home by 1) multiplying the daily room rate by the number of days you plan to stay and, 2) multiplying that total by 1.11. (For example, multiply one night at the All-Star Resort, $69, by 7 nights to get $483. Second, multiply $483 by 1.11 and you get $536.13, your total outlay. Total taxes paid: $53.13.)

Disney allows two adults per room and children under 18 stay free. For every additional adult, however, there is a charge as follows: At the campground, $2 per person; at Wilderness Homes, $5; at All-Star Resorts, $8; at Caribbean Beach, Dixie Landings, and Port Orleans, $12; at all other WDW resorts, $15.

All hotel rooms share the same rules: a reservation must be followed by a one-night deposit within 21 days of confirmation, though the deposit will be refunded if the room is canceled within 48 hours of arrival. Check-in is 3:00 p.m., though early arrivals may check bags at the front desk, pre-register, buy tickets, and hit the parks. Check-out time is 11:00 a.m. Guests receive ID cards upon check-in that act as room key, resort credit card, and pass to board Disney transportation. All resorts offer bus transportation either directly, or with connections, to all other Disney areas. If specialty transportation exists, i.e., boat or monorail service, it's listed under the individual hotel descriptions. Additionally, all offer some type of room service, though limited to pizza delivery at the most inexpensive resorts.

All Disney-owned resorts have rooms accessible for the handicapped and convenient to the main lobby. Make sure to specify your needs when making a reservation, even if your health troubles cause little problem in day-to-day living. Many mild medical problems, for example, may be aggravated by extra walking and a change in schedule. Anytime you can save a few steps, do it. For more information on guests with special needs, refer to the chapter on handicapped travelers or call the resort directly.

When making a reservation, it's not unusual to find certain days unavailable. For example, if you request seven days at the Polynesian, you may be told that it's sold out on the final night. In this case, you can either look at other hotels or, if you only want the Polynesian, reserve the first six days and keep trying to book the final one. As soon as Disney takes a reservation, the computer registers the room as unavailable, but a) some people reserve a room and never send in a deposit, b) some people with a deposit cancel, and c) some tour operators decide they have too many rooms to rent. The result? Rooms constantly go back into inventory. To reserve that last night, try calling every day shortly after 8:00 a.m. Then ask Central Reservations to pull up your booking and see if that final night has become available. This usually works.

All resorts have laundry facilities and dry cleaning services; all rooms feature a clock radio and voice messaging. In the following examples, resort details, including room rates, were correct at press time. Expect changes.

SHADES OF GREEN

Formerly the Disney Inn, this hotel was recently purchased by, and now falls under the control of, the U.S. Army Community and Family Support Center. It is, officially, an "Armed Forces Recreation Center," one of four in the world and the only one located within the continental United States. Rooms are rented only to active and retired military personnel, including those who served in the Reserves and National Guard, as well as all appropriated and nonappropriated fund civilians and their guests. Located just beyond the Polynesian Resort, Shades of Green is not on the monorail system but has one of the most picturesque and relaxing locations on property. Bus service connects the resort to the Transportation and Ticket Center where guests may connect to the rest of "the world."

Operated by non-Disney staff, resort guests still enjoy most of the on-site perks including early park admission, guaranteed admission on busy days, and unlimited use of the transportation system. Each room is large by hotel standards at 365-square feet and each includes a sleep/sofa, two queen-sized beds, and a small table. Management quickly points out that no tax money supports Shades of Green, only nonappropriated funds, meaning money earned in military stores, bowling alleys, and movie theaters. Essentially, all those leisure services on U.S. posts are profitable and self-serving. Shades of Green is their latest acquisition.

Located beside Disney's Magnolia Golf Course, the 287-room hotel is more intimate than other properties. Rates do not fluctuate seasonally and are based on current military rank or the rank held at the time of retirement. As an added benefit, military personnel can, with proof of status, buy discounted park admissions unavailable to the general public. While the hotel offers modest discounts on all types of Disney passes, it offers substantial savings on Length of Stay passes that include unlimited admission to all major parks, water parks, Pleasure Island, and Discovery Island. Adult ticket prices range from $84.00 for a two-day package to $277.72 for an eight-day pass, a savings of $11.40 for the former and $40.72 for the latter. Military guests with valid ID do not have to stay at Shades of Green to get these discounted tickets, but they must stay at a Disney resort and purchase them at Shades of Green.

But, there's always a down side. First, as a non-Disney managed resort, a few of the special Disney touches are absent, such as visits by Mickey, which may be important if traveling with children. (Of course, you can always stay here, save $700, and spend it on a character breakfast.) Also, with only 287 rooms, great rates, and on-site privileges, demand is high. Rooms must be booked early.

For more information or to make reservations, military guests must call Shades of Green directly. They will mail information if requested, but allow six weeks for delivery.

Prices: E-1 through E-5 pay $57.00 per night; E-6 through E-9, O-1 through O-3, WO-1 to CW-3, GS-1 through GS-10, and NF-1 through NF-3 pay $81.00 per night; O-4 through O-6, CW-4 and CW-5, GS-11 through GS-15, and NF-4 and NF-5 pay $89.00 per night; O-7 through O-10, Foreign Military, Retired DoD Civilians, and NF-6 pay $98.00 per night.

Services: The Garden Gallery serves an inexpensive ($5.95) breakfast buffet as well as dinner. Evergreen Sports Bar offers lighter fare as well as cocktails, as does The Back Porch Lounge.

- Lighted tennis courts
- Two heated swimming pools
- Children's pool and play area
- Exercise room
- Gift shop
- Gameroom
- Laundry facilities

Transportation: Bus service links guests to the Transportation and Ticket Center with connections to all other WDW destinations.

Phone: (407) 824-3600

MAGIC KINGDOM RESORTS

The Grand Floridian

Gazebos, grand pianos, turn-of-the-century gas lamps, and afternoon high tea are resurrected in Disney's Grand Floridian. Only the sheer size of the resort — 905 rooms — belies the fact that oil and steel barons do not vacation here in the winter. The Victorian atmosphere suggests a genteel era, a time when a woman blushed if her ankle showed; when a gentleman held the door for a lady; when not tipping your hat to strangers smacked of bad breeding.

Decorated in white, off-white, off-off-white, and pastels, the 14,800-foot central lobby rises five stories and is illuminated by grand chandeliers. Potted plants accent the area; a classical piano player gives the Victorian fantasy depth. Outside, gardens are immaculate, suggesting more relaxed times when the "little people" took care of maintenance. Latticework and ornate balconies recreate the early 1900's.

While Disney's Yacht and Beach Club might arguably be rated

equal to the Grand Floridian in services offered and attention to detail, the Grand Floridian feels more formal because of its setting. It costs marginally more and, most important, it's considered the creme of the Disney resort crop. The rich, of course, do not parade, and most Grand Floridian guests spend their day rubbing elbows with other tourists as they watch country bears sing. But the Victorian theme gives the resort an other-world feel, as if it exists in a different time and place.

Rooms are spacious — about 400-square feet. Two queen-size beds and a day bed accommodate up to five people. Larger suites are available.

Prices: Value season rates start at $284 for a garden view room and range upward to $350 for a lodge tower room. During regular season, rates begin at $309 and go to $375. During holiday seasons, rates run from $324 to $390. In addition, the Grand Floridian has specialty and concierge rooms. Concierge rooms run $375 to $495 per night value season, $395 to $515 regular season, and $410 to $530 over the holidays. Suites start at $560 per night. Most rooms at the Grand Floridian sleep five with room for a crib.

Services: Six restaurants/snack bars sell food ranging from light, fast food at the Gasparilla Grill and Games, to jackets-required, formal service at Victoria & Albert's. Inbetween, 1900 Park Fare serves meals buffet style and the Garden View Lounge specializes in afternoon tea. Three lounges serve cocktails.

- Tennis on clay courts
- Boat rentals
- Swimming, both in a large hotel pool and also lakeside on the hotel's white sand beach
- Children's program available in the evenings
- Fitness. St. John's Health Club offers standard exercise fare with both sauna and massage, for Grand Floridian guests only
- Beauty salon
- Shopping
- Game room

Transportation: Direct monorail service to the Magic Kingdom, TTC, Polynesian, and Contemporary Resorts. Monorail to Epcot with a transfer at the TTC.

Phone: (407) 824-3000

The Polynesian Resort

In the volcanic islands of the Pacific, balmy sunshine and thundering storms create perfect conditions for thick jungle foliage, towering waterfalls, and lifestyles at one with nature. This entire island effect is recreated at the Polynesian Resort with bright native fabrics, ornamental designs, and the sound of drums in the distance. When crossing the main lobby, it's easy to believe in mysterious gods that live in trees and rocks and water.

The central building of the Polynesian, called the Great Ceremonial House, surrounds an indoor tropical garden centered by a two-story waterfall and dense jungle plants. Just outside, large goldfish swim under a wooden bridge that, on the first floor, leads to the parking lot. Thatched roofs cover wood walls, highlighting bright colors and bamboo furnishings.

While the Grand Floridian makes an elegant hotel feel even more elite, the Polynesian theme makes a moderately upscale hotel feel more relaxed. A "jacket required" restaurant cannot be added to a barefoot, run-on-the-beach resort and Disney does not try. It's tough to imagine a more realistic island hotel this side of Hawaii. For those people who book a hotel for its theme, the Polynesian transports imaginations geographically farther than any other Disney owned property. In addition to theming, the lay-out of the resort — 11 two- and three-story buildings amid lush landscaping — makes the Polynesian the most relaxing place to stay while still enjoying direct access to the monorail system.

Rooms can accommodate five people in two queen-size beds and a day bed. Larger suites available.

Prices: During value season, rates start at $249 for a standard room (parking lot view) and go up to $305 for a lagoon view. Regular season rates run $264 to $320. Holiday rates begin at $279 and go up to $335. Concierge rooms, in the value season, start at $305 and run to $380; in regular season they're $325 to $395; over the holidays, $340 to $410. Suites available.

Services: The Polynesian has five different eating spots serving everything from sit-down dinners to fast food. It also has one indoor lounge and one poolside lounge. A theater on the western side of the resort houses the Polynesian Luau and Mickey's Tropical Revue.

- Swimming available in the Seven Seas Lagoon or the resort's two pools
- Boat rentals
- Children's program
- Game room
- Shopping

Transportation: Monorail service to the Magic Kingdom, Contemporary, Grand Floridian, and TTC. Connecting monorail service to Epcot by way of the TTC. Guests can walk to the TTC and save time by avoiding monorail connections. Depending on room location, the walk takes from five to fifteen minutes and those who wish to use this option should request a room on the eastern side of the resort, specifically in the Pago Pago, Moorea, or Oahu wings.

Phone: (407) 824-2000

The Contemporary Resort

Twenty-five years ago, the Contemporary rose as an architectural marvel, each room built off-site, transported en masse, then plugged into a metal skeleton slot by slot. But, like everything else in life, what's new one year is old the next. That's not to say the Contemporary is a bad hotel choice, only that the A-frame idea no longer awes guests with its style or concept.

Still intriguing is the way the monorail enters one end of the building and exits the other, offering a panoramic view of the hollow inside. On the main level, one floor below, restaurants wind down the center with shops and lounges off to the side. In the center, a 90-foot high mural commemorates the American Southwest and personalizes the lobby. Recently refurbished, designers took this once-futuristic-but-then-dated-looking-resort and moved it into the 21st century. Like Tomorrowland in the Magic Kingdom, it no longer strives to look like the real future, but rather, a fictional future reminiscent of Buck Rogers or Jules Verne or The Jetsons.

Two things to note if planning to stay at the Contemporary Resort: One, the monorail, while indoors and convenient, is not accessible by wheelchair. All riders must take an escalator to reach the boarding platform. Two, when booking the Contemporary, most people think they'll stay in the main A-frame structure, but "Garden

Wings" — three story buildings not architecturally connected — extend outward between the Seven Seas Lagoon and Bay Lake and, on the other side of the A-frame, between Bay Lake and the parking lot. While these Garden Wings have nice views from both sides, guests must walk to the main building to catch the monorail. Depending on exact room location, that distance can be considerable.

All rooms have a day bed. Some have two queen-size beds; others have one king. Larger suites available.

Prices: In the Garden Wings, value season rates start at $199 for a standard room and $260 for a garden or water view; regular season rates start at $219 and go to $280; holiday rates run $234 to $295. Accommodations in the Tower (the A-frame with monorail access) run $280 to $350 in value season, $299 to $379 in regular season, and $315 to $395 over the holidays. Suites available. Many times, garden wing rooms are the first to be discounted.

Services: The Contemporary has four food spots ranging from 24-hour fast food service to all-fresh food prepared to order in the California Grill, a restaurant that replaces their long-running Broadway at the Top dinner show. While eating at the California Grill, guests also enjoy a panoramic view of the Magic Kingdom. Three lounges serve cocktails.

- Boat rentals/water-skiing
- Swimming, both in Bay Lake or two swimming pools
- Tennis, including private lessons
- Fitness Center, including massage
- Children's Program
- Gameroom
- Beauty salon
- Shopping

Transportation: Monorail service (from inside the hotel but inaccessible by wheelchair) to the Magic Kingdom, Grand Floridian, Polynesian, and TTC. Connecting monorail service at TTC to Epcot Center. The Magic Kingdom is a ten- to fifteen-minute walk. Boats also commute from the dock to Fort Wilderness, River Country, and Discovery Island.

Phone:(407) 824-1000

Wilderness Lodge

The charm at Wilderness Lodge comes from its style and natural construction. Historically, the lodge steps back to the 1900's and reproduces the great hotels of America's national parks, most notably Yellowstone. Aesthetically, it's built of wood and stone with a rustic decor.

Wilderness Lodge looks like a log cabin that grew up, a nature reprieve that ignores the social conventions of the Grand Floridian and the Yacht Club, exchanging it for the mountain heritage of our backwoods pioneers. Guests do not, however, "rough it." Today's Disney pioneers enjoy heated pools, central air, and bellhops. But you can ignore all that if you want.

With nary a palm tree in site, Wilderness Lodge sits on Bay Lake, a short distance from the Contemporary but, separated by an island, a world away. Close to the lakeshore, a hot steam geyser spouts water every hour. Moose prints cross the sidewalk leading to the main entrance. The building's roof is forest green, the exterior massive logs. Inside, the lobby towers six stories, matching the other resorts in size. Designers went out of their way to include artistic elements representative of the West. Massive lights that hang above the lobby are Native American teepees decorated with torch-cut pictures of buffaloes. An 82-foot tall fireplace burns year-round with plenty of rocking chairs in front; striated layers of rock in the chimney represent the colors of the Grand Canyon. Fifty-five foot, hand carved totem poles edge the lobby. A smaller totem pole — carved with Mickey and friends — graces the entrance to the gift shop.

The building is U-shaped and parallel to Bay Lake, creating an enclosed garden within the "U". A bubbling hot spring forms inside the hotel lobby and can be crossed by a small wooden bridge. The stream then runs outside into the "U", gaining strength as it flows toward Bay Lake, cascading over rocks and flowing around trees. It's all fake, but well done and who cares anyway?

As a hotel, Wilderness Lodge is on par with the Contemporary and Polynesian; a cut below the Grand Floridian and Yacht and Beach Club. But at Disney, theme is more important. While not on the monorail system, Wilderness Lodge is an excellent choice for adults who seek a relaxed environment. A concrete walkway connects the hotel to Fort Wilderness and River Country and guests can walk the shores of Bay Lake for a distance before turning inland. In minutes, Wilderness Lodge guests can escape the crowds and see Florida as it existed pre-Disney.

Most guest rooms have two queen-size beds, writing table, two chairs, and a balcony. Some rooms have one queen-size bed and bunk bed. Larger suites available.

Prices: In value season, rates start at $165 for a standard view and go up to $280 for a courtyard view. In regular season, rates run $180 to $299. Over the holidays, rates start at $195 and go up to $315. Suites available.

Services: Four areas offer food service, from sit-down dinners to quick snacks. All feature a rustic American theme. Two lounges sell firewater, one indoors and one poolside.

- Swimming
- Boat rentals
- Bicycling/walking paths lead to River Country and Fort Wilderness
- Children's program
- Gameroom
- Shopping

Transportation: Boats sail from the Wilderness Lodge dock to the Magic Kingdom. All other transportation — outside of walking or biking to Fort Wilderness — is by bus.

Phone: (407) 824-3200

EPCOT CENTER RESORTS

Yacht and Beach Club

From a management perspective, the Yacht Club and the Beach Club are two separate hotels. Each club has its own lobby, its own costuming, and its own employees. From a guest's perspective, however, they're two similar fantasies — two viewpoints on the same theme. Both share Stormalong Bay, a pool area so detailed that it's almost a water park in itself.

In many ways, the resorts appeal to the same type of people who might stay at the Grand Floridian but with different vacation goals. Turn-of-the-century folks might dress to the nines at the Grand Floridian because life goes on even when wintering in Florida. But during the summer, they leave their elegant apartments in New York

City and travel to the Jersey shore, staying at either their Yacht Club or their Beach Club. Here they're still rich, but more relaxed and on vacation, unwinding between multi-million dollar deals. For a moment, they might loosen their ties or let down their bustles.

Guests who enjoy the Grand Floridian also enjoy the Yacht and Beach Club, but many have a distinct preference for one over the other. The Grand Floridian feels more formal, as if guests are always at their best. The Yacht and Beach Club feels more relaxed, as if rich guests are among friends and can let their hair down. That's not to say any Disney resorts actually are formal. Shorts, Mickey ears, and crying kids can be found everywhere at Walt Disney World and only one restaurant in the entire complex requires jackets (not coincidentally at the Grand Floridian). But they feel different.

The Yacht Club carries a nautical theme throughout all decor. Clapboard exteriors, hardwood floors, brass, and external boardwalks imply that somewhere, unseen, a huge fleet of private yachts awaits your arrival. Rooms are sailing colors of blue accented by white furniture. The Beach Club, a bit more subdued, is framed by croquet courts, sand beaches, and palm trees. Rooms are light green. Accommodations at both resorts are spacious with two queen-sized beds and a small table. Larger suites available.

For the exclusive use of Yacht and Beach Club guests, Stormalong Bay is the nicest swimming area of all the Disney resorts. For adults who enjoy swimming but prefer to avoid the teenagers at the Disney water parks, Stormalong Bay combines the best aspects of a water park without the expense and inconvenience. One of two lagoons has whirlpools, jets, and rising sands. A second lagoon, offering less activities, is more relaxing. Beautifully landscaped and created, the swimming area sits on the shore of Crescent Lake. For those who prefer standard swimming pools, one can be found at each end of the complex.

Prices: During value season, rooms start at $229 per night for a standard room and go to $295 for a water view. During regular season, rooms run $244 to $315; over the holidays, $259 to $330. Concierge rooms are available at the Yacht Club only. In value season, they start at $380 and go to $395 for a lagoon view; regular season rates run $399 to $415; holiday season rates $415 to $430. Suites available.

Services: Six different places to eat — two under the auspices of the Yacht Club, two under the Beach Club, and two shared between them — offer a range of dining, from casual to elegant. Four lounges guarantee an unending supply of alcohol.

- Swimming
- Boat rentals
- Fitness Center
- Tennis
- Gameroom
- Children's Program
- Shopping

Transportation: Epcot Center is within walking distance, though accessed in World Showcase rather than by the main entrance. The Boardwalk Resort can also be reached on foot. Boats travel to Disney-MGM Studios.

Phone:(407) 934-7000 for the Yacht Club; (407) 934-8000 for the Beach Club

The BoardWalk Resort

The BoardWalk Resort is Disney's newest and includes both hotel rooms, a nighttime club area, and a selected number of time-share resort rooms booked through Disney's Vacation Club. As such, it's difficult to classify. Is it a resort to be placed in this chapter or a minor Disney park to be included elsewhere? Tough question, but since admission is free to the boardwalk (though not all the clubs), it's included here. The resort, opened in early 1996, completes the Epcot Resort area's Northeastern beach theme.

The main access to the Boardwalk Resort shops and restaurants is, of course, a boardwalk that fronts Crescent Lake, located across from Disney's Yacht and Beach Club. Three clubs offer a range of entertainment, all directed at adults over thirty. Viewed by Disney Imagineers as the mature traveler's Pleasure Island, the shows are more sophisticated than others found on property. The ESPN Club, for example, moves the usual corner bar and grill into the big time, signing on with the biggest name in sports broadcasting and offering virtual reality games as well as 70 television monitors. Jellyrolls, a piano bar specializing in "dueling pianos," is half-piano bar, half-comedy club with an emphasis on the latter. Of particular interest to mature travelers is the Atlantic Ballroom, a dance hall with an architectural slant circa 1930. The Atlantic Ballroom Orchestra — a permanent live band performing nightly — plays tunes from the '40s to the '90s. Admission costs $5 per person.

41

The Boardwalk's decor captures the feel of the beach, including a mismatched group of furnishings. Of course, in a real boardwalk hotel, mismatched means one object might actually clash with another. At a Disney boardwalk hotel, mismatched pieces flow together in some strange and interesting way. With 378 rooms, the BoardWalk Inn is about 1/3 the size of the Grand Floridian or the Yacht and Beach Club, the smallest upscale resort on property.

Rooms are spacious, comparable to other top-of-the-line Disney hotels.

Prices: While the Boardwalk appears to be a single hotel complex, it's actually two: the Boardwalk Inn and the Boardwalk Villas. The Boardwalk Inn compares to most other Disney resorts while the Villa is part of the Disney Vacation Club. For now, however, you may book a room in either area. To avoid confusion, look at it this way: the Boardwalk Inn has "normal" hotel rooms and the Boardwalk Villas are "furnished suites."

Boardwalk Inn rooms start at $229 per night for a standard room during value season and go up to $295 for a water view. In regular season, rooms run $244 to $315; over the holidays, $259 to $330. Standard concierge rooms start at $390 during value season and go up to $440 for deluxe accommodations. The same rooms cost $410 to $460 during regular season and $425 to $475 over the holidays. Suites available.

The cost of a Villa results from both size and view, with deluxe room categories enjoying a better skyline. In value season, standard studio rooms start at $229 with deluxe rooms costing $260. A one bedroom villa runs $295, one bedroom deluxe villa $340, a two bedroom standard $395, two bedroom preferred $445, and a three bedroom garden villa that sleeps twelve, $985. Regular season rates start at $244 standard studio, $280 standard studio preferred, $315 one bedroom villa, $350 one bedroom villa preferred, $415 two bedroom villa, $465 two bedroom villa preferred, and $995 three bedrooms. During the holidays, expect to pay $259 for a standard studio, $295 preferred studio, $330 one bedroom, $375 preferred one bedroom, $430 two bedroom, $480 preferred two bedroom, and finally, $1045 for twelve people in a three bedroom.

Services: In addition to the three clubs, four restaurants serve everything from sit-down dinners to ice cream and baked goods. Five sites serve cocktails.

- Tennis
- Professional grass croquet
- Swimming, with Coney Island slide and theme
- Biking
- Fishing
- Muscles and Bustles health club
- Children's Program
- Game room
- Shopping

Transportation: Epcot is accessible on foot, not far by Disney standards but a bit of a hike by couch potato standards. A water taxi connects to Disney-MGM Studios and Epcot.

Phone: (407) 939-5100 for the Boardwalk Inn; (407) 939-6200 for Boardwalk Villas

Walt Disney World Swan

The Swan and the Dolphin — independently owned and operated — have a symbiotic relationship. Both have the same style architecture and the same design scheme, unusual enough to have its own description — "entertainment" architecture. They face each other, both with gigantic sculptures on top. Both offer similar connections to parks. And, finally, both rely more on style than theme.

The Swan, managed by Westin and crowned by two gigantic blue swans weighing 14 tons each, relies on color, artistry, and unusual architecture. The theme might be described as waves and water and flowing designs. While not symbolic of anything specific, it's a fun, campy style that fits at Disney World but would be painfully out of place in New York City or Atlanta. It has a cartoon feel, as if *Alice in Wonderland* might be at home here.

The architectural design is cutting-edge and winner of national awards. Colors are bold, the lines of the buildings large and imposing. The style is carried through into the rooms, though on a smaller, more manageable scale. Each room has two queen size beds or one king in a variety of configurations. Suites are available.

Both hotels discount rates below those listed, based on anything from AAA membership to age. Because they are not Disney owned, however, you will find different deals. If not satisfied with the prices offered by Disney's Central Reservations, call both hotels directly.

Prices: Off-season, rates run from $250 to $290 for two adults. In high season (Christmas, Thanksgiving, and February through Easter), rates run from $280 to $320. Extra person charge $25 year-round. Concierge rooms costs $340 in value season and $370 regular. Suites available.

Services: Four restaurants feed almost every budget, from 24-hour service to Oriental cuisine and poolside snacks. A lobby lounge converts from morning breakfast to evening cocktails.

- Swimming in several spas, large lap pool, and themed grotto pool
- Boating
- Tennis
- Fitness Center
- Children's Program
- Gameroom
- Shopping

Transportation: Watercraft commute to Epcot and Disney-MGM Studios. Epcot Center can also be reached on foot, though it's a healthy hike.

Phone: (800) 248-SWAN or locally (407) 934-3000

Walt Disney World Dolphin

Sister to the Swan, the Dolphin is managed by Sheraton Hotels. Giant fish sit atop the building, an architectural balance to its neighbor's gargantuan swans. Similar in style and substance, the Dolphin's strongest visual image is hundreds of seven-story banana leaves painted across the building. Bright colors, stripes, designs, and walkways, give the building a larger-than-life feel.

Rooms sleep four.

Prices: In the off-season, rates run $245 to $305 for two adults. High season (early February through Easter), rates run from $285 to $365. Extra person charge an additional $15 per night. Concierge rooms cost $365 low season and $395 regular season. Suites available.

Services: No less than seven different locations serve food, though only four are true restaurants including one buffeteria and one specializing in Mexican cuisine. Three lounges serve cocktails.

- Swimming in three pools as well as a lakefront beach
- Boating
- Tennis
- Fitness Center including sauna and massage

- Gameroom
- Shopping

Transportation Epcot Center can be reached on foot. Watercraft commute to Epcot and Disney-MGM Studios.

Phone: (800) 227-1500 or locally (407) 934-4000

MODERATELY PRICED RESORTS

The Caribbean Beach Resort

The Caribbean Beach is fun. It's an island party, a reggae jam.

Located not far from Epcot, the resort sits by itself, too far to walk to any park, yet close enough to Epcot to be considered an "Epcot area resort." Two-story buildings circle a 42-acre lake, called Barefoot Bay. Five separate areas — thematically classified as different "islands" — include Aruba, Barbados, Jamaica, Martinique, and Trinidad. Walking from island complex to island complex is comparable to a Caribbean cruise that stops in a different port-of-call each day. While each section has identical accommodations, each reflects the architectural styling of their home island. Nuances of color and pattern change, reflecting the origins of an island's early settlers and the building materials found nearby. But all have bright paint and warm weather styling. The island theme is carried over to the food court and even the swimming pool.

Incoming guests register at the Custom House, a reception area near the main entrance. Old Port Royale, a food court located roughly in the center of the complex, was designed to look like a farmer's market and has seven different vendors. The main swimming pool surrounds an old Spanish fort, with sliding boards and other kid activities.

Because of the Caribbean Beach Resort's swimming pool with a slide and waterfalls, proximity to theme parks, and party atmosphere, it tends to be the favorite moderately priced accommodation for people traveling with children. Dixie Landings or Port Orleans is a better choice for those who want a sedate environment. In addition, the resort has a wide-open feel thanks to the lake, but by definition, guests must sometimes walk a long way to reach the front desk or food service. (The promenade around the lake is a full 1.4 miles. Even active adults might find this difficult after theme-parking all day.)

Busses stop at seven spots around the outside of the complex. When compared to Disney's high-rise hotels that have a single bus stop, you walk less but, thanks to the extra stops, spend more time on the bus.

In size, all moderately priced resort rooms at WDW are identical. All include two double beds, a double sink, and table with chairs. At the Caribbean Beach, the interiors, while colorful, are softer and more restful than the outside architecture. Price differences are based on view rather than size.

Prices: In value season, rates start at $114 per night for a standard view and go to $129 for a water view. In regular season, rates run $124 to $139; over the holidays, $134 to $149.

Services: One full service restaurant and a separate food court with six specialty areas. Pizza and light items available through room service. One lounge serves cocktails.

- Swimming in large themed pool, plus each "island" has its own pool
- Boat rentals
- Bicycling
- Jogging
- Gameroom
- Shopping

Transportation: Bus only.
Phone: (407) 934-3400

Dixie Landings

Dixie Landings and Port Orleans, built at the same time and existing side-by-side, share a similar theme and similar (Disney created) legend. Just as the Mississippi River winds through the old South before emptying into the Gulf of Mexico at New Orleans, the Sassagoula River (which is not really a river) winds through Dixie Landings and past Port Orleans where it empties into Downtown Disney.

Disney Imagineers worked overtime on the legend of Dixie Landings. The registration area resembles a steamship sitting on the river, with new guests booking passage on a cruise rather than into a hotel room. Across the water, Ol' Man Island is home to the swimming pool, playground, and fishing hole, and was built, according to legend, years ago for the kids by the original owner. Sidewalks bear the imprint of palms. From some mysterious location, banjos pick and guitars strum.

Rather than one large building, Dixie Landings is a series of smaller buildings sitting among the magnolias and Spanish moss. Styled after the plantation system somewhere around the time when Scarlett O'Hara attended parties at Twelve Oaks, the buildings closest to the river resemble large, pre-Civil War mansions. But as you travel deeper into Dixie Landings — into the "parishes" — the buildings become more impoverished, reflecting the poorer areas of the deep South.

The mansions sport massive columns and staircases along with stately decor. The more rustic rooms have weathered wood exteriors and tin roofs — no less accommodating but much less ornate. All rooms are fitted with brass and pedestal sinks, hickory bedposts, and quilted bedspreads. Because Dixie Landings is made up of separate buildings, it covers a lot of territory. If making a reservation, request a room close to the steamship (the main building) and explain that you need it for ease of walking. Disney folks are generally happy to help you.

The atmosphere at Dixie Landings closely matches that of the deep South, but with those Twentieth century touches — like air conditioning and flush toilets — that modern man cannot live without. Guests hailing from north of the Mason Dixon line particularly enjoy the change of pace.

Minus the decor, rooms are identical to those at the Caribbean Beach and Port Orleans with two double beds, two sinks, and small table with chairs. Selected rooms have king size beds and some have trundle beds. Price variations are based on view rather than room size.

Prices: In value season, rates start at $114 per night for a standard view and go to $129 for a water view. In regular season, rates run $124 to $139; over the holidays, $134 to $149.

Services: Guests enjoy either a sit-down restaurant or a food court with five separate counters. Pizza and light items available through room service. Cocktails are served both in the Cotton Co-Op Lounge and poolside.

- Swimming; five pools in addition to Ol' Man Island
- Fishing
- Bicycling

- Boat rentals
- Gameroom
- Shopping

Transportation: The Sassagoula River Cruise, a fifteen-minute trip that might include a retelling of the legend of Ol' Man Island and Dixie Landings, makes a stop at Port Orleans and continues on to Downtown Disney. All other transportation is by bus.

Phone: (407) 934-6000

Port Orleans

Jazz floats through the air and Mardi Gras decorations are in place. Guests discover the French influence everywhere — in decor, in music, even in the food. Walkways recreate the brick streets of New Orleans and the three story structure looks more like row houses than a single building. Colors are bright. The swimming pool — not the largest at Disney's moderately priced hotels but certainly its most original — relies on a sea serpent for decoration. Part of the serpent's back includes steps that cross the pool. Part of the serpent is a slide. Part is just decoration. Pool, walkway, and the street celebrate Mardi Gras, in a Disney-fied way.

The main building includes restaurants, stores, and check-in. Guest registration, like that at Dixie Landings, looks like something else. In this case, it's a bank. In a separate food court, giant masks float overhead with court jesters and Mardi Gras leftovers.

Port Orleans feels a bit more elegant than Dixie Landings and certainly more so than Caribbean Beach. Like other choices between Disney hotels, there's no actual difference between the three resorts — all offer similar amenities, restaurants, etc. — but the theme itself adds to the formality. The jazz at Port Orleans gives it a slight foreign feel (to those not from Louisiana) and an exciting push, as if a gathering of musical intellectuals awaits in each nook and cranny. Dixie Landings — from the guitar pickin' to the stately elegance — suggests a more genteel existence.

Port Orleans, with a mere 1,008 rooms, is also about half the size of Dixie Landings or the Caribbean Beach Resort. In addition, the three-story, row house style of architecture allows each room to be relatively close to the main entrance and centralized bus transportation, meaning a fair compromise between convenience and efficiency.

Port Orleans' rooms are identical to those at Dixie Landings and Caribbean Beach, though styled with pedestal sinks and Cajun motifs. Each room has two double beds, twin sinks, and table with chairs. Selected rooms have king size beds. Room price variations based on view only.

Prices: In value season, rates start at $114 per night for a standard view and go to $129 for a water view. In regular season, rates run $124 to $139; over the holidays, $134 to $149.

Services: A sit-down Cajun restaurant and a food court serve guests, plus pizza and light fare can be delivered to your room. Cocktails are served in the lounge and poolside.

- Swimming pool
- Bike rentals
- Boat rentals
- Gameroom
- Shopping

Transportation: The Sassagoula River Cruise makes a trip upstream to dock at Dixie Landings, and it travels downstream to Downtown Disney. Other WDW destinations are served by bus.

Phone: (407) 934-5000

Coronado Springs

Slated for a late September 1997 opening, Coronado Springs does for the American Southwest what the Caribbean Beach did for the islands southeast of Florida. Themed around a 15-acre lake, Coronado Springs has three areas that reflect the oceanfront, urban, and country areas of the American Southwest and Mexico. A new mid-priced hotel on par with Dixie Landings, Port Orleans, and the Caribbean Beach, it will be the first mid-priced Disney hotel to also have extensive convention facilities.

Prices: In value season, rates start at $114 per night for a standard view and go to $129 for a water view. In regular season, rates run $124 to $139; over the holidays, $134 to $149.

Services: A single sit-down restaurant and separate food court for fast food. Cocktails served in an indoor lounge and poolside.

- Swimming pool
- Bike rentals
- Boat rentals
- Fitness Center

- Gameroom
- Shopping

Transportation: Bus only to all destinations.
Phone: (407) 939-1000

BUDGET HOTELS

All-Star Resorts

These are the smallest, cheapest, and brightest Disney resorts to date. Certain Disney standards — cleanliness and friendliness, for example — are found everywhere at Disney. But the two All-Star resorts appeal to the budget hotel crowd, offering slightly smaller rooms and economy accommodations.

If you could take away the All-Star Resort's bigger-than-life decorations, you'd find row after row of hotel rooms identical in shape, style, and function. To make money in the hotel business, builders have to minimize their per-room construction cost. Disney accomplished that by using the same three-story floor plan over and over and over again.

But they disguised it. They pretend each building is unique by hiding it behind over-sized decorations. In the All-Star Resorts, giant Coke cups, enormous football helmets, monstrous cans of tennis balls, and a three-story jukebox overshadow the accommodations. A giant cowboy boot fits a size 270 foot, a monstrous top hat would please Paul Bunyan. In other words, the big decorations make you overlook the extra touches they don't include — namely, the amenities that cost money. The main lobby is functional — no wall-to-wall carpeting, no intricate architectural lay-out. (They have line drawings on the walls.) No bellboys. No beautifully decorated lounge area.

But rooms cost from $69 to $89. For those on a tight budget who plan to spend most of their time at theme parks, the All-Star Resorts make an on-site vacation possible. They're also a good choice for active people that do no more than sleep in a hotel room, dragging their tired patooties home from a park every day and then collapsing in total exhaustion. While some things are limited at the All-Star Resorts — the only food service is fast food and the only bars poolside, for example — there's still swimming in the large themed pools.

Although Disney carries the cartoonish theme into individual rooms — bedspreads are sports-decorated and bureaus resemble lockers — the in-room decor is more subtle than that found outside. Functional-sized rooms (meaning not very large) leave little space for ballroom dancing once you add in two double beds and a small table with chairs.

Because it's a budget hotel, expect more families with small children. But also because it's a budget hotel, fewer people spend a whole day at the pool, opting for other diversions instead. While other Disney resorts have larger rooms and more exotic themes, money saved by staying at the All-Star Resort can buy quite a few five-star dinners. Everything in life is a trade-off and many people skimp on hotel accommodations so they can spend their cash elsewhere. Future plans call for a third All-Star resort, perhaps themed to the movies.

Prices: A standard room costs $69 and a courtyard/landscape view $74 in value season; $79 to $84 regular season; $84 to $89 over the holidays.

Services: Both All-Star Resorts have a food court, each featuring several different choices, mainly simple fare like burgers, barbecue, and pizza. The only cocktail service is at the outdoor, poolside bars.

- Swimming
- Gameroom
- Shopping.

Transportation: Bus service only.

Phone: (407) 939-5000 for All-Star Sports; (407) 939-6000 for All-Star Music

FORT WILDERNESS

Camping means more than trees, barbecues, and an occasional deer. Camping means a different attitude about vacationing. While people staying in other Disney areas may never meet their next door neighbors, much less get to know them, campers usually introduce themselves, ask people where they're from, and lend sugar to the folks nearby. Each evening in Fort Wilderness, there's a campfire in the central meadow, free to all Disney guests. Chip 'n Dale show up and lead the crowd — mostly parents and children — in a camp song. Guests toast marshmallows and, after the singing, watch a classic Disney movie under the stars. It's not high entertainment, but it's a nice place to meet folks from around the world.

The good thing about Fort Wilderness is the amenities and woods. More activities are offered here than at any other resort on site. The bad thing about Fort Wilderness is traveling to other locations on Walt Disney World property.

Fort Wilderness has one main road that winds through the campground. Connected to that road are secondary paved roads that form small loops, home to the campsites and at least one air-conditioned restroom/shower. To travel somewhere on the Disney transportation system, campers must walk to the main road — a bit of a hike if you have a site in the back — and wait for a bus. In addition to picking up campers at each small loop, the bus stops at major recreation areas and Pioneer Hall, the campground's heart that includes a trading post, restaurant, and the Hoop-De-Doo Review, one of Disney's two dinner shows. Depending on which bus you board, it may also travel off-site to Wilderness Lodge and/or the Transportation and Ticket Center

Simple, really. However, depending on destination, the journey can require two (and sometimes three) modes of transportation. In some cases — traveling to the Grand Floridian, for example — you might take a bus to Pioneer Hall, then a boat to the Magic Kingdom, then a monorail to the Grand Floridian. That's fun the first time but gets old fast.

For new arrivals, the bus system can be confusing. Every Disney bus looks alike, but in most cases, has its destination displayed in front as well as on the side. But campground busses stop a number of places. For example, they can't call a bus "Transportation and Ticket Center" if it also stops at Pioneer Hall and every campsite loop. So at Fort Wilderness, they name their three bus routes "Crockett," "Boone," and "Internal." Posted signs list which busses go where. Internal busses make continuous loops around the campgrounds, a safe choice for on-site destinations, but Boone and Crockett service both on-site and off-site destinations and, adding to the where-the-hell-do-I-go confusion, they service different campsite loops.

The easiest advice: Consult the Disney Transportation Guide and follow the directions exactly. Or two, study the signs by the bus stop and wait until the appropriate bus shows up. Or three, wait until a bus pulls up, tell the driver where you want to go, and take their advice.

Given the lay-out of the campground, the system is as efficient as it can get, but still confusing. A Crockett bus, for example, may go where you want with only a stop or two along the way. But the same bus, boarded for your return trip back to the campsite, may spend a half-hour cross-Disney trekking before getting there. Further muddying the waters, an "internal" bus goes two different directions, meaning a trip from a campsite close to Pioneer Hall may take as little as two minutes or as long as twenty. On the positive side, memorizing the bus names and getting a working knowledge of the campground roads makes it easier. After just a few days, most campers become experts.

By driving or renting a car, you can avoid the hassle of waiting for buses and boats when traveling to outside-the-campground places. And, when driving your own car, the campground is actually more convenient than other resorts since you can park just a few feet from your front door. Note that you cannot drive around Fort Wilderness. They do, however, rent electric carts for approximately $25 per day, a smart option for those who hate waiting once they're ready to go somewhere. To book campsites close to Pioneer Hall, Settlement Trading Post, restaurants, beaches, and the petting zoo, request a spot in loops 100, 200, 300, or 400. For quieter camping farther from the action, request 1500 to 2000.

Campsites

Compared to other campgrounds, Fort Wilderness is top-of-the-line with private showers, spacious lots, clean accommodations, and landscaped grounds. There's a campsite available for every type of camper made, including some for those sleeping in a tent. No open fires are allowed in Fort Wilderness campsites, though marshmallows can be roasted over wood during the evening campfire in the Meadows. Preferred campsites have electric hook-ups, water, sanitary disposal, and cable TV; partial hook-ups only electricity and water. Pets are welcome in selected sites for an additional $3 per day charge.

Campsite Prices: Sites start at $35 in value season and go to $49. During regular season, $44 to $58. Over the holidays, $49 to $64. A separate tent-only area costs $15 per person and $10 for a screen-house. Weekly and monthly rates available.

Wilderness Homes

Disney's Wilderness Homes allow non-campers to enjoy the same camaraderie as those with tents and motor homes. Comparable in price to the Contemporary or Polynesian, these trailer homes come with kitchen supplies (dishes, pots, pans, etc.) and daily maid service. While not as stylish as staying elsewhere, the homes are comfortable and relaxing. In addition, preparing a meal yourself, especially breakfast, can save more than a few dollars when vacationing. One type of trailer home sleeps four adults and two children; another style sleeps four adults.

It's almost unfair to compare a Wilderness Home with other on-site accommodations. It's not as pretty. It's not as convenient. But it's also friendlier. In some ways, it's a different type of vacation — one that includes more human interaction and time with nature. Folks who never considered a Wilderness Home many times find it the preferred alternative. Selected homes accessible to the handicapped.

Wilderness Home Prices: Rates run from $185 value season to $215 regular season and $230 over the holidays.

Fort Wilderness Services: In addition to the Hoop-De-Doo review, a dinner show, one place currently serves food — a buffeteria. Crockett's Tavern, located in the same building and accessible to the restaurant, serves cocktails only.

- Swimming; in addition to the Fort Wilderness pools and a private beach on Bay Lake, guests may swim at River Country (with separate admission)
- Bike Rentals
- Petting Zoo
- Campfires (Complimentary, featuring Chip 'n Dale and followed by a Disney movie)
- Horseback riding
- Boat rentals (Both on Bay Lake and canoe rentals on the canals that wind throughout the campground)
- Tennis
- Camping sports — horseshoes, tetherball, volleyball, etc.
- Gameroom
- Shopping

Transportation: Bus to other parts of the campground. Watercraft also connect to the Magic Kingdom and the Contem— porary from Pioneer Hall. Bus service travels to other destinations with sometimes complicated connections at the TTC or theme parks.

Phone: (407) 824-2900

OTHER ON-SITE RESORTS

Disney's Old Key West Resort

A Disney-ized version of a timeshare resort, the Old Key West Resort is part of Disney's Vacation Club, but unsold timeshare rooms can be rented by weekly guests. Featuring a Grand-Floridian-meets-the-Caribbean-Beach decor, a wide range of room sizes can accommodate almost any number of people.

More an apartment than a hotel room, suites are stocked with essentials for cooking meals, cleaning dishes (in a dishwasher, of course), and relaxing. Optional luxuries might include a whirlpool tub in the master bedroom, terraces, and coffee makers. If traveling with children, these suites can be a blessing, allowing you to keep different hours by putting kids to sleep while you watch TV or read. You can also save money by preparing some meals yourself.

The themed atmosphere at Old Key West is relaxed, but not as much as at the Polynesian. Guests experience a sense-of-community, thanks to a full-time activities director in Conch Flats Community Hall, and a group clubhouse loaded with indoor activities such as table tennis and movie rentals. Outside, there's a sense of elegance lurking somewhere about, even though most guests wear the traditional tourist costume of shorts, cotton shirts, and cameras. Two adults with no intention of preparing meals in their hotel room might be better served staying at a different Disney resort. Those traveling with another couple or who enjoy cooking while on vacation will find Old Key West a good choice.

Note: Membership in the Disney Vacation Club is promoted heavily, with information stations set up all around Walt Disney World. Salespeople are not rude or pushy like many timeshare salesmen, nor is there a danger that they'll rip you off. The Vacation Club is even worth considering if you plan to regularly visit Disney and/or leave a vacation legacy for your children should you meet an untimely end. Still, Disney does not refer to its program as a "timeshare," and denies any similarity. While there are some subtle differences between Disney's Vacation Club and traditional timeshare resorts, in the real world, they're too similar to call anything else.

Within the Vacation Club, timeshare slots are exchangeable with 200 other premium resorts nationwide, including nearby Disney owned resorts in Vero Beach and Hilton Head Island in Georgia. In addition to purchasing a piece of Disney (though it expires in the year 2042), Vacation Club members enjoy other discounts including park admission for the duration of their stay. If interested, Disney cast members will be more than happy to fill you in on the details during your vacation or before you leave home.

Prices: In value season, a studio goes for $209 per night, a one bedroom for $285, two bedroom for $390, and a three bedroom, grand villa for $825. During regular season, a deluxe room costs $229, a one bedroom $305, a two bedroom $410, and a grand villa $845. Over the holidays, a deluxe room goes for $244, a one bedroom for $320, a two bedroom for $425, a three bedroom for $860.

Services: There are three ways to get food: a sit-down restaurant, a snack bar, and pizza delivery to your room. The Gurgling Suitcase serves cocktails.

- Swimming
- Sauna
- Baseball, shuffleboard, volleyball
- Tennis
- Fitness center
- Game room
- Shopping

Transportaion: All transportation by bus.

Phone: For Old Key West, call (407) 827-7700; for Vero Beach Resort, call (800) 359-8000; for Hilton Head, call (800) 453-4911

The Villas at the Disney Institute

The most hotel-like resort owned by Disney, the Villas at the Disney Institute are actually a couple different hotel styles located in the same place. The Disney Institute, which premiered in February of 1996, initially siphoned off two hotel areas — the Bungalows and Town Houses — for the use of Institute guests, though bookings have been weaker than Disney hoped. A unique type of Disney vacation package described in the chapter on "Other WDW Attractions," the Disney Institute operates somewhat independently from the rest of Disney World. Currently, the Villas house both Institute and non-Institute guests.

Staying here involves a trade-off. The smallest rooms have at least a wet bar and refrigerator, the largest a full kitchen. In other words, these can literally be a "home away from home." On the down-side, they're farther from the theme parks and other activities than their sister Disney resorts. Located next to Downtown Disney, however, shopping is convenient. In addition to nearby Typhoon Lagoon, guests may enjoy the Institute's restaurants and luxury items (such as massage) for an additional fee.

While all Disney resorts have immaculate landscaping, the architectural style of the Villas fit easily into the lay of the land, incorporating nature into the overall design. Its theme — if it had one — might be "Florida Wilderness" thanks to location and brown, earthy decor. While locals may find it routine, it appeals to those from out-of-state. The Lake Buena Vista Golf Course winds around selected villas and mature trees shade many of the other buildings. Some accommodations sit under a thick forest, their views spanning Disney waterways.

Accommodations at the Villas vary. The smallest units have an L-shaped construction with a sitting area on one end and a bedroom area on the other. Small one bedroom accommodations have a living room with pull-out bed and a king-size bed in the bedroom, sleeping four comfortably. Treehouse Villas — one of the most unique and attractive accommodations on Disney property — feature second-floor living in a private "treehouse." Individual treehouses sit in the woods with land separating one from the other. A wide balcony circles the exterior and the view includes wildlife, Disney canals, and lots of trees.

The Villas at the Disney Institute are a good choice for those who don't care to spend time at a themed hotel and for those most concerned with golf or other resort amenities. Because of its far-from-the-action-location, it's not the preferred choice for families with small children, but many stay here anyway since it's also one of the few accommodations that offers full kitchen facilities and sleeping space for more than five people. For those taking the entire family, four Grand Vista Homes are also available. These spacious homes come ready to go, featuring stocked kitchens. Bikes and golf carts are included in the cost.

Prices: Rates run from $195 per person value season for a Bungalow, to $285 for a one bedroom vacation villa, $320 for a two bedroom villa, $355 for a treehouse, and $375 for a two bedroom fairway villa. During regular season, rooms cost $215 for a one bedroom club suite, $305 for a one bedroom vacation villa, $340 for a two bedroom villa, $375 for a treehouse, and $400 for a two bedroom fairway villa. Over the holidays, a one bedroom club suite runs $230, a one bedroom vacation villa $320, a two bedroom vacation villa $355, a treehouse $390, and a two bedroom fairway villa $415. Grand Vista Homes run $975 to $1,150 value and regular season, $995 to $1,185 over Christmas.

Services: There are no private resort restaurants, but Downtown Disney and the Four Seasons restaurant in the Disney Institute fill the void. Depending on villa location, however, Downtown Disney ranges from "somewhat convenient" to "way over there." Many people cook for themselves and groceries can be delivered to your door. The Seasons' Lounge is the sole site for cocktails, but nearby Pleasure Island has a huge selection. Many on-site activities are also part of the Disney Institute and unavailable at certain times.

- Swimming in one of five pools
- Golf
- Biking
- Fitness Center
- Tennis
- Gameroom
- Shopping

Tranportation: Certain sections are close enough to Downtown Disney that able-bodied visitors can walk. Other WDW destinations are serviced by bus. Due to the size of the resort, the buses stop at various points along the way.

Phone: (407) 827-1100

DISNEY VILLAGE HOTEL PLAZA

Living in the gray area between on-site and off-site hotels, the seven Hotel Plaza resorts offer some of the on-site amenities enjoyed by other guests, but not all. Many hotels were recently refurbished and all now sport coordinating pastel colors that make them appear more homogenous. Guests can walk to Downtown Disney though it's a long hike from some properties. Each has some kind of transportation service to at least the major parks, but guests do not have complete access to all Disney areas nor unlimited use of Disney's own transportation system. And, since the individual hotel's relationship to

Disney is based on contractual obligations, the figures keep changing. If considering one of these hotels, refer to the questions in the next chapter on off-site hotels and use them as a guideline when booking. While these hotels are on-site, and therefore more convenient, they are still fairly far from the three major parks.

Remember that the day-to-day running of these hotels comes under the control of private management and not the Walt Disney Company. That in no way means they're a bad choice, only that they must be analyzed separately. Deposit rules, check-in time, check-out time, and other details are established by individual properties and may differ from Disney-owned resorts.

For specific information, telephone the hotels directly. While those affiliated with a national chain can be reserved through an "800" number, dialing the hotel directly may net you a lower room rate using the booking suggestions covered in the chapter on off-site hotels. Currently, many now concentrate on convention business.

Buena Vista Palace

With over 1,000 rooms, this is the largest hotel in the Village area. It has suites, nonsmoking rooms, rooms for guests with disabilities, restaurants, lounges, and other resort amenities. Rates run about $150 to $250 per room; $240 to $455 for suites.

Address: Buena Vista Palace, 1900 Buena Vista Drive, Lake Buena Vista, FL 32830

Phone: (407) 827-2727 or (800) 327-2990

Grosvenor

With a slight Caribbean feel, the Grosvenor has all the standard amenities: swimming pools, tennis courts, etc. Restaurants and a lounge are located on site, plus a Sherlock Holmes Museum. Rooms for the disabled available. Rates from about $115 to $175 year round, $195 to $495 for suites.

Address: Grosvenor, 1850 Hotel Plaza Boulevard, Lake Buena Vista, FL 32830

Phone: (800) 624-4109 or locally (407) 828-4444

Doubletree Guest Suites

Doubletree Guest Suites is a fairly small, all-suite hotel located a fair distance from Downtown Disney. With a two-story aviary and one restaurant, the hotel enjoys a small-time atmosphere that is lost in some of the bigger hotels. Rates from about $130 to $239.

Address: Doubletree Guest Suites Resort, 2305 Hotel Plaza Boulevard, Lake Buena Vista, FL 32830

Phone: (800) 222-8733 or locally, (407) 934-1000

Hilton

The main entrance sports palm trees with thousands of miniature white lights. Sitting on 23 acres, rooms are upscale and tasteful. No less than seven restaurants and lounges serve those with a gnawing hunger and those with a taste for spirits. Rates range from about $195 to $255, suites $459 to $759. A number of rooms are handicapped accessible.

Address: Hilton at Walt Disney World Village, 1751 Hotel Plaza Boulevard, Lake Buena Vista, FL 32830

Phone: (800) 782-4414 or locally (407) 827-4000

Courtyard by Marriott

Featuring a glass elevator and towering atrium, the Marriott (formerly Howard Johnsons) sits between I-4 and Hotel Plaza Boulevard. It features three swimming pools, playground, exercise rooms and a restaurant. Rooms for the disabled available. Rates run about $79 to $169 year-round.

Address: Courtyard by Marriott 1805 Hotel Plaza Boulevard, Lake Buena Vista, FL 32830

Phone: (800) 782-4414 or locally (407) 827-4000

Royal Plaza

Every room in the Royal Plaza has a balcony or patio, including ten suites and two celebrity suites. It has all resort amenities, including a men's and a women's sauna. Restaurant and lounges on property. Recently renovated. Rates run about $99 to $159; suites from $139 to $189. Rooms for the disabled available.

Address: Royal Plaza, 1905 Hotel Plaza Boulevard, Lake Buena Vista, FL 32830

Phone: (800) 248-7890 US or locally (407) 248-7890

Travelodge

This tower hotel has two restaurants and a top-floor lounge that offers a panoramic view of Lake Buena Vista. It features a gameroom, pool, and playground. Rooms about $99 to $169, suites $199 to $299. A limited number of rooms for the disabled are available.

Address: 2000 Hotel Plaza Boulevard, Lake Buena Vista, FL 32830

Phone: (800) 348-3765 or locally (407) 828-2424

OFF-SITE HOTELS

64 Major Hotel Areas "Outside The World"
US 192/Kissimmee • Lake Buena Vista •
International Drive • Orlando • Orange Blossom
Trail

66 Elderhostels

67 Questions to Ask When Booking an
Off-Site Hotel

Chapter Five

OFF-SITE HOTELS

There are a number of reasons to stay off Disney property. Many guests, especially those visiting for the second, third, or even tenth time, may include one Disney day in their vacation itinerary, but otherwise, they plan to see other things in Orlando. Off-site hotels are not only less expensive, but they also offer easier access to non-Disney destinations. Some hotels, the Hyatt Grand Cypress and the Peabody, for example, rival the best accommodations within Walt Disney World, with luxury amenities in a self-contained resort. Other hotels offer rates as low as $35.00 per night in the off-season, a weekly savings of almost $250.00 compared to a one-week stay at Disney's least expensive resort.

But be wary when booking "a deal." The Disney name guarantees a high level of cleanliness and service, not to mention employees that bend over backwards to satisfy a complaining guest. Should you book a room at the All-Star resort and, once there, wish for something grander, you can easily transfer to another other Disney-owned property. No such guarantee comes with most off-site accommodations, even if the hotel is affiliated with a major chain.

If booking an inexpensive hotel, refer to an independent source for a referral, either a friend who visited recently or an unbiased guide, such as AAA's (Automobile Club of America) TourBook for Florida. The book is free to AAA members. Many budget hotel deals come from small, independently owned places not affiliated with a national chain nor with access to an international reservation system. Most are located along US 192 near Kissimmee or Disney's Maingate and were built when Disney first opened. Some even predate the attraction (and some look it). While cheap rooms can be found, however, an inexpensive hotel with a low guidebook rating is not worth your time unless money is extremely tight.

There is one rule-of-thumb when booking off-site hotels: The closer you are to Disney World, the higher the price. A few years ago, one hotel near US 192 and Florida's turnpike offered a $25.00 per night rate for "as many people as you can fit into the room." Unfortunately, to get to Disney World you had to go through downtown Kissimmee and a number of red lights during the busiest times of the day. In this case, the room was clean, but not worth the added inconvenience for anyone other than poor college students on spring break.

MAJOR HOTEL AREAS "OUTSIDE THE WORLD"

US 192

US 192 runs east to west, intersecting I-4 on the south side of Walt Disney World. World Drive, the main artery into Walt Disney World, begins as an exit off US 192. Twenty-five years ago, when the Magic Kingdom was Disney's only theme park, the US 192 entrance served all traffic and was referred to as Disney's "maingate." This "maingate" designation, while historically accurate, is a bit misleading since there are now other entrances, specifically an I-4 exit leading directly to Epcot. But to keep crowds flowing smoothly, the Disney people try to divide traffic evenly between all entrances. In truth, all Disney World roads can access each other just as you can take twenty different routes to get to the grocery store from your home. One way may be faster or more direct, but other routes still get you there.

A few US 192 hotels are actually closer to Disney-MGM Studios and Epcot Center than some on-site hotels. When booking a US 192 hotel, determine how close it really is to Disney. Many hotels on US 192 include the word "maingate" in their name, such as the "Days Inn Maingate West" or "Econo Lodge Maingate Hawaiian Resort." Some are close to the maingate entrance; others are not.

In general, commute times to Disney World property are reasonable if the hotel is located west of Kissimmee. Even if you stay a few miles away, you will face only a few red lights and moderate traffic. If the hotel is located within, or east of, Kissimmee, plan to face some congestion and red lights as your drive through town.

Lake Buena Vista

Close to Disney property, the Lake Buena Vista (LBV) hotels offer easy access to Downtown Disney and Typhoon Lagoon. Located across the street (US 535) from the on-site Village Resorts, hearty guests can even walk to Downtown Disney from selected hotels. However, it's a long haul, and trying to cross busy US 535 makes the task too challenging to consider it an asset.

Lake Buena Vista is not as close to the major Disney parks as some US 192 hotels, though most LBV hotels offer complimentary shuttle buses to the Magic Kingdom, Epcot, and the Disney-MGM Studios. The LBV area is not a major entrance to WDW nor a main artery that other tourists pass through nor home to any minor Orlando attractions. For those reasons, it's less congested and cleaner than other off-site hotel areas.

The Lake Buena Vista designation is confusing because it's not only an area, it's a town. To the US Postal Service, Walt Disney World's mailing address, regardless of resort, is Lake Buena Vista. But even though the Grand Floridian and the Comfort Inn both have a Lake Buena Vista address, don't assume that you can walk from one to the other or that they're both Disney-owned. For the purposes here, Lake Buena Vista refers only to the off-site area to the north of US 535, directly adjacent to WDW property.

International Drive

Running parallel to I-4, International Drive (referred to as "I-Drive" by locals) has a heavy hotel concentration and a few non-Disney attractions, including Belz Factory Outlet Mall, Wet 'N Wild, Ripley's Believe It Or Not Museum, and an array of dinner shows. Located at the southern end of International Drive (by the Beeline Expressway — State Road 528 — that connects I-4 to the Orlando International Airport) is the Orange County Convention Center. A few blocks farther south is Sea World.

International Drive is difficult to navigate during slow seasons and downright impossible during busy ones. Thanks to thousands of driveways leading into the hotels and attractions, cars constantly exit and enter the highway. Add to that a number of traffic lights and people who "don't really know where they're going," and you may decide to avoid this area. It's certainly not closest to Disney World. On the plus side, International Drive has good hotels, including some all-suite resorts as well as mammoth budget hotels with inexpensive rooms. The closeness of the hotels and shops, while a visual disadvantage, aids people who like to walk to dinner and shopping.

If considering an International Drive location, ask the reservation agent where the hotel is located and try to book something on the southern end. Hotels south of the Sand Lake Road intersection don't experience as much bumper-to-bumper congestion or that pushed-together feeling as hotels to the north. They are, however, closer to the Orange County Convention Center, so ask if any large conventions will be in town over your stay.

Orlando

As a medium-sized city, Orlando has a number of downtown hotels used mainly by business travelers. While "Orlando" and "Walt Disney World" are synonymous to many people, they're actually 15 miles apart. Downtown hotels, an excellent choice for adults who wish to visit Church Street Station on a regular basis, are inconvenient for those planning extensive theme park excursions. Traffic in downtown Orlando, while no match for New York City, is still thick over rush hours and should be avoided if possible.

Orange Blossom Trail

This Orlando road runs north to south and connects to US 192 east of Walt Disney World. The few hotels here offer good rates year-round because they're located in what can euphemistically be called Orlando's red-light district. While hotels tend to be fenced-in and many have 24-hour security, the trade-off in safety is not worth the savings.

ELDERHOSTELS

Not a hotel, per se, the Elderhostel program offers adults over 60 (a spouse must be at least 50) an educational vacation and a few operate within driving distance of Walt Disney World and Orlando. None, however, can be considered extremely convenient. Two Elderhostels — one in Oviedo and one in Wekiva Springs — are slightly less than an hour from Walt Disney World.

The Elderhostel program is a camp for intelligent adults. Instead of stringing beads in a craft shop, however, campers expand their horizons and share ideas with fellow seniors, tapping into the resources of nearby universities as they take college-level, Liberal Arts courses. A non-profit organization, Elderhostels can be found throughout the U.S., Canada, and in 49 foreign countries. Tuition ranges from $350 to $500 per person and includes all meals and instruction; transportation to and from the Elderhostel is not covered though it can be arranged.

While Elderhostel may not be the most convenient way to see Walt Disney World, it stands on its own in value and style. For more information, contact Elderhostel through their headquarters at:
Elderhostel
75 Federal Street
Boston, MA 02110
Phone: (617) 426-8056

QUESTIONS TO ASK WHEN BOOKING AN OFF-SITE HOTEL

1. Is that your least expensive room?

To obtain the lowest possible rate, call the hotel directly, even if they're affiliated with a national company that offers an "800" number. Most hotels are franchised, meaning that local reservation agents may be empowered to offer lower rates than those quoted by a national reservation agent.

When you first call, expect reservation agents to quote their most expensive room rate, hoping you will immediately accept. Push them until they reveal the absolute cheapest room, no matter its location or condition. Even if you're willing to pay a little more for a good view or a larger room, first determine their lowest price and use it as a baseline for comparison. Once you know the baseline, you can decide if an upgrade is worth the extra cost.

Second, ask about discounts. Hotels routinely discount room costs to any group or affiliation member. Just being a senior citizen is often enough; sometimes AARP works; many times, membership in AAA is enough. Some hotels save their best discounts for corporations but have extremely lax rules on the requirements to get this "corporate discount." In the end, don't be afraid to ask the reservation agent, "What is your lowest discounted rate and who is eligible for it?" The only time you should pay full rack rate (hotelier's term for full price) for any room, anywhere, is in a time of high demand, such as Christmas or when the Olympic Games are in town.

When making a reservation and confirming a rate, note the name of the person who booked you, the date, and that person's department. While most agents guarantee your reservation with a confirmation number, computers are still imperfect machines. A few extra details are worth their weight in gold if, upon arrival, you're told that they're "sorry, but there's nothing in the computer."

2. How close are you to Disney?

A hotel advertising "two miles to Walt Disney World" means exactly that — two miles until you set foot on Disney-owned land. But since the Disney resort covers 43-square miles, it may be a long haul from your hotel to the Magic Kingdom or Epcot. Still, distance-from-Disney is the best way to judge convenience. If the hotel reservation agent gives you a driving time to Disney, such as "it's only ten minutes by car," press for specifics. If they don't know the actual mileage, book elsewhere. Almost everyone wants to know the distance to Disney World and, unless it's the reservation agent's first day on the job, he's hiding something.

3. Can I park my car right outside the room?

On the positive side, a convenient parking space saves steps. On the negative side, hotels with convenient parking are more accessible to thieves. If it's a long trek from car or bus to your room, then it's a long way for a thief to run too.

4. What kind of locks are used — credit card or key?

As hotels update, they move to the credit card locks. These cards don't carry your room number on them, meaning that if lost, a thief would still not know which room was yours. In addition, the code can be changed making each key, in effect, your own. Previous occupants cannot lie and say they lost their key, only to return later to steal from the next renter.

5. When was the hotel refurbished last?

It's best if a) it's not being refurbished during your stay, or b) it's not scheduled for refurbishment right after you leave. Some hotels, notably along the US 192 corridor but also elsewhere, are over 25-years old. Some are in great shape. Some are not. If they have recently refurbished some rooms, request one of the "new" ones, receive a guarantee, and note the name of the person you talked to. Make sure loud construction will not interfere with your vacation.

6. Do you have a (fill in the blank)?

As a great crime detective once said, assume nothing. If you like a big breakfast, ask about a buffet or special. Many hotels offer deals. Almost all hotels have a pool, but ask anyway if you plan to swim. If traveling during the winter months, ask if the pool is heated or even open. Is there a shuttle to Disney World? Is it complimentary? Many hotels have no shuttle or, if they do, they charge for the trip.

Note that many hotels do not serve lunch in their restaurants. Most guests eat breakfast and then head out to the theme parks, returning in time for dinner. If you expect to spend time relaxing at the hotel, ask what restaurants are located nearby.

7. What are the cancellation penalties?

Most hotels have no penalties if you cancel the reservation within one to three days prior to arrival. However, ask. Bargain rooms many times carry substantial cancellation penalties since the hotel works on a slim profit margin.

8. Would you please mail me a brochure?

After reading the brochure, if the hotel is not what you hoped for, make other arrangements.

MONEY QUESTIONS

71   Allocating Vacation Dollars: What Do You
       Want to See?

72   Walt Disney World Tickets: Options, Costs
       Options For Everyone • On-Site Guests •
       Magic Kingdom Club Members • Florida Residents •
       Military Guests

79   Tickets: Where to Buy

80   Discounted Tickets

81   Discounted Coupons to Other Area
       Attractions

Chapter Six

MONEY QUESTIONS

The Walt Disney World Resort accepts American Express, Visa, MasterCard, and the Disney credit card at most locations. They accept only cash at a few small sites, notably some fast food restaurants.

In addition, Disney prints its own money, with cartoon character's faces in the center spots usually occupied by Washington, Lincoln, and Hamilton. These "Disney dollars" add to the fantasy of a different "world" — one that even prints its own currency. And, of course, it's a big money maker for the Disney corporation. Disney dollars are exchangeable with U.S. dollars on an equal value (i.e., a $5 Disney dollar equals $5 U.S.). If you want an expensive souvenir, take one home. If not, exchange them for U.S. currency before you leave.

ALLOCATING VACATION DOLLARS: WHAT DO YOU PLAN TO SEE?

In dreams, the perfect vacation involves little planning beyond choosing a destination. Once you arrive, you go to bed when you want, rise when you want, decide over breakfast what you feel like doing, and when good and ready, you do it. The problem in converting this "dream plan" to reality is that, by the time you're ready to do something in Orlando, you pay top dollar for it and, upon arrival, find that it's crowded. To make things worse, once you return home, you discover from friends that you missed "the most beautiful garden in the world," or "the greatest ride," or "the best darn seafood anywhere" — all because you didn't plan.

A Walt Disney World vacation is a little like life. You plan for the future in case you live to be a hundred, but you also live for today in case you drop dead tomorrow. If money is limited, you must balance your desire for a good hotel against your desire to have four or five top-of-the-line dinners. Would you prefer to spend time golfing or swimming by the pool? If swimming, you may want to pay for a better hotel. If golfing, you may want to book a location close to a course.

By not planning at all, your commute time from hotel to attraction may be inconvenient. Or you may have a rental car that you don't need because you're staying on Disney property and using their transportation system. Or you may stay on Disney property and still wish that you had a car because you want to drive to Cypress Gardens. Most people don't want their vacation planned day-by-day, but by formulating a general plan of attack, you can cut expenses for things you don't care about and spend more money on things you do.

WALT DISNEY WORLD TICKETS: OPTIONS, COSTS

The Disney ticket prices listed below are probably wrong. They were correct as we went to press, but a great man once said that change is the only sure thing in life. Never-the-less, the listed prices (which do not include tax of 6%) should at least serve as a guideline. Assume a 5% increase overall and budget accordingly.

Each type of ticket allows one full day's admission, meaning you may leave the park and return the same day without paying again. If planning to return, make sure you get your hand stamped at the exit (they use invisible ink that can be seen only under a black light) and be prepared to show both your stamped hand and your pass or ticket when you return. This works if returning to the same park you left and also if you transfer to a different Disney park — assuming you have a pass that allows you to park hop.

Disney sells no two- or three-day park passes to the general public, only one-, four-, or five-day passes. Many people think this is unfair, that Disney has only three parks (temporarily) and, if not a two-day, they should at least sell at a three-day pass. (In Disney lan-

guage, a "pass" is a single admission price paid for multiple days at
the parks and a "ticket" is good for only one day.)

Realistically, Disney *should* sell a three-day pass. For many people
— especially those visiting the resort for the second or third time — a
two- or three-day, all-three-parks pass would be ideal. But Disney
exists to make money and, like any profitable corporation, certain
Disney executives keep a close eye on the bottom line. If purchasing a
four-day pass, guests have a financial incentive to spend their tourist
dollars within Disney World rather than visit the competition. That
helps Disney's bottom line. A lot. While not ideal, it's best to look
upon the pass system as a necessary — and understandable — evil.

In other words, you don't get world class attractions without
someone, somewhere, finding the money to pay for them. In Walt
Disney's day, his brother, Roy, took care of the boring financial
details, freeing Walt to explore creative endeavors. Today, others handle it. In the future, expect even more confusion with the 1998 premiere of Disney's Animal Kingdom and a whole new array of ticket
packaging.

If you want to enjoy the magic, you gotta pay the magician.

Disney Ticket Options Available to Everyone

1-Day/1-Park-Only Ticket: $38.50 plus tax; Child (3-9) $31.00
plus tax. The simplest ticket option, this covers one park for one-day.
(Either the Magic Kingdom, Epcot, or Disney-MGM Studios.)
Guests may leave and return to the chosen park but they may not
visit other parks on the same ticket. Price includes limited use of the
WDW transportation system.

4-Day Value Pass: $129.00; Child pass (3-9) $103.00 plus tax.
Like buying four separate 1-day/1-park tickets, this includes a one-
day admission to the Magic Kingdom, one-day to Epcot, and one-day
to Disney-MGM Studios. The fourth day's admission is a wild card,
exchangeable at any one — and only one — of the three parks. In
other words, you visit your favorite park twice. The pass also includes
limited use of the WDW transportation system.

Passes never expire, so if you use only three-days, keep the pass
for your next trip. Passes state that they are not exchangeable and,
contractually, you agree to those rules when you buy the ticket. That
makes it *unethical* to use a pass purchased by someone else or to sell

remaining days to other visitors. With that said, however, it's done all
the time. People who want three days at a Disney park buy a 4-day
pass and sell or give the remaining day to others.

4-Day Park-Hopper Pass: $144.00; Child pass (3-9) $115.00
plus tax. Allows four days of park admission but without the only-
one-park-per-day rule. You may visit Epcot in the morning, the
Magic Kingdom in the afternoon, and MGM in the evening. (And
then have a mild coronary somewhere around midnight.) The pass
also includes unlimited use of the WDW transportation system and
unused days are good forever. If you're 60-years-old and plan to ride
Splash Mountain on your 100th birthday, save that pass with the
remaining days. You won't be required to buy a new ticket in the year
2037.

5-Day World-Hopper Pass: $196.00; Child pass (3-9); $157.00
plus tax. The theme park visitation privileges are identical to the 4-
day Park-Hopper pass but with a) another day of unlimited park-
hopping and b) admission to Disney's minor parks. For those who
wish to see all of Disney in one week, this pass puts the "world" at
your feet. Admission to the smaller parks — Typhoon Lagoon,
Blizzard Beach, Pleasure Island, River Country, and Discovery Island
— is valid for seven days only, from the day of the first stamp. In
other words, if you plan to visit the Magic Kingdom on a Monday,
you have seven days, starting on that Monday, to enjoy the smaller
parks. The five major theme park days are valid forever. Pass also
includes unlimited use of the WDW transportation system.

Since the cost of a 5-Day World-Hopper Pass reflects the small-
parks perk, make sure you want to take advantage of it. (Each smaller park is described in the chapter "Other WDW Attractions.") If
planning to only visit Pleasure Island, for example, you may find it
cheaper to buy a 4-Day Park-Hopper pass and a single admission to
Pleasure Island.

Annual Pass: $236.00; Child pass (3-9) $205.00 plus tax. Unlimited
admission to the three major parks for an entire year. Also includes
parking fees.

Premium Annual Pass: $329.00; Child pass (3-9) $289.00 plus tax.
Unlimited admission to the three major parks for an entire year, along

with unlimited admission to Discovery Island, Pleasure Island, River Country, Blizzard Beach, and Typhoon Lagoon. Also includes parking fees.

Discovery Island: $11.95; Child pass (3-9) $6.50 plus tax. Expect Discovery Island to close in 1997 due, in part, to the premiere of Disney's Animal Kingdom.

River Country: $14.75; Child pass (3-9) $11.50. Annual pass $55.25; child $55.25

Blizzard Beach or Typhoon Lagoon: $23.95; Child (3-9) $17.95. Annual pass $84.95; child $67.95.

Pleasure Island: $16.95 (must be 18 or older). Annual pass $40.95.

Disney Ticket Options Available Only to On-Site Guests

"**Length of Stay**": For those who want all of Walt Disney World at their fingertips, on-site guests can visit the parks of their choice — both major and minor — the entire time they stay within Walt Disney World. The pass is good from the moment they arrive through the day of departure, including the time after check-out.

For those who plan to visit a Walt Disney World park every day, the cost of a Length of Stay pass compares favorably to a five-day World Hopper Pass, though the difference is not substantial. Whether or not it's a good value depends on how much time you spend at the major and minor parks. If you don't use one day on a World-Hopper Pass, that day is still valid for a future admission. With the "Length of Stay" pass, that day is simply lost.

From a psychological stand-point, (in other words, if money is no object), the Length of Stay pass bestows spontaneity. Using simple math skills, a one-day admission from a four-day World Hopper pass costs $34.25 plus tax. Most people will not spend $34.25 to enter Epcot at 8:00 p.m., only to enjoy dinner in a French restaurant. But Length of Stay guests, able to go where they want when they want, can do what they want. Prices start around $175 for four-day's admission and go up to $300 for ten-days; children (3-9) run about $140 to $250.

Magic Kingdom Club (MKC)

The Magic Kingdom Club is a Disney subsidiary that markets vacations through a membership plan that is either free through company personnel departments or sold directly to members who pay a fee to join. Many government branches and large private employers participate, though individual workers are sometimes unaware of it.

The Magic Kingdom Club works to Disney's advantage in several ways. For one, it's a marketing tool — a way of publicizing the theme parks at a relatively low cost. Disney gets free advertising on company bulletin boards and through flyers. Two, it appears that these other companies endorse Disney. If AT&T, for example, offers all employees a Disney World discount, it logically follows that AT&T considers WDW a place worth visiting. (Not only do children pressure their parents to take them to Disney World at home, now their employer nudges them to go when they're at work.)

Three, the Magic Kingdom Club is a Disney-owned travel agency. When people book their trip directly, Disney saves money on commissions normally paid to travel agents — generally 10% on the cost of a hotel room. You get a cheaper vacation; Disney makes more money. The only loser is your travel agent.

Since large companies offer a smorgasbord of benefits, contact your company's personnel office for more information and to find out if you're a member. Magic Kingdom Club benefits may also be extended to retired workers. For people not working in a member company, anyone can join the Magic Kingdom Club at a cost of $65 for two years, or $55 for travelers 55 and over. Travel benefits are the same, but paid membership also includes a two-year subscription to *The Disney Magazine,* a quarterly publication focusing on new developments in the Disney parks and inside information on company movies. If planning a Disney trip, the cost of MKC admission is worth the price.

Applications to join the Magic Kingdom Club may be picked up at any Disney Store. To order by phone, call (800) 41-DISNEY. Allow at least two weeks for delivery.

Savings for MKC members are subject to change. On the price of admission, the Magic Kingdom Club currently saves members 4% to 15% off the amount paid by non-members. Passes in high demand — specifically the four-day or five-day park hopper pass — net the smallest discount, 4% and 5% respectively. The three water parks, Discovery Island, and Pleasure Island save 7% to 9%, and MKC members can save almost 15% on a Pleasure Island admission. Through the Magic Kingdom Club, selected hotel rooms and restaurants are discounted 10% to 15%, along with selected merchandise in the Disney Village Marketplace and Pleasure Island. (*Selected* is the key word here, though it is not deceptive advertising. Most merchandise, hotel rooms, and restaurants charge slightly cheaper rates to Magic Kingdom Club members — non-discounted exceptions are top-of-the-line products.) This benefit alone saves many vacationers the price of MKC membership.

In addition, MKC members who live in Florida can share in the Florida resident discounts. While percentages vary, the deals are usually similar to other Florida specials (see next section), but discounted an additional 5% or so.

Florida Residents

Walt Disney World offers a number of discounts to Florida residents. All require proof of residency. While a driver's license works best, "proof" is a somewhat flexible concept and can include electric bills, property leases, etc. (Showing up with a great tan, however, is not enough.)

Generally, Florida residents enjoy cheaper prices in the off-season. For adults with flexibility, that's the best time to visit anyway. Most deals are short-term and change from year-to-year. The year Blizzard Beach opened, for example, Disney offered a two-for-one plan where residents could enjoy a theme park one day and visit River Country the next, all at a rate lower than the regular price for a one-day park admission. River Country, Disney's oldest and smallest water park, expected few guests during the off-season thanks to competition from Blizzard Beach. Recognizing that River Country's day-to-day costs run about the same whether the pools are full of guests or completely empty — and that most visitors also spend money on food and souvenirs once there — Disney made money on the deal by increasing costs only marginally. A number of in-state visitors who live over four hours away, such as those in the Miami/Fort Lauderdale area, spent extra money staying in a Disney hotel.

Another time, Disney offered a discounted park rate for one day, but allowed Florida residents to visit all three parks, a luxury not available to out-of-staters with a one-day admission. Locals who didn't want to spend an entire day in one park now had an incentive to return and see the new attractions in all three parks. Everybody won.

In addition to these seasonal specials, the following passes are available for Florida residents. Prices are correct at press time, but subject to change.

- **Epcot After 4:** $69.00; Child pass (3-9) $59.00 plus tax. Allows admission to Epcot after 4:00 p.m. for a full year. Valid every day except New Year's Eve.
- **One Park Annual Pass:** $99.00; Child pass (3-9) $79.00 plus tax. Allows unlimited admission to the Magic Kingdom all year long, with limitations over Christmas, Easter, and the 4th of July.
- **Seasonal Pass:** $149.00; Child pass (3-9) $127.00 plus tax. Unlimited admission to all three major parks, except during the busiest travel times of Easter, Christmas, and most of the summer.
- **Annual pass.** $229.00; Child pass (3-9) $195.00 plus tax. Unlimited admission to all three major parks, any day of the year. Also includes parking fees.
- **Premium Annual Pass:** $319.00; Child pass (3-9) $271.00 plus tax. Includes all three major parks plus Discovery Island, Pleasure Island, River Country, Blizzard Beach, and Typhoon Lagoon. Price includes parking fees.
- **Senior Pass:** $77.00; Equals two one-day, one park tickets.

Military Guests

Veterans, active duty military, dependents, and Department of Defense civilians can buy two kinds of discounted Disney admission packages for themselves and their guests. Discounted length-of-stay passes must be purchased at Shades of Green, the military-owned resort found on site, and are sold only to guests at on-site Disney resorts. Standard passes can be purchased at Shades of Green or any other Disney ticket outlet.

The dollar amount for a length-of-stay pass varies. Compared to a full-fare cost, a two-day pass saves an adult $11.40, a three-day pass $21.74, a four-day pass $41.96, a five-day pass $49.58, a six-day pass $49.08, a seven-day pass $47.46, and an eight-day pass $40.72. Children (3-9) slightly less. On the standard Disney admission packages, savings are less dramatic. One-day admissions run $3.81 less, four-day park hoppers $16.14, and five-day world hoppers $21.76. Again, children slightly less.

Military guests enjoy one perk unmatched by any other discounted group (except Florida senior AAA members) — two- and three-day admission tickets. Guests can purchase a two-day admission for $73.50 (only one park per day) or a three-day pass for $109.50.

TICKETS: WHERE TO BUY

Most people buy their tickets after arrival at Disney World. Off-site guests line up at ticket windows located at the entrance to the three major parks, shuffle credit cards, and spend their early park hours standing stomach-to-back with fellow guests also parting with their vacation savings.

In other words, you'd be wise to purchase your tickets before you arrive. Tickets may be purchased ahead of time at:

• **Disney resorts.** On-site guests can purchase tickets in their hotel.

• **The Disney AAA Ocala Information Center.** Those driving to Walt Disney World by way of I-75 — and that's just about everyone coming from America's Heartland by car — can stop by the Disney AAA Ocala Information Center, exit 68 at State Road 200. In addition to tickets and knowledgeable sales people, they also reserve on-site hotel rooms, many times at substantial savings for those brave individuals brazen enough to set out on a vacation without reservations. Florida resident tickets may also be purchased here.

• **Disney Stores.** Those driving down the East coast and relying on I-95 have no Information Center to stop at, but can purchase tickets at any Disney Store. If already in Central Florida, Disney Stores can be found in the Orlando Fashion Square Mall, the Altamonte Mall, or at Seminole Towne Center. For those arriving by car and traveling I-4, the Seminole Towne Center is most convenient, located just off exit 51 in Sanford, 30 miles north of Walt Disney World. The stores sell all passes but not one-day admissions.

• **Orlando International Airport.** Disney operates an Information Center/Disney Store in the main terminal. Tickets (except special Florida resident tickets) may be purchased here. Located in the main terminal, buying tickets before claiming your luggage avoids back-tracking and suitcase-juggling.

• **By mail.** For the super-organized with at least four weeks before departure, tickets can be ordered by mail, though the service is not free. Send check or money order for the exact amount of the tickets [confirm prices or order by phone at (407) 824-4321], plus $2.00 for shipping and handling, to:

Walt Disney World
Box 10,030
Lake Buena Vista, FL 32930-0030
Attention: Ticket Mail Order

DISCOUNTED DISNEY TICKETS

There are none. At least, none of significance.

The Walt Disney Company offers small discounts to those groups listed above, but otherwise, everyone pays full price. You will, however, see stands in the Disney area offering inexpensive admission tickets. The dealers fall into three categories: 1) ticket resellers who buy up unused days on a departing guest's four- or five-day pass, 2) ticket consolidators that may offer better deals to other area parks but not to Disney, or 3) timeshare salesmen.

Of the three, timeshare salesmen are the pushiest, though their presence has waned in recent years. They pay full price for their Disney tickets and sell them to you for less. The only thing you need do is preview their timeshare property. They say that you're under no obligation to buy. They say that a sales presentation only takes a couple hours. While the discounted tickets are a legitimate bargain, the savings are not worth the time or emotional strain. These guys crank up the pressure as their sales presentation runs on. Avoid them.

Ticket resellers have a tougher time with Disney's latest ticket options. Working with a reseller, you will get a discount, but it's not above-board. You won't get caught. No one checks I.D.'s at the front gate nor do tickets have anything that states who bought them. Still, the money saved is not worth the ethical trade-off.

Consolidators either buy a large number of (non-Disney) discounted tickets or work on a commission arrangement, making a set amount for every ticket sold. For example, they might go to a non-Disney attraction and buy 2000 tickets at a 40% discount, add 20% back in for profit, and still sell them to the public for 20% less than their face value. From the non-Disney attraction's stand-point, they receive cash for those 2000 tickets and they now have an independent businessman pushing their park to people who stopped by to purchase Disney tickets. Consolidators sell Disney tickets, but without enthusiasm, since they make no profit. They sell them only because they have to; because without the sign saying, "Get Your Disney Tickets Here," no one would talk to them. In other words, they *say* they sell Disney tickets — and they do — but they're really pushing other attractions.

There's nothing wrong with this. In fact, if you want to visit another Orlando attraction, they can save you money. (But check for discount coupons in local ads first.) Do not, however, allow them to talk you into something just because they recommend it. While some ticket sellers listen to you and offer wise advice, many recommend attractions that have a high profit margin.

One final note: Orlando ticket booth sales are currently volatile. Thanks to International Drive's new five-day Vacation Value Pass (Universal Studios, Sea World, and Wet 'n Wild together) and Universal Studios' whirlwind expansion, the competition heated up. The attractions wheel and deal with hotel owners, offering perks and money to make sure they gain favor with guests. If your hotel's ticket desk says "Destination Universal," for example, the hotel does not run it, Universal Studios does — not the place for unbiased theme park advice. In addition, the parks have cut the commissions they pay vendors, forcing them to raise rates. There are no good guys and bad guys here, just independent and corporate-owned ticket vendors trying to make a buck. To be safe, decide what you want to see and do first, then check rates at a ticket desk. If given advice, take it with a grain of salt. Then buy your ticket and have fun.

DISCOUNTED COUPONS TO OTHER AREA ATTRACTIONS

You rarely pay full price for attractions other than Disney. Universal Studios, for example, has a list three pages long, detailing every group that gets a discount. Ask about senior discounts, AARP discounts, AAA discounts, corporate discounts, and anything else that might net you a few bucks off. Even mentioning your rental car company or your airline might be enough to shave dollars off the admission price. In addition, check the cheap hand-outs found in every hotel and restaurant within ten miles of Disney. Not only do they stock brochures for the different attractions, but most have newspaper quality booklets that call themselves "guides," but you won't find anything other than ads with coupons.

The following attractions, at presstime, offer discounts to adults over 55:

Attraction	Regular Rate	Senior Rate	Phone
Cypress Gardens	$27.95	22.95	(941) 324-2111
Gatorland	12.67	10.13	(800) 393-JAWS
Movie Rider	8.95	7.95	(407) 345-0501
Ripley's Believe It or Not!	9.95	8.95	(407) 363-4418
Sea World (12 month pass)	69.95	59.95	(407) 363-2249
Universal Studios	38.50	32.72	(407) 363-8217
Church Street Station	16.95	13.95*	(407) 422-2434
A World of Orchids	9.58	8.51	(407) 396-1887

* *With AARP membership only.*

List courtesy of The Orlando/Orange County Convention & Visitor's Bureau, Inc.

HANDICAPPED TRAVELERS

7

84   General Information

89   Hearing Impaired Guests

90   Sight Impaired Guests

Chapter Seven

HANDICAPPED TRAVELERS

GENERAL INFORMATION

Overall, Walt Disney World is a handicapped-friendly place where people with physical limitations can still enjoy the magic, though that depends a bit on the degree of those physical limitations. At the risk of over-generalizing, people who walk short distances with help have little difficulty boarding the attractions and enjoying the parks and resorts. Those who cannot walk on their own face a greater challenge and an occasional problem, but Disney goes the extra mile to accommodate handicapped guests and deserves credit.

Question: Who is handicapped?

Answer: This is philosophical. Some people saying we're all handicapped in some way. At Walt Disney World, however, everyone who *chooses* to be handicapped (i.e., rents a wheelchair to get around) *is* handicapped. At home, many people can clean the house, drive to market, and shop for groceries. But these same people may not be able to walk 1.3 miles around Epcot's World Showcase Promenade. Or, if they do make the trip, they find little energy left to explore Future World or enjoy the 9:00 p.m. showing of IllumiNations. In their home town, these folks are not handicapped. At Epcot, they are.

Most people underestimate the physical demands of long hours and days of walking. For some mature adults, using a wheelchair conserves energy; others would not be caught dead in a wheelchair. Some want to tour for only five or six hours, then return another day; others like the arrive-early/stay-late/recuperate-tomorrow style of visit. Decide which kind of touring you're comfortable with — none are wrong. The bottom line: have a good time. If riding in a wheelchair bothers you, don't do it. If leaving the park early to fight exhaustion bothers you, don't do it. But be realistic. Don't spend 16 hours on your feet if it turns your last four hours into a stress-filled endurance test. The goal is to leave happy, not to "see everything."

All resorts on Walt Disney World property have rooms accessible to the handicapped, most close to the main lobby and elevators. If in doubt about your physical capabilities, ask for one. If you don't require a handicapped room but don't "get around as well as you used to," request a room close to either the hotel lobby, the nearest transportation station, or, both. While reservationists rarely guarantee a room location, requests are added to your reservation and, most times, granted. For help finding a room, call Central Reservations and ask for the Special Requests Department, (407) 934-7639. A non-Disney company, Holiday Assistants, helps handicapped travelers in the Orlando area. For more information, contact them at (800) 945-2045, (407) 397-4845, or write them at: Holiday Assistants, 7798 Indian Ridge Trail North, Kissimmee, FL 39749.

Depending on specific resort, the following is a limited list of available Disney resort services that can be requested when making a reservation.

- wheelchair transportation
- rails in bedroom and bathroom
- wide bathroom doors
- wheelchair-accessible showers with benches
- wheelchair-sized vanities
- hand-held shower heads
- rubber bed pads
- lower beds
- close captioned television
- strobe light smoke detectors
- knock and phone alerts
- double peep holes in doors
- TDDs
- Braille on the telephones, elevators, and selected menus
- voice-activated room controls
- accessible kitchen appliances and cupboards
- insulin refrigeration

In addition, Disney reservationists can make arrangements for special needs such as oxygen, individualized transportation, etc.

All three parks and the resorts give service animals access to everything except rides — Space Mountain, for example — where it's not safe for the animal. And all rides accept guests who can walk from wheelchair to ride vehicle, though some action rides warn against specific problems. For these "action" rides, handicapped visitors are *discouraged* from riding through warning signs, recorded announcements, and sometimes verbally by Disney cast members. But they are not usually *prohibited* from riding. (There are exceptions. Disney, like all other theme parks, walks a fine legal line. They don't discriminate against the handicapped by denying access, yet they must cover their legal rear ends in case of an accident. By over-warning people of the possible dangers, guests can make an informed decision and not legally blame Disney if something goes wrong.)

Many attractions can be accessed by non-ambulatory guests who lift themselves from a locked wheelchair into the ride vehicle, the ease of which depends on the size and shape of the vehicle. While many rides can be stopped to prop a locked wheelchair next to an unmoving car, the size of a ride vehicle's leg opening can still make boarding difficult. In the end, each handicapped guest must decide how much work they want to do and whether an attraction is worth the effort.

Special note: Guests who need to transfer directly from a wheelchair to a ride vehicle must rely on friends, relatives, or "the kindness of strangers." Disney prohibits cast members from helping. From a legal perspective, it's easy to understand this hands-off policy resulting from a fear of lawsuits. Disney is big, rich, and ripe for suing. One small mistake on the part of an employee — nothing more than simple human error — could result in millions of dollars in damages and court costs. But by not helping handicapped guests, Disney loses a small piece of the magic. This lack of courtesy is out-of-character for a park that oozes kindness and love. It's understandable but sad — more a problem with our sue-anyone-for-anything society than Disney. At any rate, handicapped individuals requiring extra help should travel with someone they trust.

Since Epcot and Disney-MGM Studios rely heavily on shows and visual rides — plus they're newer — they have a greater number of handicapped accessible attractions. The Magic Kingdom — because under the glitter it's actually an amusement park with thrill rides — is less accessible. That's not to say a quadriplegic cannot enjoy the Magic Kingdom. There are many adapted rides and high quality shows. It just means that, when touring the Magic Kingdom, prepare for a few disappointments.

In each of the chapters outlining the major parks, a handicapped notation follows a ride's description. At the entrance to most attractions, Disney cast members scope out those traveling in a wheelchair and guide them to the handicapped entrance, generally providing shorter wait times in shaded areas.

The following information specifically relates to handicapped travelers and those with special needs:

• Disney publishes the *Walt Disney World Guidebook for Guests with Disabilities* and distributes it free of charge inside the parks. The guidebook describes accessibility for all WDW attractions, though many times the physical demands of a ride fall into gray areas. For example, the guide tells Space Mountain riders that they should be able to "maneuver across catwalks and down a series of ladders," an activity many disabled people cannot perform. But only when the ride is stopped for an emergency is this "catwalk crossing" required. In other words, almost never. If you're a gambler who likes to play the odds, go for it. But in defense of the guidebook, it warns handicapped riders of potential dangers. If you're extremely unlucky and Space Mountain shuts down because of a technical glitch — and you must walk across that 100-foot-in-the-air catwalk — you can blame no one but yourself. Anyone wishing to experience a ride should weigh the risks against the benefits, then make a decision on the understanding that they're in charge of their personal safety. For legal and ethical reasons, Disney warns of the dangers. Now it's up to you.

To receive a copy of the *Walt Disney World Guidebook for Guests with Disabilities* before your arrival, call: (407) W-DISNEY. For TDD access: (407) 345-5984. Or send a request, in writing, to:

Walt Disney World Guest Communications
Box 10,000
Lake Buena Vista, FL 32830

• **Wheelchair/stroller rentals**. Available at all three major parks and the Transportation and Ticket Center. At the Magic Kingdom, they're located on the far right, immediately after entering the park and before walking under the railroad station that leads to Main Street, U.S.A. If someone walks off with a rented wheelchair, they can be replaced (with receipt) at the Merchant of Venus in Tomorrowland, Tinker Bell's Treasures in Fantasyland, and the Frontier Trading Post in Frontierland.

At Epcot, wheelchair and stroller rentals are on the left after passing through the entrance gates and just before Spaceship Earth, at the Gift Stop on the right side of the main ticket booths, or at the International Gateway in World Showcase. Replacement wheelchairs can be found at the same locations.

At Disney-MGM Studios, they're found at Oscar's Super Service Station (an old-fashioned gas station), located on the right after passing through the entrance gates. Replacement chairs may be found at The Costume Shop toward the rear of the park.

Wheelchairs and strollers rent for $5.00 per day plus a $1.00 deposit. (The deposit encourages you to return the wheelchair rather than just leave it somewhere in the park.) Electric wheelchairs rent for $30.00 per day plus a $2.00 deposit. If touring more than one park in a day, you need to rent only one wheelchair. Return it when you leave your first park, keep the receipt, and show it to an attendant at the next park. While selected rides have vehicles that accommodate wheelchairs, note that only standard wheelchairs may be used — not ECV's. Also, ECV's can sell out fast. If you need one, plan to arrive at the park early in the day.

• **First Aid.** Each park has a First Aid station staffed by a registered nurse. In the Magic Kingdom, it's located at the end of Main Street beside The Crystal Palace restaurant. In Epcot, it's in Odyssey Center, the final area of Future World — on the left — as you enter World Showcase. At Disney-MGM Studios, it's next to Guest Relations, located on your left directly inside the entrance gates.

• **Medical Attention.** Sand Lake Hospital is the closest hospital to Walt Disney World and can be reached by driving east on I-4 and following the signs with a large "H" (for hospital). The hospital can be seen from I-4 since Sand Lake Road runs parallel to the highway. Guests traveling from Disney World (going northeast) should use exit 27A. From the other direction (heading southwest), take exit 29. Sand Lake Hospital phone numbers: (407) 351-8550 Emergency Room, (407) 351-8500 Main switch board.

For non-emergencies, MediClinic operates close to Disney's main-gate entrance at the corner of I-4 and US 192. For house-calls (or is it resort-calls?), MediClinic also runs HouseMed. By calling (407) 239-1195, you can make arrangements for a HouseMed physician to visit your hotel room. For prescriptions, a Gooding's Pharmacy is located directly across from WDW property, near the Village Hotels and Downtown Disney.

• **Parking**. Each park has handicapped parking close to the main entrance. If needed, inform an attendant at the main entrance to each park. He will issue a special parking pass and give directions.

• **Telephones**. The parks have wheelchair accessible telephones located throughout.

• **Restrooms.** Available everywhere.

SERVICES FOR GUESTS WITH HEARING IMPAIRMENTS

Assistive listening devices amplify the sound of selected attractions for guests hard-of-hearing. In the Magic Kingdom, seven presentations benefit; in Epcot, thirteen; in Disney-MGM Studios, seven plus the Sci-Fi Dine-In Theater. At Epcot and MGM, these assistive listening devices are available at Guest Relations; in the Magic Kingdom, at City Hall. All are free but require a refundable $25 deposit.

Telecommunications Devices for the Deaf (TDDs) are offered at the same locations. Additionally, many phones throughout the parks are equipped with amplified handsets. TDDs may be used when calling Walt Disney World information by dialing (407) 827-5141.

In the parks, each show and attraction also has a written script available for those who wish to read along. Ask any cast member for a copy. Guests are asked to return the script at the end of the show.

SERVICES FOR SIGHT IMPAIRED GUESTS

Braille guidebooks are available at City Hall in the Magic Kingdom and Guest Relations/Services at both Disney-MGM Studios and Epcot. In addition, sight impaired guests can tour-by-cassette with equipment found at the same three locations. The service is free but requires a refundable $25 deposit.

PARK TOURING TIPS

8

93 Always Go Left

94 Disney Style of Queuing

95 Get to the Park Early

95 Park Early-Entry Days

96 Which Day of the Week Is Best?

97 Theme Park Dining

Chapter Eight

PARK TOURING TIPS

The three major Disney theme parks exist on a variety of levels and can entertain many types of folks. Some people never consider a Walt Disney World vacation because they envision only a cartoon character and some high-tech rides, but the cartoon character and high-tech rides are only a small part of the WDW smorgasbord.

For those unimpressed with the fantasy, WDW lives on a technological level. How do they make 3-D, see-through ghosts in the Haunted Mansion? How do they make speakers above Main Street synchronize perfectly to the passing SpectroMagic parade? How do they make Epcot attractions *smell* like the scene they're portraying?

For other people unimpressed with fantasy *and* technology, there's the business aspect of Walt Disney World. Crowd control, marketing, food service, and electrical engineering at WDW impress even the experts. Anyone working in a personnel department knows that you never get a perfect work force, but Disney employees are all friendly (on "Disney drugs" according to locals). How do they do it?

And for those not interested in fantasy, technology, or business, something else will catch their attention. Gardens at all three parks are immaculate, a big draw to horticulturists. Yearly events include a teddy bear convention, car shows, and art exhibits, among hundreds of other things. World Showcase countries are not just building facades, but showcases for a country's culture. Many include museums.

In other words, everyone finds something they like.

The following chapters detail the three major parks: the Magic Kingdom, Epcot Center, and the Disney-MGM Studios. Chapter descriptions are based on the following assumptions:

• *All attractions are worth seeing, but people have different levels of tolerance.* To some visitors, for example, the fun of Splash Mountain (over 11-minutes of AudioAnimatronic figures singing songs from the Disney movie, *Song of the South*) is not worth the horror of a ten-second, 52-foot fall at 40 m.p.h. The description of Splash Mountain will explain the fall and enough about the 11-minutes of entertainment to allow you to make an intelligent decision. Armed with information, you can decide if the "fun" is worth the "fall."

• *You want information about an attraction, but don't want to know everything.* Walt Disney decided long ago that rides should evolve like a movie and a story line should lead viewers through the action. Hence, many attractions follow that formula with a plot that slowly unfolds and builds up to a conclusion. Giving away too many details is like saying "The butler did it," as your friend reads a mystery novel you just finished. It's not fair.

• *Disney World is more than rides.* Adventureland in the Magic Kingdom, for example, is home to Pirates of the Caribbean and the Jungle Cruise. But Adventureland has exotic plant life, native drums, steel bands, jungle-style shops, mysterious native carvings, and unique food. Everything comes together to create a rain forest atmosphere. For anyone with a functioning imagination, it's a fun place to visit even without the rides.

• *Some rides are worth a long wait. Others are not.* If traveling off-season, this shouldn't be a major problem, but if it is, know what to expect. Everyone loves the Country Bear Jamboree in the Magic Kingdom, but is it worth an hour wait? If you're a country music fan, it probably is. If the entire queue is air-conditioned, it definitely is. But if you hate country music and you must wait in direct sunlight, you may well decide to move on. Read the descriptions and decide for yourself.

ALWAYS GO LEFT

Some touring tips apply to all three parks. "Always go left" when waiting in a line is the worst kept secret of Disney touring, appearing even in Disney's guides. Sometimes it's true; many times, however, it's not. A better one is "don't follow the crowd."

Sometimes a line begins single file and then splits along the way in order to move guests to two separate loading areas, such as it does at Small World. Other times — Space Mountain, for example — there are actually two different rides. If left to their own devices, most Americans go right. We drive on the right. We push our grocery carts to the right. We're just right-minded people.

Here's the rule: Unless a lane is roped off, it is open. Many times, an unused lane is on the left because of our natural propensity to go right, but sometimes the opposite is true. Once a crowd chooses one line and leaves another empty, people following behind don't venture into the open-but-empty side, either because they feel guilty moving ahead of others or because "It might not really be another line and the people in front of me know that." At Disney, line-waiting is an exact science. If there is a vacant line to one side, it's meant to be there. They've designed no mistakes.

An addendum to this rule is: If in doubt, go left. This rule doesn't always save steps, but it won't make you walk farther. Besides, if the lines are too short to see people waiting ahead of you, you picked a good day to visit.

DISNEY STYLE OF QUEUING

Many things affect how long you wait for a ride. Certain rides — Spaceship Earth at Epcot, for example — have a connected set of cars that move constantly. These rides handle the same number of people, per hour, all day long. They cannot add space during busy season nor subtract space on slow days.

Other rides — Thunder Mountain Railroad in the Magic Kingdom, for example — handle different numbers of guests at different times because they adjust the number of trains. In the morning, the ride might start off with only one or two trains, adding others as crowds pick up, eventually having five on line. On these types of rides, a crowd of 100 people waits twice as long at 9:00 a.m. as they do at 3:00 p.m., even if the line is equally long. Most attractions that rely on trains, boats, or unattached cars operate this way.

Still other attractions require a long down time (meaning a period of time while the ride is not operating) while passengers load, notably amusement-type rides like the Mad Tea Party or Dumbo the Flying Elephant. Long down times can make a short line drag on forever.

Finally, waiting times for every ride are influenced by the attraction's popularity. For repeat guests, a handful of attractions will be new. Expect long wait times on the ExtraTERRORestrial Alien Encounter, for example, no matter how great it is, simply because it's new and repeat visitors never experienced it before. The same is true for Honey, I Shrunk the Audience at Epcot. Disney promotes new stuff to encourage repeat visitors. Of course, some rides are popular simply because they're great rides.

Because wait times can vary tremendously based on when you arrive, the number of cars operating, and the season of the year, guidelines presented here can help you make an intelligent choice, but the final decision sits squarely in your lap.

Some attractions have signs at the entrance detailing the wait time. Expect your actual wait time to be shorter. Disney learned long ago that people are very forgiving if the wait time is ten minutes less than expected, but not so forgiving if it's ten minutes longer.

GET TO THE PARK EARLY

If a park opens at 9:00 a.m. and gates stayed locked until that second, a crowd of angry people would extend clear back to the Goofy Parking Lot, already frustrated with their day. So, rather than face an angry mob of people, Disney opens their parks early.

If a park officially opens at 9:00 a.m., arrive at least half an hour earlier, preferably more. By arriving early, it's entirely possible to get four or five attractions under your belt before the crowds show up. On days when the park only opens for nine hours, it also gives you more time on a one-day admission.

An entire park does not open early, however. Disney planners estimate attendance and open enough to hold the crowd, varying it from day-to-day. At the least, Main Street opens in the Magic Kingdom with ropes blocking access to the other lands. Opening time and areas also change daily at the Disney-MGM Studios and Epcot.

Some people prefer a late arrival, staying until the park closes. This works during the busy season, though lines are never as thin late at night as they are early in the morning. In slower seasons, there is no advantage to arriving late.

PARK EARLY-ENTRY DAYS

As a benefit for guests staying at on-site Disney hotels, one of the three parks opens 1 1/2 hours early every day for their exclusive use, a selling point advertised heavily when persuading travelers to stay within Walt Disney World. If you're staying on-site, there are two sides to this coin. Assuming you visit during a slow season, the early opening gives you an extra hour of touring. On the flip side of that coin, that early-arrival perk goes out to every on-site guest and many stay at the "early opening" park all day. In other words, while the park may be open longer, the added crowds make that park the busiest one of the day, forcing you to use your "free" hour waiting in afternoon lines.

Assuming that all three parks open at 9:00 a.m., a perfect touring plan would get you to the early-opened park at least a half hour before the "early" opening. Tour whatever section is open and then relocate to another park once the crowds get thick. For this plan to work, you must have a World Hopper or Length of Stay pass.

If you want to spend an entire day at one park, whether you're an on-site guest or someone staying off property, it's best to avoid the park with an early opening day. To find out the early admission schedule — and this program goes through constant changes — call WDW at (407) 824-4321. Currently, the Magic Kingdom opens early on Monday, Thursday, and Saturday. Epcot opens early on Tuesday and Friday. Disney-MGM Studios opens early on Wednesday and Sunday.

WHICH DAY OF THE WEEK IS BEST?

The average Walt Disney World visitor arrives on a weekend and tours the Magic Kingdom on Monday, Epcot Center on Tuesday, and Disney-MGM Studios on Wednesday. On Thursday, he or she returns to the Magic Kingdom. Weekends — generally transit times from home to Orlando — are the best days to visit during busy seasons. During slower seasons, however, Disney offers special rates to Florida residents, making the weekends less advantageous. In slow season, visit on the week days listed below. If you must visit over a weekend, Sunday crowds are usually thinner than those on Saturday.

Best days:
Magic Kingdom. Wednesday or Friday; avoid Monday
Epcot. Thursday or Monday; avoid Tuesday
Disney-MGM Studios. Friday or Monday; avoid Wednesday

THEME PARK DINING

The number of sit-down restaurants is limited in the Magic Kingdom and Disney-MGM Studios, but since they appeal to many mature travelers, they're described in greater detail in the following sections. Epcot has many.

Note on fast food restaurants in all parks: The Disney system puts a cashier behind a podium with a line formed on both sides. The cashier takes an order from the person on their right, gives change, then takes an order from the person on their left. Once you order, you step forward and pick up your food. To save time, first look for a short line. Sometimes the line may be six persons deep on one side and nonexistent on the other. Remember that Disney knows what it's doing — if that empty line is not roped off, it's open. Second, avoid lines with a worn-out 30-something man standing alone. He probably has six kids waiting for him to return with food. Best bet: get behind teenagers who tend to order only for themselves, or mature adults, who tend to order for no more than two people at once.

In general, Magic Kingdom food costs are reasonable. A Magic Kingdom burger is not, however, as cheap as one at McDonald's. Served together with French fries and/or fruit, a fast-food meal for two, including drinks, is about $15.00 plus tax. When charging for food, Disney price-setters walk a fine line. With a captive audience and rules against bringing food into the park, they can pretty much charge what they want. People pay to eat. But if Disney gouged the public, nickel and dime-ing them to death, it would leave a bad taste in people's mouth (no pun intended) and they might not return, harming future profits. So Disney Execs charge as much as they can up to, but not crossing, the amount that guests will consider exorbitant.

The Disney folks walk that line well. The prices certainly turn a profit, but the quality matches many fast-food restaurants and is better than some. Compared to outside competitors, the atmosphere cannot be beat. Most guests accept Disney prices as reasonable, though high.

At press time, reservations or preferred seating could be made sixty days in advance for many full-service restaurants by calling (407) WDW-DINE. Reservation policies have changed more than once, so check before leaving home.

THE MAGIC KINGDOM

101   Getting to the Magic Kingdom

102   First Things First

104   Touring Tips

105   Guidelines For Those Who Don't Mind
a Lot of Walking

107   Lands and Rides

> Main Street • Adventureland • Frontierland •
> Liberty Square • Fantasyland • Mickey's Toontown
> Fair • Tomorrowland

131   Parades and Shows

136   Magic Kingdom Restaurants

140   Shopping

142   Don't Miss...

Chapter Nine

THE MAGIC KINGDOM

The cornerstone of all Disney theme parks, the Magic Kingdom (MK) literally defines Disney. The symbol of a Disney World vacation — after Mickey Mouse himself — is the towering skyline of Cinderella's Castle cutting the ice-blue Florida sky or framed in the nighttime darkness by a spray of fireworks. At Christmas, America watches Santa Claus float down Main Street; in spring, the Easter Bunny.

While you might learn a thing or two in the Magic Kingdom, it exists for pure entertainment. At a time when little boys fantasized about the wild west, Walt Disney gave it to them in Frontierland. Fairy tales, the favored reading for generations of children, became a three-dimensional reality in Fantasyland. The future took shape in Tomorrowland.

For mature adults, some of the Magic Kingdom's attractions are silly — dressed-up carnival rides made for children. The Dumbo ride, for example, adds a colorful touch to Fantasyland. But unless adults have a small child in tow, her eyes wide, her heart pounding, they won't wait an hour to sit inside a fiberglass elephant and spin in a small circle.

Thankfully, most rides appeal to both kids and adults, whether on a dream level or because of futuristic technology. A few attractions — the Hall of Presidents, for example — leave children far behind. Adults with only one or two days to visit Walt Disney World may prefer Epcot or Disney-MGM Studios. But if staying a week, consider the Magic Kingdom. It has a lot of things to keep mature adults happy.

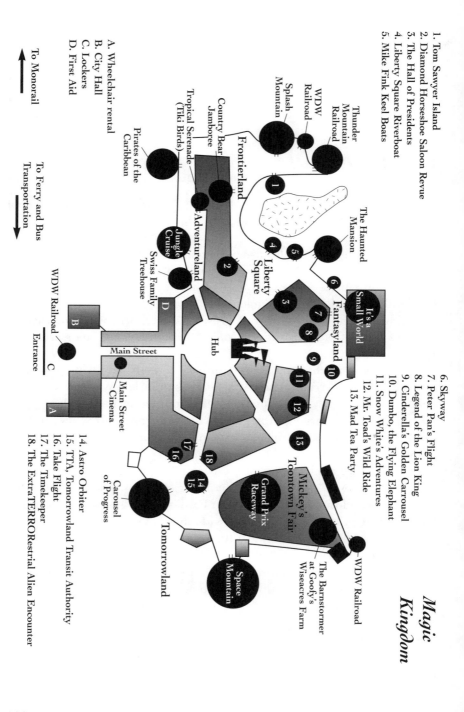

GETTING TO THE MAGIC KINGDOM

On-site guests travel by monorail, boat, or bus. The standard route for off-site guests is to take exit 25 off I-4 and head west on U.S. 192. Immediately after the I-4 exit, signs direct traffic right and onto Disney property, the maingate entrance. After entering Disney property, you'll pass Disney MGM-Studio's Earful Tower and continue on until you reach the Auto Plaza. Pay for parking and follow the signs.

If you're heading west on I-4 (from Orlando, the International Drive area, or Lake Buena Vista), you can save a few miles by taking I-4 exit 26B, officially the route to Epcot. Once on Disney property, signs will direct most of the traffic to Epcot, but a second road will continue on to the Magic Kingdom, merging shortly with World Drive, the main drag leading to the parking lot described above. Pay close attention to signs since most lanes lead to Epcot.

At presstime, parking was $5 per day, free to resort guests. Save your parking ticket if traveling to other Disney parks since a single daily payment is valid at all three.

Once you park your car, you're still not close to the Magic Kingdom. To guarantee complete control over his new "world" — something he didn't have in California — Walt Disney made the Magic Kingdom hard to reach by car. Once parked, you're still a tram ride away from the Transportation and Ticket Center, and a boat or monorail ride away from the main entrance to the Magic Kingdom. While this far-away parking lot makes getting inside difficult and time-consuming, it also adds to the fantasy, as if the MK is truly a foreign land.

At any rate, memorize where you parked. The rows are numbered and the lots named after Disney characters. If you forget the location, check in City Hall before leaving. Parking attendants keep a daily record, logging the times when each parking area filled. If you remember the time you arrived, they can tell you approximately where you parked. In addition, parking attendants can deal with any minor emergency, from keys locked inside the vehicle (they have a master set for every car made) to dead batteries (using built-in jumper cables the length of a van).

To get to the Transportation and Ticket Center (TTC) after you park, board a complimentary tram. While not a wild ride, hold on if you sit on either end. Tram trips run nonstop in the morning but stop frequently at the end of the day. At the TTC, purchase tickets if you haven't already done so and then proceed north toward the Seven Seas Lagoon. (If unsure of the direction, use your herding instinct and follow the hundreds of people flowing the same way.) At the turnstiles, a cast member may glance at your ticket, then let you through.

Across the Seven Seas Lagoon stands the entrance to the Magic Kingdom. To cross the lake, choose either the WDW monorail (straight ahead) or the ferry (to the left). If the crowds aren't too thick, the monorail provides an aerial preview of the monorail resorts, a trip through the center of the Contemporary, and a slightly faster commute time. The ferry, modeled after the Staten Island Ferry, has thinner crowds and a relaxing ride. The ferry also takes slightly longer, but not enough to forego the trip. Wheelchair guests may use either monorail or ferry, though the entrance leading to the monorail is somewhat steep.

FIRST THINGS FIRST

Once you exit the monorail or ferry, pass through the entry turn-stiles and walk under the WDW Railroad Depot, still flowing with the crowd. Once through, you're in the heart of Disney World — Main Street. U.S.A. Now break away from the crowd, bear left, and visit City Hall. Once inside, request a park map and schedule for the day's live entertainment if you do not yet have one. Thus armed, begin your day.

While nothing substitutes for a map, people with a rudimentary sense of direction can visualize the Magic Kingdom's lay-out in their head. Visitors enter the Magic Kingdom at one end of Main Street, called Town Square, and then walk down the street to the Central Plaza, or Hub. Main Street is shaped like a giant Q-tip, with a central garden at each end. If you walk straight and stand in the center of the Hub, the street circles you, Main Street is behind and Cinderella's Castle directly in front. Almost every land is accessible from the Hub. As you face the castle, Tomorrowland is at 3 o'clock, Mickey's Toontown Fair at 2 o'clock, Fantasyland straight ahead (through the castle), Liberty Square at 10 o'clock, and Adventureland at 8 o'clock. Rather than return to the Hub to visit each land, however, walkways also connect one land to another, so visitors may start in one land and wind their way through, visiting each land in turn.

Simple, right?

Here are the exceptions: First, Mickey's Toontown Fair, the only land added since the Magic Kingdom first opened, sits off the main walkway. Second, the wheel circling the Hub grows flat off to the left. While Tomorrowland, Fantasyland, and Liberty Square circle the Hub, Adventureland does not, extending to the left in a straight line. Behind Adventureland (back-to-back) runs Frontierland, which connects to Liberty Square.

In other words, the lands do not form a perfect circle, but look more like a comma with a tail off to your left. They are connected, however, and can be visited (except Mickey's Toontown Fair) without backtracking.

If starting in Adventureland, you can flow into Frontierland, then Liberty Square, then Fantasyland, Mickey's Toontown Fair, and Tomorrowland. By entering Tomorrowland, you can do it in reverse. Or start anywhere else, circle toward either Tomorrowland or Adventureland, then cross the Hub to visit lands as yet unseen, ending your journey where it began.

The following services are offered in the Magic Kingdom:

• **Wheelchair and Stroller Rental.** Located on the far right immediately after passing through the Magic Kingdom turnstiles and before passing under the WDW Railroad Station. Wheelchairs also available at the TTC for those who cannot make the journey unaided.

• **Money.** SunTrust operates a cash machine on Town Square, the first building on the left as you enter the Magic Kingdom after passing under the WDW Railroad Station. Open 9 a.m. to 4 p.m., SunTrust also cashes checks and advances money off a credit card, along with other services. Two other ATM's can be found near the Tropical Serenade in Adventureland and in Tomorrowland's Light & Power Company (the exit for Space Mountain).

• **First Aid**. On the Hub, beside the Crystal Palace. (Near Adventureland.)

• **Baby Care**. Next to First Aid, on the Hub, beside the Crystal Palace

• **Post Office**. There is no post office in the Magic Kingdom, but stamps may be purchased at City Hall. Mailboxes can be found on poles along Main Street.

- **Lost and Found**. In City Hall, at the entrance to Main Street. For losses discovered after you leave the park, phone (407) 824-4245.
- **Storage Lockers**. Located under the WDW Railroad Station at the entrance to Main Street. These are ideal for rain gear or a light snack (though officially you cannot take food into the parks). Additional lockers located at the TTC. Anything too large for a locker can be stored at City Hall inside the Magic Kingdom or at Guest Relations in the TTC.
- **Information.** For directions or general questions, ask any cast member. For specific information, stop at City Hall. For park-wide ride information, a Tip Board in front of Cinderella's Castle lists the wait time for the most popular attractions.
- **Guided Tours**. Tours change in style and substance. Currently, a four-hour tour departs City Hall at 10:00 a.m., lasts four hours, and costs $45 in addition to regular park admission. Participants do, however, see things the ordinary visitor does not, including the famous Disney underground tunnels that run under Main Street and throughout the park. For more information, call (407) WDW-TOUR or stop by City Hall.
- **Pets**. Except for service animals, pets are not allowed in any Disney parks. It is also against Florida law to leave animals unattended in a vehicle (and down-right cruel). The Magic Kingdom Pet Care Center is located outside the entrance and charges about $6 per day.
- **Disabled Guests**. Sight impaired guests receive complimentary tour cassettes at Guest Relations. At the same location, hearing impaired guests can rent TDD's or Assistive Listening Devices which amplify selected attractions. In addition, written scripts are available at the entrance to individual attractions.

TOURING TIPS

- Arrive early if you can, at least a half hour before the park opens. If you're a night owl and waking early makes a day at the Magic Kingdom feel like work more than pleasure, by all means sleep in. You will, however, spend more time in line unless crowds are extremely thin.
- Guests staying off-site should avoid the Magic Kingdom on days when on-site guests are allowed to enter the park one hour earlier than the general public. (See Chapter 8: Park Touring Tips).

• Skip Main Street until later in the day. Main Street has no major attractions, but lots and lots of shopping best enjoyed in the afternoon. Also, Main Street shops stay open later than the rest of the park. The plus side to shopping after the park closes: you essentially add time to your day, buying merchandise only after the rides have shut down. The downside to shopping after the park closes: elbow-to-elbow crowds.

• Use the WDW Railroad for transportation. The three stops — at the entrance to Main Street, the outskirts of Frontierland, and Mickey's Toontown Fair — represent the farthest reaches of the Magic Kingdom. Boarding in Frontierland, for example, takes you to Main Street with relative ease.

• Start touring in the land with the longest/slowest lines. For most, this is Fantasyland. For roller coaster enthusiasts, Frontierland or Tomorrowland.

• Plan to visit on two days, if possible, riding attractions with long lines on two separate mornings. Also, pick traditionally slow days (See Chapter 8: Park Touring Tips).

• Try to eat at non-traditional times, avoiding 11 a.m. to 2 p.m. and 5 p.m. to 8 p.m. In other words, eat while others ride; ride while others eat.

GUIDELINES FOR THOSE WHO DON'T MIND A LOT OF WALKING

One, arrive early.

Two, enjoy popular rides first. The only problem with rule two: The Disney folks, extremely efficient at crowd control, place their anchor attractions at opposite ends of the park. You can't "hop" on Space Mountain and then "hop" on Splash Mountain. Between "hops," you hike from one end of the Magic Kingdom to the other.

The task is simpler for those who don't like roller coaster attractions. Space Mountain, Thunder Mountain Railroad, and Splash Mountain are the three favorite rides for early morning guests, and all get crowded early. Sedate rides such as the Jungle Cruise have long lines later in the day, but shorter ones in the early hours. Find your personality-type in the following descriptions and choose the touring plan that suits your needs. Unfortunately, the first itineraries have a "see as much as you can" mentality rather than an "enjoy it as much as you can" one. There's nothing wrong with that. However, at some point, you will find yourself waiting in line. Expect it and roll with the punches. It's all part of the Disney experience.

For those who love roller coasters: Head for Splash Mountain first, then nearby Thunder Mountain Railroad in outer Frontierland. Cut across the park and ride Space Mountain and Alien Encounter in Tomorrowland. Then walk across the Hub to Adventureland and ride the Jungle Cruise.

It's now 10:30 a.m. and you're probably ready for that first nap.

To make the above itinerary slightly easier, arrive early and board the WDW Railroad on Main Street. The train will pull out when the park opens. Get off at the first stop, Frontierland, and ride Splash Mountain and Thunder Mountain Railroad. Reboard the train (a pleasant ride in and of itself) and disembark at the next stop, Mickey's Toontown Fair, and walk to Space Mountain.

For those who hate roller coasters: Head directly to Fantasyland and ride the three minor attractions: Snow White's Adventures, Mr. Toad's Wild Ride, and Peter Pan's Flight. If lines have not yet formed, take the Skyway to Tomorrowland and enjoy Alien Encounter, then walk across the Hub to Adventureland and the Jungle Cruise.

For those who hate roller coasters and think the Fantasyland rides are dumb: From the Hub, make a hard left into Adventureland and ride the Jungle Cruise. Cut across the Hub to Tomorrowland and Alien Encounter. Ride the Skyway to Fantasyland and explore Haunted Mansion, then circle the Rivers of America (keeping the water on your right) and visit the Country Bear Jamboree.

For those who only want to know where to start: Frontierland if you love roller coasters, Fantasyland if you want to do it all, Adventureland if you want to take it as it comes.

For those who plan their own itinerary but want a list of the rides with the most uncomfortable waits:

Adventureland: Jungle Cruise

Frontierland: Splash Mountain, Thunder Mountain Railroad

Liberty Square: Haunted Mansion

Fantasyland: Peter Pan's Flight, Mr. Toad's Wild Ride, Snow White's Adventures, Dumbo the Flying Elephant, Mad Tea Party, and Skyway to Tomorrowland.

Mickey's Toontown Fair: None

Tomorrowland: Grand Prix Raceway, Space Mountain, and the ExtraTERRORestrial Alien Encounter.

LANDS AND RIDES

How to Read the Attraction Descriptions

Each attraction is followed by a letter from "A" to "E". Before Walt Disney World switched to a one-price admission policy, each ride required a ticket. "E" tickets were the most expensive, required for all top-of-the-line attractions. "A" tickets worked only on the simplest rides, like the horse-drawn trolley on Main Street. "B", "C", and "D" fell somewhere inbetween.

Note — Background information on the ride. For example, if the ride is an "E" ticket in substance, but not entertainment value, it's noted here. Also, designers based many rides on Disney movies. If plot information helps you understand the ride, it's explained.

Movement — Describes all motion on the ride along with anything else that might make adults uncomfortable. Disney "surprises" en route are not described unless they move you fast, throw you around, or jump in your face.

Line — Describes the queue line, whether it's inside or outside, air-conditioned or not, long or short.

Wait time — Judges the waiting time in relation to other attractions. For example, a wait time listed as "long" does not necessarily mean hours standing in line. The Jungle Cruise, for example, has a long wait time. That means that, when the park is very busy, expect to wait as long as an hour. On a less-crowded day or early in the morning, when some rides have no wait at all, expect ten or fifteen minutes. In other words, "long" is a relative term based on all other operating rides and not an exact estimate of time.

Wheelchair Access — Notes any special problems encountered by those in wheelchairs. Remember that WDW cast members will not help a guest transfer from wheelchair to ride. If you cannot transfer alone or with the help of a companion, sigh and move on to a ride that accommodates you. If you can ride, look for a cast member at each attraction's entrance. Most times, they'll find you.

The following descriptions assume you tour Main Street first, then make a hard left at the Hub and begin your tour in Adventureland, continuing to circle clockwise and enjoying each land as you come to it.

MAIN STREET, U.S.A.

On a design level, Main Street is turn-of-the-century America, right down to the street lights, gingerbread moldings, hanging flower baskets, and Victorian architecture. On a fantasy level, it's more. Main Street is home. It lives in the nation's collective unconscious as a better time, a time when boys stole kisses as they walked their best girl home from the malt shop (and it wasn't sexual harassment); when apple pies cooled on Widow Jones' windowsill; when five-year-old boys in knickers rolled giant hoops down the street; when no one locked their doors because crime only happened in "the big city."

Everything backs up this Main Street fantasy. The music — almost imperceptible unless you concentrate — comes from turn-of-the-century-themed films. The smell of baking cookies wafts from the bakery, an aroma created by Disney Imagineers rather than fresh baking cookies. The local movie theater plays the latest film.

It all fits.

Offering more shopping than entertainment, Main Street is the best place to find Disney souvenirs, though smaller stores can be found throughout the park. The few Main Street attractions add to the Victorian atmosphere. They're fun diversions but none a "must see."

Escape Spots: In the center of Main Street, two side streets intersect, appearing to lead to other parts of town. Either side provides shelter from the crowds with a few benches for relaxing. One, on the "Main Street Emporium" side, is filled with flowers and is a favored picture spot. Directly off the Hub, another get-away spot sits at the bottom of the hill, on the water, and to the left of the main entrance to Tomorrowland. The original home of Swan Boats, a water ride which only lasted a few years, this covered pavilion may host special shows during busy times but in slow seasons, it's one of the best get-away spots in the entire park.

Main Street Cinema

TICKET: A

NOTE: Shows a range of silent films in air-conditioned comfort, notably, Mickey Mouse's first cartoon, Steamboat Willie. Movies run continuously and guests enter and exit at their leisure. Unlike most cinemas, this one has no seats.

MOVEMENT: None.

LINE: None.
WAIT TIME: None.
WHEELCHAIR ACCESS: Complete.

Main Street Transportation
TICKET: A
NOTE: Different modes of transportation — from horseless carriages to horse-drawn trolleys — transport guests from one end of Main Street to the other. As transportation, they don't travel far and even a short wait time takes longer than walking the same distance. Ride if they bring back memories.
MOVEMENT: Nothing unusual.
LINE: Short but outdoors.
WAIT TIME: Short to medium, depending on season.
WHEELCHAIR ACCESS: Limited. Must be able to transfer out of a wheelchair without a cast member's help.

Walt Disney World Railroad
TICKET: C
NOTE: If taken full-circle, this 21-minute, 1 1/2 mile trip touches on most lands in the Magic Kingdom. A favorite of Walt Disney, the engines are antiques but almost entirely rebuilt. The trip includes a stop in Frontierland and Mickey's Toontown Fair. Length of the ride is not monitored, meaning you can board on Main Street and disembark at the first stop in Frontierland or, if you love trains, ride all day long. The antique arcade games — Kiss-O-Meters and the 1¢ "movin' pictures" — once housed in the Main Street Penny Arcade (pre-1995) are now located in the WDW Railroad Station.
MOVEMENT: Gentle.
LINE: Longer first thing in the morning, growing shorter as the day wears on. The opposite is true for the Frontierland and Toontown Fair stations. Queue is sheltered, but not air-conditioned.
WAIT TIME: Medium in the morning; short in the afternoon. Many times, you simply wait for the next train.
WHEELCHAIR ACCESS: Wheelchairs can ascend an exit ramp located within the station. Guests must be able to transfer from wheelchair to train; wheelchairs may then be folded and taken aboard. Nonambulatory guests will find boarding easier in the Frontierland or Toontown Fair stations where they may remain in their wheelchairs.

ADVENTURELAND

From the jungles of darkest Africa to the palm studded coast of the Caribbean, Adventureland exists as a hodge-podge of geographic areas where modern luxuries cease to exist. The land is moist with plants that grow thick and dark. Ceiling fans spin on brightly painted porches, drawing heavy air across native islanders. The goods sold in most local stores are basic — straw hats, printed shirts, wind chimes, and ceramic turtles; most feature an ecology theme. Many are imported from India, Africa, the Caribbean, and Thailand. Somewhere in the Adventureland distance, native drums beat; cannons thunder; parrots screech.

The tropical array of Adventureland plants surprises many avid gardeners. More than any other land in the Magic Kingdom, Adventureland relies on its greenery for atmosphere. To your right as you enter, Caribbean styled architecture houses gift shops and eating places. To your left is the jungle. It's all too organized — and beautiful — to really be the fringes of civilization. But it's the perfect fringe of a Disney civilization.

Escape Spots: Immediately after crossing the bridge under Adventureland's main entrance, on the left, there's a row of shaded seats. While part of the walkway, it's separated by planters, not a direct route to anything, and rarely used. Also, nooks and crannies within the Pirates of the Caribbean building are perfect for resting, especially for non-shopping spouses who must wait for a loved one to finish browsing.

Swiss Family Treehouse

TICKET: B

NOTE: Based on the 1960 Disney movie, Swiss Family Robinson, the film family's treehouse home is recreated. More exciting to those who saw the movie, it is none-the-less interesting, most notably to kids who dream of having the perfect treehouse in their backyard. The tree itself is fake. Every few years, the leaves — all 300,000 of them — are taken down and cleaned.

MOVEMENT: This is a walk-through attraction, viewed by climbing up and down many stairs, all outdoors but shaded. The line moves continuously, though some people go slower than others. No air-conditioning.

LINE: Shaded but outdoors. Visible from the walkway.

WAIT TIME: Short.

WHEELCHAIR ACCESS: None. As a stairs-only exhibit, there's no way to make it accessible. Much is visible from the ground, however, and those confined to a wheelchair can at least watch.

Tropical Serenade

TICKET: D

NOTE: Usually referred to as the Enchanted Tiki Birds, this is Disney's first AudioAnimatronic attraction. Most of the 17-minute show takes place above your head, with no seat better than another. For some, it's too cute. For others, it's beautiful.

MOVEMENT: None.

LINE: There is a simple preshow with standing room only. Seats are counted and if you're admitted to the preshow, which is shaded but outdoors, you will soon be admitted to the air-conditioned main show. The outside line moves into the preshow all at once, so a long line does not necessarily mean a long wait. Length is completely visible.

WAIT TIME: Short

WHEELCHAIR ACCESS: Complete. Guests may remain in their wheelchairs.

Jungle Cruise

TICKET: E

NOTE: Like many of the Magic Kingdom's best attractions, technology does not substitute for good writing. A boat tour of the world's wildest rivers, the Jungle Cruise is dismissed by many mature adults as "too childish." The sights are secondary, however, to the dialogue from the captain. While children marvel at the elephants and deadly jungle natives, adults enjoy jokes too corny to make you laugh — but you laugh anyway. Because the ride takes place outdoors, try to visit before the sun goes down.

MOVEMENT: Boat ride; nothing sudden or violent. At one point, the guide shoots a loud cap gun at a hippopotamus.

LINE: Deceptive. Length of the wait depends, in part, on the number of boats in service, something you can't determine from the outside. Also, the line weaves around and behind walls, making it difficult to see. If possible, ride in the morning, but check the posted sign near

the entrance for an estimated wait time and subtract five or ten minutes. Line is shaded with overhead fans, but not air-conditioned.
WAIT TIME: Long.
WHEELCHAIR ACCESS: Possible. Riders sit on a seat that wraps around the outside of the boat or a single seat that runs down the middle. To board, a piece of padding is lifted off the outside seat and the wood is used as a step. Wheelchair-bound guests must transfer from their wheelchair, onto this step, then down into the boat, leaving their wheelchair on the dock. Those who cannot walk short distances must rely on a companion for lifting.

Pirates of the Caribbean
TICKET: E
NOTE: Everyone from kids to the almost-deceased enjoys Pirates of the Caribbean. All ages have a good time, hum a nonsensical song as they exit, and talk about the hair on a man's leg. (You must ride to understand.)
MOVEMENT: Little. The boat slides down one small hill early in the ride, similar to a long sliding board. Only the extremely faint-of-heart should object.
LINE: Invisible. Much of it winds through a recreated Spanish fort, making it pleasant and air-conditioned. If both sides are open, go left.
WAIT TIME: Medium. While this is one of the Magic Kingdom's most popular rides, it runs continuously and a large number of boats can accommodate many guests at once.
WHEELCHAIR ACCESS: Possible. Guests must transfer themselves from wheelchair to boat, at roughly floor level. Boat seats can be used as a step.

FRONTIERLAND

Welcome to the old west, home of gun slingers, saloons, and those lovely dance hall girls. In this cleaner-than-real Disney version, bad guys fight good guys, mine trains run out-of-control, bears sing, a steamboat navigates the river, local cowpokes chew on giant turkey legs, and dance hall girls do nothing but dance. Somewhere, a banjo picker scratches out a tune.

When Walt Disney built California's Disneyland, a western craze was in full swing both in movies and on television. All boys and girls wanted to rope cattle and ride horses. Frontierland wasn't meant to represent the actual west, but the romanticized west of a kid's fantasies. It's the West that never was, but the West that everyone knows.

Escape Spots: Aunt Polly's Landing on Tom Sawyer's Island is the best place in WDW to watch the action, yet feel a bit removed. You've got to travel — by raft — to the island first, but for a casual, picnic-style lunch, it can't be beat.

Walt Disney World Railroad

TICKET: C

NOTE: The same train described under Main Street. Trip includes stops at Main Street and Mickey's Toontown Fair.

MOVEMENT: Gentle.

LINE: Queue is sheltered but not air-conditioned. Length is visible from the entrance.

WAIT TIME: Short to medium.

WHEELCHAIR ACCESS: Riders may remain in wheelchairs if entering or exiting at the Frontierland or Mickey's Toontown Fair stations. At the Main Street station, nonambulatory guests must be able to transfer to their wheelchair.

Splash Mountain

TICKET: E

NOTE: One of the Magic Kingdom's best. Based on the Disney film, *Song of the South*, over 100 AudioAnimatronic figures trace the story of Brer Fox and Brer Bear as they try to catch Brer Rabbit during the 11-minute ride. Using reverse psychology, Brer Rabbit begs them not to throw him into the briar patch, swearing it would be a fate worse than death. The none-too-bright captors laugh and immediately throw him into the briars, not knowing that rabbits live in briar patches. The drop at the end of the ride — if you stretch your imagination — represents Brer Rabbit's fall into the briar patch.

The final hill — a 40 m.p.h., 52-foot drop at a 45° angle — can be previewed from the outside. Note to the squeamish: the splash of water you see after each log boat touches down is actually created by giant water cannons and not the boat's impact at the bottom of the hill.

MOVEMENT: The main hill is visible from the outside. Two viewing levels allow you to watch either the disappearance into the briar patch or, from the lower level, the harried riders return to a normal speed. Judge for yourself if you can stand it. There are three other drops inside the mountain, but none nearly as exciting (scary?) as the final one. If you think you can take it, ride. The inside show makes a scare worthwhile.

Folks in the front definitely get wet; those farther back probably get wet. Riding toward the rear and lowering your head at the bottom of the hill allows you to leave the ride relatively dry, with cameras and hair-dos intact. Minimum height requirement 44 inches.

LINE: The main part of a long line winds through an outdoor courtyard — visible if you walk under the WDW Railroad Station, though it cannot be seen from the main entrance. After the courtyard, the line enters a barn, goes up stairs, and through a cave. If the line starts after the entrance to the barn, the wait is not bad. Check the sign at the entrance for specifics.

A small section is air-conditioned, with cool vents blasting air in other locations. Part of the ride itself is air-conditioned.

WAIT TIME: Long.

WHEELCHAIR ACCESS: Possible. To ride, a guest must transfer from wheelchair to log boat, which requires either upper body strength or a companion willing to lift. In addition, most guests need to hold themselves upright during the final hill to keep their body from bouncing around. In the unlikely event the ride shuts down, guests are warned that they must be able to "negotiate stairs and walk through narrow passageways." Guests with "heart conditions, motion sickness, back or neck problems, or other physical limitations" are advised not to ride.

Thunder Mountain Railroad
TICKET: E

NOTE: Once upon a time in early Disneyland, a peaceful little train chugged through America's frontier. But it changed and grew up. Now it's a run-away train that moves just fast enough to put a small scare into feeble hearts. For roller coaster lovers, it's mild stuff. For people who consider a merry-go-round heart-stopping excitement, it knocks your socks off. If you have doubts about riding any Disney roller coasters but hate to miss attractions, ride this one first. It's the tamest. If you're chicken, however, many of the sights can also be seen from the WDW Railroad or the Liberty Square Riverboats. Pay attention to the antique mining equipment — it costs Disney $300,000. Also, consider a ride after dark when selected indoor scenes are more dramatic.

MOVEMENT: The ride can be previewed by walking part way up the exit. There are no big hills. Most thrills come from small hills and quick turns, unlike traditional roller coasters. At the end, prepare for a sudden stop. Guests with "heart conditions, motion sickness, back or neck problems, or other physical limitations" are advised not to ride; must be 40 inches tall.

LINE: Impossible to tell. While a long line may wind up the hill to the ride's entrance, once inside, the line may move directly to the boarding area — or it might loop back and forth, back and forth, winding through the building. In addition, it's impossible to know how many trains are operating. Check at the ride's entrance for a sign estimating the wait time and assume it takes a few minutes less. Once inside, the entire queue line is covered but not air-conditioned.

WAIT TIME: Long.

WHEELCHAIR ACCESS: Possible. But guests must be able to board the ride unaided, transferring from wheelchair to train car. In addition, some upper body strength is needed throughout. The ride warns those who suffer from "motion sickness, back or neck problems, or other conditions that may be aggravated by this ride" to think twice before boarding. Wheelchairs should enter through the main exit found to the right of the entrance.

Tom Sawyer Island
TICKET: B

NOTE: Both a get-away on crowded days and a playground for kids, Tom Sawyer's Island is the closest thing to a natural wilderness inside the Magic Kingdom. Most attractions — teetering rocks, barrel bridges, and fake caves — cater to the Elementary school crowd. Island sights follow the story of Tom Sawyer (who probably lived on Main Street) and Huck Finn. Aunt Polly's, a water-front restaurant on the island that sells light, picnic-style fare, is one of the park's best spots to relax. Eat on the porch and watch the crowds amble through Frontierland or the giant Liberty Square Riverboats that ply the waters of the Rivers of America. Note that the island is only open during daylight hours.

MOVEMENT: Certain walkways are unsteady, such as the barrel bridges. To get to the island, guests ride rafts across the Rivers of America. Rafts are fairly steady, but akin to standing in a bus and holding handrails for support.

LINE: If waiting for a raft to cross the water, lines are fully visible, mostly shaded, but not air-conditioned. Remember that if a line forms on the mainland, there's a good chance another will form on the island when it's time to return, doubling your total wait time.

WAIT TIME: Short to Medium

WHEELCHAIR ACCESS: Poor. Wheelchair-bound guests can cross in the rafts, but will find it difficult to get around. Steps and dirt paths make it challenging. Some things — the barrel bridges, for example — are impossible.

Country Bear Jamboree

TICKET: E

NOTE: Even if you hate country/western music, see this one. If you enjoy country/western, visit twice. Destroying the notion that all bears look alike, the show relies on technology, but entertains thanks to good writing and tap-your-foot tunes. Unlike most Audio–Animatronic attractions, this one changes during different seasons. At Christmas, for example, the bears sing carols and dress for the ice and cold.

MOVEMENT: None — a theater presentation

LINE: While one group enjoys the 16-minute show, a second enters an air-conditioned (though you stand elbow-to-elbow) room directly inside the entrance. When the doors open, the new group fills the theater as the old group files out the other side. Queue lines are outdoors. Most areas are shaded but not air-conditioned.

WAIT TIME: Medium to long.

WHEELCHAIR ACCESS: Good. A cast member (get their attention) directs wheelchairs to the left side of the waiting line and on to a special seating area within the theater.

Frontierland Shootin' Arcade

TICKET: A

NOTE: The only Magic Kingdom attraction not included in a general admission, new-fangled Hawkins 54-caliber buffalo rifles shoot infra-red beams that cause strange reactions when they connect with a tar-

get. Graves spin, ghosts fly, and coyotes howl if you hit them exactly right. Popular with kids, it's one of those things that mature adults seldom try — but should.
MOVEMENT: None.
LINE: None.
WAIT TIME: Short.
WHEELCHAIR ACCESS: Easy by ramp. Two guns accommodate wheelchair guests.

Diamond Horseshoe Saloon Revue
TICKET: D
NOTE: A real live stage show in a real live saloon with real live can-can girls. In these thirty air-conditioned minutes, you laugh at jokes so G-rated that they shouldn't be funny — but they are. The atmosphere is bawdy, best-of-the-West stuff.
MOVEMENT: None. Guests are seated at tables with limited food and beverage service available.
LINE: The Diamond Horseshoe Revue is now a first-come, first-served show. Guests wander in and out both during the show and at other times. Its western-style architecture, air-conditioning, and food service make it a good spot to rest if the crowds aren't too thick.
WAIT TIME: Short.
WHEELCHAIR ACCESS: Good. Guests may remain in wheelchairs throughout. Entrance ramp located to the right of the main doors.

LIBERTY SQUARE

Smaller than the other lands, Liberty Square recreates a Northeastern American city, circa 1776. While four attractions have a Liberty Square address, only the Hall of Presidents completely fits the theme. The Liberty Square Riverboat and Mike Fink Keelboats board by Liberty Square, but once moving, spend most of their time touring outer Frontierland. The Haunted Mansion, set back from the square, fits uneasily into the Revolutionary War motif.

But in Liberty Square itself, the spirit of the U.S.A.'s founding comes into focus. The Liberty Tree grows in the middle of the square and recreates the spirit of 1776, when the Sons of Liberty hung lanterns on trees to celebrate American Independence. In the background, playing from invisible Disney speakers, march music — heavy with fifes and drums — creates an 18th century atmosphere.

Shops sell pewter and crafts. Architecture duplicates the style of the period, though no specific building is represented. Cast member costumes — floor length dresses and below-the-knees knickers — complete the fantasy.

Escape Spots: The Sleepy Hollow Restaurant, located by the gate leading from Liberty Square to the Hub at the end of Main Street, has secluded seating in the rear. This covered, outdoor area is a perfect get-away — ideal for a fifteen-minute soda break or a light meal.

The Hall of Presidents

TICKET: E

NOTE: Two things astound first-time visitors to The Hall of Presidents: First, the 42 presidents look eerily alive as they quietly chat with each other, scratch an itch, and stare at the audience. Second, it's graphically obvious that our forefathers are part of us and not a group of strangers that lived decades ago. The style of hair and dress change subtly as each President — starting with George Washington and ending with Bill Clinton — is introduced. Seeing these men introduced in chronological order shows how close the United States is to its roots, something easy to forget when we look back on our pre-Internet/inside restroom days.

MOVEMENT: None. A theater presentation.

LINE: Inside and air-conditioned. If possible, see it in the afternoon when other lines are long. Since it's a 25-minute show, however, the wait could be 25 minutes long if you're unlucky enough to arrive just as the doors close.

WAIT TIME: Short.

WHEELCHAIR ACCESS: Good. Guests may remain in wheelchairs.

Liberty Square Riverboat

TICKET: B

NOTE: The real frontier, Disney World style, exists behind Tom Sawyer's Island and can be seen either by train, Liberty Square Riverboat, or Mike Fink Keelboat. The riverboat, named for Disney designer, Richard F. Irvine, is a true working steamboat, but the ride is so smooth, it's difficult to believe you're really floating. (You are, but relax and enjoy it. You're also connected to a track under the water.) To view the scenes on both sides of the boat, find a centrally

located seat near the front or the back.
MOVEMENT: Almost none.
LINE: Short. The boat handles hundreds of people and usually takes everyone who is waiting. No air-conditioning.
WAIT TIME: Short.
WHEELCHAIR ACCESS: Complete. Wheelchair guests may remain in their chairs.

Mike Fink Keelboats
TICKET: C
NOTE: Circling Tom Sawyer's Island and the Disney frontier, the Mink Fink Keelboats cover the same territory as the Liberty Square Riverboat. The riverboat is bigger, less cramped, and smoother. The Mike Fink Keelboats, however, are more intimate and have a guide who gives a comic spiel en route. During slow seasons, the keelboats don't operate. In any case, choose either the keelboats or the riverboat, but not both.
MOVEMENT: Very little except for slight boat rocking.
LINE: Outdoors though covered.
WAIT TIME: Medium. Line may not get extremely long, but it doesn't move very fast.
WHEELCHAIR ACCESS: Poor. Guests must transfer from wheelchair to keelboat, usually requiring assistance. Most handicapped guests prefer the Liberty Square Riverboat.

The Haunted Mansion
TICKET: E
NOTE: Don't assume this is 1) scary, or 2) for kids. Anyone who's seen an old Topper movie or even Casper cartoons knows that ghosts look a lot like people, only they can disappear at will and, when present, are a white, see-through apparition. And, of course, they live in a haunted mansion. The Disney ghosts don't disappoint. They're 3-dimensional, disappear, and fly. Hallways stretch to infinity, rooms expand, and pictures follow you with their eyes. It's comic book stuff, but high quality entertainment.
MOVEMENT: The first, very short part of the attraction involves walking and standing. The second and longer portion takes place in a "tomb buggy," a two-person ride vehicle that moves at a steady, even pace throughout. The cart turns to the left and right to make sure

guests can see all the ghostly delights. At one point, the "buggy" turns completely around and guests almost lie on their backs as they go down a short hill. In all, there's nothing to deter anyone from enjoying The Haunted Mansion.

LINE: The waiting line is outdoors but shaded, most visible from the street. On a busy park day, people at the end of the line must stand in direct sunlight. To board the ride portion of the attraction, guests step onto a conveyer belt moving at the same speed (somewhat fast) as the tomb buggies.

WAIT TIME: Medium to long.

WHEELCHAIR ACCESS: Fair. Look for a cast member. Handicapped guests board at the ride's exit. Cast members will stop the ride, if necessary.

FANTASYLAND

Sometimes as people age, they forget the fantasies of childhood. A five-year-old fears the wicked witch that wants to eat Hansel and Gretal. He listens with baited breath to the story of Peter Rabbit, sure that Mr. McGregor will kill him. He sighs when Prince Charming kisses Snow White.

Sadly, it's harder to touch that childlike part as you age. After many years of not believing in Santa Claus and the tooth fairy, it's hard to remember how you felt as you waited for their arrival. But if you can still tap that part of your childhood — that part that believes in dragons and fair maidens and talking frogs — you'll love Fantasyland. If you can't resurrect that child within yourself, you'll still enjoy the color and the technology and the music, but you won't want to spend much time here.

When Walt Disney first built California's Disneyland, many of the rides were traditional, carnival-style attractions. While today's new rides are big budget, high-tech extravaganzas, a few simple ones still exist within the Magic Kingdom, and most are in Fantasyland. Of course, Disney's carnival rides hide behind beautiful paint jobs and intriguing themes. Flying teacups are not run-of-the-mill cups — they're the ones from Alice in Wonderland. Under different decor and paint, the Dumbo ride is, at other amusement parks, a cheap helicopter ride. But it feels somehow grander inside the Magic Kingdom.

Three of the Fantasyland attractions, Snow White's Adventures, Peter Pan's Flight, and Mr. Toad's Wild Ride, last less than five minutes and have none of the technological thrills found elsewhere. Still, they're fun if the line is not long. Try to visit first thing in the morning. The 20,000 Leagues Under the Sea attraction officially departed after numerous will-it-open/won't-it-open rumors, but the crystal clear lake still exists, waiting for an Imagineer to decide what to put there. New in '96, Ariel's Grotto features a small kids-can-get-wet playground plus cave where, after waiting in line, they can meet the little mermaid herself.

Escape Spots: Fantasyland has few escape spots. There's a semi-shaded piece of walkway near the 20,000 Leagues Under the Sea lagoon. Also, on the second floor of the castle, you can eat in King Stefan's Banquet Hall, perhaps the most interesting restaurant in the Magic Kingdom and one of the few offering table service. Its medieval atmosphere softens considerably when Cinderella visits.

Skyway to Tomorrowland
TICKET: C
NOTE: No special effects or surprises here. The aerial view is serene as you float above the Fantasyland hub-bub in quiet comfort and see what the rides really look like behind their facade. The ride is one-way. All guests — except the disabled — must disembark in Tomorrowland.
MOVEMENT: Smooth, but with a small amount of swinging.
LINE: Outdoors, not air-conditioned, and possibly long since it cannot move a large number of people at one time. The line's length is not visible from the walkway, but it's easy to turn around if you walk part way up and decide it's not worth the wait.
WAIT TIME: Medium to long.
WHEELCHAIR ACCESS: Fair. Disabled people must be able to transfer to a stationary Skyway gondola from their wheelchair. While it is a one-way trip for most, disabled people may ride round-trip. For wheelchair-bound guests, this is the only way to enjoy the Skyway since the Tomorrowland station is inaccessible.

It's A Small World
TICKET: E
NOTE: Singing the same song for over 30 years, this celebration of international harmony first debuted at the 1964-65 New York World's Fair. Doll collectors love it; children love it; first-timers lover it. Some

locals and repeat visitors are finished with it now, finding that after they ride, they can't get the song out of their head. Internationally famous, it's a must-see attraction for the uninitiated.

MOVEMENT: The entire ride is by boat, but with little to no rocking. Suitable for anyone.

LINE: Semi-air-conditioned and shaded, it moves quickly. One thick line of people breaks down into smaller lanes as you get close to boarding. Pick the line with less people, generally the one to the left.

WAIT TIME: Short to medium.

WHEELCHAIR ACCESS: Good. Selected boats have ramps with wheelchair access. Board from the exit ramp.

Peter Pan's Flight

TICKET: C

NOTE: Peter Pan's flight is slightly confusing to those unfamiliar with the movie, but visually intriguing anyway. Scenes loosely follow the plot of Disney's *Peter Pan*. Ride vehicles — small boats — connect to overhead rails, with action taking place below. Riders view scenes as if they're actually flying. If you ride only one "C" ride in Fantasyland, make it this one.

MOVEMENT: Slight tilts left or right, but nothing wild.

LINE: Not air-conditioned, but covered. Guests hop on a conveyer belt moving at the same speed as the ride vehicles. Ride can be stopped momentarily for those who need extra time boarding.

WAIT TIME: Long.

WHEELCHAIR ACCESS: Fair. Riders must transfer from wheelchair to vehicle by themselves.

Legend of the Lion King

TICKET: D

NOTE: Another show that takes a hit Disney movie and retells it in *Reader's Digest* form. Those who have not seen *The Lion King* may miss a few plot points, but they'll enjoy it anyway. Performed entirely by puppets (though it's unfair to call them puppets given their size and styling), the production includes state-of-the-art special effects, sound, and lighting. Both a waiting area and the theater are air-conditioned, making it a good choice for the middle of the day.

MOVEMENT: None. Theater presentation. Pre-show with standing room only.

LINE: Outdoors. It will not move at all until the doors open, then everyone enters the waiting area at once.
WAIT TIME: Short to medium.
WHEELCHAIR ACCESS: Good. Wheelchair riders may remain seated.

Cinderella's Golden Carrousel
TICKET: B
NOTE: A merry-go-round, but it's Disney perfect and plays classic movie melodies. Built in 1917, it's one of the few Disney attractions created by someone else.
MOVEMENT: Up and down; up and down.
LINE: Ride and line are outdoors, though mostly shaded.
WAIT TIME: Medium.
WHEELCHAIR ACCESS: Poor. Riders must be able to transfer out of a wheelchair and support themselves on a wooden horse.

Dumbo, The Flying Elephant
TICKET: C
NOTE: A kid's ride, but visually attractive.
MOVEMENT: Spins in a circle, but riders control the height of the cars (the elephants?) from within the ride.
LINE: Outdoors and not shaded.
WAIT TIME: Long. In the morning, many parents and children head for this one first before the wait becomes unbearable. That, in turn, makes it unbearable before any other Magic Kingdom attraction.
WHEELCHAIR ACCESS: Poor. Riders must be able to transfer from wheelchair to elephant.

Snow White's Adventures
TICKET: C
NOTE: The ride loosely follows the movie. Recently updated, it was originally a dark ride, meant to scare kids with scenes of the witch. Toned down, it now includes happy scenes. Fun for those who enjoyed the 1939 movie, it makes the animation three-dimensional.
MOVEMENT: Carts move evenly and without hills.
LINE: Shaded but not air-conditioned.
WAIT TIME: Long.

WHEELCHAIR ACCESS: Fair. Riders must be able to transfer from wheelchair to ride.

Mr. Toad's Wild Ride
TICKET: C
NOTE: Antique cars wind through scenes from the classic story, *The Wind in the Willows*. Most characters are not three-dimensional, but flat drawings on wood that bounce or retreat as the out-of-control ride vehicle races around the English countryside. Pleasant but uneventful, there is one scene with a train that is psychologically unnerving.
MOVEMENT: It just calls itself "wild." Anyone can ride.
LINE: Shaded but not air-conditioned.
WAIT TIME: Long.
WHEELCHAIR ACCESS: Fair. Riders must be able to transfer themselves from wheelchair to ride vehicle.

Mad Tea Party
TICKET: C
NOTE: Cute ride with the potential to make you sick. Great for kids. Most adults ignore it.
MOVEMENT: You spin round and round, in tiny circles, big circles, and cup-sized circles.
LINE: Outdoors but shaded.
WAIT TIME: Medium
WHEELCHAIR ACCESS: Must be able to transfer from wheelchair to teacup.

MICKEY'S TOONTOWN FAIR

Home to Mickey and Minnie Mouse and the best place to meet the famous mammal, Mickey's Toontown Fair has little else directed at adults. Upgraded in time for Disney's 25th Anniversary celebration, most attractions are hands-on activities rather than shows, though a small roller coaster, The Barnstormer, debuted. While the area is designed for kids, it can be a pleasant sojourn for adults, as long as it's not too crowded. On busy days, many adults content themselves with viewing this land from the stopped train as they wait for it to continue its journey to Main Street. For them, that's enough time in Mickey's Toontown Fair.

Both Mickey and Minnie have a home here, both designed in a what-if-cartoons-were-real motif, and both toured by foot. After exiting Mickey's house, crowds flow toward the Judge's Tent where, after waiting in another line, you can meet the famous mouse. Adults wishing to forego the event can beat a retreat through his garage. In Minnie's home, a number of surprises enchant kids. Once outside, three more lines form to visit with classic characters (Goofy, Pluto, etc.), princesses (Jasmine, Cinderella, etc.), or villains (Captain Hook, Jafar, etc.)

Minor Toontown Fair attractions include Donald's Boat, a place for kids to get wet as they play, and the Toontown Hall of Fame, where cartoon vegetables are on display.

The Barnstormer at Goofy's Wiseacres Farm
TICKET: C
NOTE: A roller coaster, this one surpasses the kiddy rides found in most amusement parks, but doesn't even touch Thunder Mountain Railroad. Sized for adults as well as children, this short ride might suit people considering Space Mountain, but who "want to get their feet wet." All others should save their wait time for more exciting venues.
MOVEMENT: No large hills. Most thrills come from curves and dips.
LINE: Outdoors; most visible from the main entrance.
WAIT TIME: Medium to long.
WHEELCHAIR ACCESS: Fair. Guests must transfer from wheelchair to coaster.

Walt Disney World Railroad
TICKET: C
NOTE: The same train described under Main Street. Trip includes stops at Main Street and in Frontierland.
MOVEMENT: Gentle.
LINE: Queue is sheltered but not air-conditioned. Length is visible from the entrance.
WAIT TIME: Short to medium.
WHEELCHAIR ACCESS: Riders may remain in wheelchairs if entering or exiting at Mickey's Toontown Fair or Frontierland stations. At the Main Street station, nonambulatory guests must be able to transfer to their wheelchair.

TOMORROWLAND

In 1995, the past finally got too close to the future. Tomorrowland had not aged well. Almost twenty-five years after the Magic Kingdom opened, Tomorrowland found itself competing with nearby Epcot Center. Unfortunately, Epcot won the high-tech contest and Tomorrowland looked like an also-ran.

So Disney Imagineers changed Tomorrowland, but not by designing the projected world in the year 2020. If they couldn't compete with Epcot, then they'd create the dream of tomorrow — but from the perspective of our ancestors. Following design successes at EuroDisney, Imagineers created a Buck Rogers-style future, one with shiny copper, chrome, and brass. Architectural designs look like they were lifted from early Superman comics, built with Erector Sets, and designed for George Jetson. Tomorrow — the Disney tomorrow — is flashy, irreverent, and fun.

For the redesign, Imagineers kept three existing attractions, upgraded one ride, replaced two others, and threw in a futuristic arcade. During the day, Tomorrowland is metallic and shiny. At night, it's electric — literally. Miles of neon frame the buildings, their colors varied, the effect dazzling. If you visit during the day, return at night just to see the difference.

Escape Spots: Both Cosmic Ray's Starlight Cafe on the Fantasyland side of Tomorrowland and the Plaza Pavilion to the right of the main entrance, have dining areas that overlook both the Hub at the end of Main Street and parts of Tomorrowland. (You may want to avoid lunch and dinnertime, however.)

Grand Prix Raceway

TICKET: D

NOTE: This one's mainly for kids.

MOVEMENT: Not too violent, it's like traveling in a riding lawn-mower, but with more style and no grass. Drivers are warned not to bump the car in front of them but the rule is not always obeyed. Cars are on tracks. Guests must be 52 inches in height.

LINE: Much of it is shaded but outdoors.

WAIT TIME: Long. Even a short line moves slowly since the ride can't accommodate many people at once.

WHEELCHAIR ACCESS: Limited. Guests must transfer from wheelchair to car and somehow work the floor pedals.

Astro Orbiter
TICKET: C
NOTE: This is the Dumbo ride without the elephants. It's also higher in the air. Great for kids. For most adults, not appealing.
MOVEMENT: Round and round and up and down.
LINE: Outdoors though shaded.
WAIT TIME: Long.
WHEELCHAIR ACCESS: Fair. Guests must move themselves from wheelchair to jet.

Tomorrowland Transit Authority (TTA)
TICKET: C
NOTE: Formerly the WEDway Peoplemover, the TTA is not high excitement, but it's great way to whiz around Tomorrowland, preview attractions, and get a feel for the area. Be sure to see the "city of tomorrow" displayed during the ride. Looking dated, it's Walt Disney's prototype for Epcot, planned as a working city rather than a theme park. Today, the Disney-developed town of Celebration comes closer to Walt's original vision. The TTA also enters Space Mountain and provides an easy way to preview the ride and analyze the length of the queue.
MOVEMENT: Suitable for anyone.
LINE: Outdoors but shaded. Guests ride a conveyer belt to the second level and ride a second conveyer belt to board the ride. Both belt and ride vehicles move at a reasonably slow speed.
WAIT TIME: Short. Not the most popular Tomorrowland attraction and able to handle a large number of guests, the wait is reasonable even during busy periods.
WHEELCHAIR ACCESS: Poor. Guests cannot take wheelchairs up the ramp leading to the second floor, meaning they must be able to stand for a while, walk a short distance, and enter the ride vehicle.

Tomorrowland Light and Power Company
TICKET: None
NOTE: The new home of Main Street's Penny Arcade, Tomorrowland Light and Power Company's latest video games tempt the eight to sixteen crowd.
MOVEMENT: None.
LINE: None.

WAIT TIME: None.
WHEELCHAIR ACCESS: Good. Selected games accessible to those in wheelchairs.

Space Mountain

TICKET: E

NOTE: Space Mountain is the best roller coaster in the Magic Kingdom. If you hate roller coasters, forget it. If you like roller coasters, plan to ride early before the onslaught of heavy crowds. Space Mountain simulates space — the lack of light, lack of gravity, and vast emptiness. It operates in almost total darkness. Stars and asteroids fly by, at times lighting the track for an uneasy minute. Sometimes you see which way you're headed; sometimes you don't. For those unsure if they should ride, first travel on the Tomorrowland Transit Authority. You'll not only preview the ride, but you can check the line and see if it's worth the wait. A non-riding companion may walk inside Space Mountain, bypass the ride, and wait by the ride's exit. Signs inside the main waiting area give directions.

MOVEMENT: Left, right, up, and down. It moves only 28 miles per hour but feels much faster. Must be 44 inches tall to ride.

LINE: Sometimes the Disney folks will back the line up at the front entrance, even though there's room inside and you're still a long way from the main waiting area. This line waits in the sun. Once allowed inside, the entire line is air-conditioned.

WAIT TIME: Long. But just because there's a long line outside the building does not mean a long wait. Sometimes a long line is inside; sometimes outside. The only way to preview the internal line is to ride the Tomorrowland Transit Authority or check the sign in front and assume a few less minutes.

WHEELCHAIR ACCESS: Fair. You must be able to move from wheelchair to rocket and have enough upper body strength to hold tight. Guests are warned that they must "be in good health and free from heart conditions, motion sickness, back or neck problems, or other conditions that may be aggravated by this ride." In case of an emergency stop (unlikely), guests may be required to negotiate catwalks.

Skyway to Fantasyland
TICKET: C
NOTE: One-way trip to Fantasyland. It's usually faster to walk, but the aerial view shows the park from a different perspective.
MOVEMENT: Smooth with a slight swing sometimes. Anyone can ride.
LINE: Shaded but outside.
WAIT TIME: Long, due to the limited number of people that can board at one time.
WHEELCHAIR ACCESS: None. Guests in wheelchairs should board in Fantasyland where they will be allowed to ride round-trip.

Carousel of Progress
TICKET: D
NOTE: Most adults love this one, perhaps because they relate to it. Premiering at the 1964-1965 New York World's Fair at the same time as Small World, it moved to Disneyland when the Fair closed and, later, to Walt Disney World. In this unique format, the audience literally rotates around four stages, seeing different scenes that trace technological progress through the years. Each scene recreates the electrical marvels of yesterday and today, from indoor pumps to virtual reality games. Remember when radio was king? When TV's were black and white and only inches wide? It's here. The final scene — the world of today — has been upgraded many times.
MOVEMENT: Anyone can ride.
LINE: Outdoors but shaded. There's not usually a real line except on the busiest days. People wait in a group as the building turns and everyone enters at once.
WAIT TIME: Short
WHEELCHAIR ACCESS: Good. Riders may stay in their wheelchairs for the performance.

Take Flight
TICKET: C
NOTE: This short ride celebrates our ability to travel and see the world. With a couple interesting effects, it's a pleasant diversion that doesn't require a long wait, though not one of Disney's must-sees.
MOVEMENT: Moving cars pivot left and right to view the scenes, but anyone may ride.

LINE: Air-conditioned unless extremely long.
WAIT TIME: Short.
WHEELCHAIR ACCESS: Fair. Guests must transfer themselves from wheelchair to vehicle from a moving conveyer belt. Cast members will stop the ride if necessary.

The Timekeeper

TICKET: D
NOTE: Brought from EuroDisney and Americanized, this attraction takes you on a journey through time, hosted by a Robin Williams-styled robot called Timekeeper. Using a 360-degree movie, the attraction includes the two traits that make Disney stand out — good movie-making and good writing. Timekeeper and cohorts entertain; the movie amazes.
MOVEMENT: None, but you must stand for the performance.
LINE: Indoors and air-conditioned unless very long.
WAIT TIME: Medium.
WHEELCHAIR ACCESS: Good. Guests may stay in their wheelchair.

The ExtraTERRORestrial Alien Encounter

TICKET: E
NOTE: Billed as the first PG-rated Disney attraction, it's still fairly tame. Those familiar with business conventions can follow the plot; those who never attended one might be a bit lost. Essentially, X-S Tech, an intergalactic business group, messes with things best left alone. The company has a booth at the Tomorrowland Convention Center displaying their newest technology that transfers people (or things) long distances, similar to Captain James T. Kirk beaming up or down from the Starship Enterprise. They're trying to sell this new technology to conventioneers, played by you, the theme park guest. At one point in the demonstration, things go very wrong.

The ride carries a warning for those with health problems, but most people can enjoy it. On a first ride, people tend to be scared because they don't know what's going to happen. Many people panic when the restraint system automatically slides down over their head, assuming that it implies rapid motion. It doesn't.
MOVEMENT: None. There are two pre-shows, both air-conditioned and both enjoyed while standing. In the main show, certain special

effects scare people. Expect blasts of air in your face, drops of water, and total darkness. You will not, however, be eaten.

LINE: Outdoors but shaded. The entire line is visible. Once inside, the first preshow begins. Minimum height of 48 inches required.

WAIT TIME: Long.

WHEELCHAIR ACCESS: Good. Guests may remain in their wheelchair for the entire show.

PARADES AND SHOWS

Parades and shows change, making them less predictable than the big-budget AudioAnimatronic attractions. Never-the-less, they're one of the Magic Kingdom's best features. It doesn't matter how well performers sing or dance when they're supported by Disney special effects, artistic fireworks, ingenious backdrops, Hollywood-perfect costuming, and a full selection of Disney songs.

A guide to the "big ones" is included here, but there's no substitute for the daily guide to shows and special events available at City Hall or the front turnstiles. Refer to it often. If you just saw the Tiki birds in Adventureland and you're ambling toward Pirates of the Caribbean, check to see what time the steel drum band plays. If soon, hold off on Pirates and find a comfortable place to stand. If half an hour away, see Pirates, then enjoy the show.

All Magic Kingdom parades begin at the Fire Station on Town Square and travel to the Main Street Hub. The parade circles the Hub, passing by the entrance to Tomorrowland and Cinderella's Castle before crossing the bridge into Liberty Square. At the entrance to the Liberty Square Riverboat, the parade turns left and continues through downtown Frontierland before ending at Splash Mountain. For some parades, the route is reversed.

Because they've seen it on TV, most people want to view the parades on Main Street or, ideally, from atop the WDW Railroad platform at the head of Main Street. From the railroad platform, Cinderella's Castle rises in the distance as the parade circles Town Square. If interested in this location, arrive up to an hour and a half before the parade to secure the position. It's not exactly a secret. To enjoy it from the curb on Main Street, arrive 45 minutes beforehand, depending on the daily crowds. While not the parade view seen on TV, Liberty Square or Frontierland viewing areas fill up later than those on Main Street. Because it takes time to walk the parade route, the first floats arrive in Frontierland ten to fifteen minutes after their Main Street debut.

Disney parades are not built for only those guests with a first row seat. Most floats rise two stories high, visible to everyone no matter how thick the crowds. Standing in front is best — it's less claustrophobic. But it's not necessary to enjoy the show. If you exit an attraction and discover a parade marching by, stop and enjoy it. Even with five people between you and the parade, you don't miss much. And, since walkways get cut off by the passing parade, you may not be able to get through anyway. If you arrive shortly before a parade begins and find thick crowds, look for a roped-off, parade crossing spot. Manned by Disney employees, these remain open throughout the parade and, even if five people are in front of you, the open space allows a decent view of an entire float.

Special areas are reserved for those in wheelchairs. Ask any cast member — they're everywhere just before a parade — for the nearest location or refer to the *Guidebook for Guests with Disabilities*.

SHOWS

Three live action shows have already been mentioned as attractions — Legend of the Lion King, Mickey's Toontown Fair Show, and the Diamond Horseshoe Saloon Revue. Refer to earlier descriptions for information.

Main Street Performers

• A Ragtime piano player, located at Casey's Corner just off the Hub to the left, belts out familiar tunes.

• The Dapper Dans sing barbershop songs, dance, and tell jokes.

• The Rhythm Rascals entertain on instruments like washboards and banjos, mixing humor into the music.

• The Flag Retreat, scheduled for shortly after 5:00 p.m., features a flock of homing pigeons.

• Walt Disney World Band performs in Town Square.

Fantasy in the Sky Fireworks

It's just like watching the Disney fireworks on TV — only better. When the Magic Kingdom first opened, the fireworks did not go off behind Cinderella's Castle. But too many people watched Walt

Disney's *Wonderful World of Color* and, every Sunday night, saw fireworks go off behind the castle. Recognizing legitimate customer complaints when they heard them, the Disney people quickly moved the fireworks to their correct behind-the-castle location. While every city from San Diego to Bangor sets off fireworks on the Fourth of July, Disney's add a third dimension — music. And Tinker Bell. The music sets off the fireworks, making the blasts and pops more dramatic. Tinker Bell adds her touch sometimes, just as she did on the TV show, flying across the sky from Cinderella's Castle.

During slow seasons of the year, fireworks are not scheduled, though they'll be presented every night during 1997. Fireworks generally go off at 10 p.m. after the SpectroMagic Parade. Since the lights of Main Street are dimmed during the display, sight impaired guests may find it difficult to maneuver if they choose not to watch.

Castle Forecourt

Performed in front of Cinderella's Castle and visible from the Hub, the Castle Forecourt performers sing and dance their way through Disney-oriented shows. For Disney fans, it's a 3-D version of favorite movie moments. For those who missed Disney's most recent offerings, it's a way to enjoy the newest songs. Depending on the show, other non-Disney pieces are also performed. Many times, two separate shows are scheduled.

Shows might be canceled in case of inclement weather and content may change based on season of the year. Check the daily show guide for specifics. Plan to arrive at least fifteen minutes early and don't forget the Florida sun.

Character Meals

Aimed directly at the elementary school crowd, Disney offers an array of meals where the characters show up, socialize, and spend quality time with youngsters. While adults can certainly attend without kids — no one from back home will recognize you, after all — the main draw is food, Mickey Mouse, and photo ops. The Crystal Palace now features Winnie the Pooh all day long, King Stefan's Banquet Hall in Cinderella's Castle hosts a "Once Upon a Time" breakfast buffet, and The Liberty Tree Tavern has a character supper. Check the daily schedule for more information. Reservations can be made ahead of time by calling (407) 939-3463.

Electrical Water Pageant

Not a Magic Kingdom attraction per se, this string of barges circles the Seven Seas Lagoon and Bay Lake, putting on a show at each scheduled stop. The forerunner of the Electric Light Parade (now in EuroDisney), it doesn't have the technological diversity of SpectroMagic, but electric lights shimmering on top of the water seem magical and, at the same time, eerily out-of-place. Each barge is lit separately and virtually invisible before turned on. The show lasts about ten minutes.

While many departing Magic Kingdom guests end up seeing the show by accident as they wait in line for the monorail or ferry, it is best viewed from the dock or beach of a Disney Resort where crowds don't detract from the show. The show's schedule changes seasonally. Stop by City Hall or any of the Disney Resorts to determine exact times during your stay. In addition to the Magic Kingdom, the Electrical Water Pageant performs at the Polynesian, the Grand Floridian, Wilderness Lodge, Fort Wilderness, and the Contemporary.

Galaxy Palace Theater

Formerly the Tomorrowland Theater, it's located between the Carousel of Progress and Take Flight. Check the entertainment calendar for times.

Very loosely based on the TV show, *Star Search*, Mickey and friends drag out alien talent in hopes of winning the grand prize. Much of the show caters to kids, but the songs make even adult feet tap. This big-budget play is a pleasant diversion in good weather. Watch the sun, however — the audience sits outdoors. Completely accessible to wheelchairs.

Caribbean Steel Drum Band

Located in Adventureland, this group appears sporadically.

The Sword in the Stone

Located in Fantasyland and aimed at children, the legend of King Arthur is reenacted when one lucky youngster pulls the fabled sword from the stone.

PARADES

25th Anniversary "Remember the Magic"

Replacing the Mickey Mania parade, "Remember the Magic" runs through December of 1997. Depending on the crowds, front row seats start to fill up from 20 minutes to 45 minutes before the parade. Don't forget the unforgiving Florida sun.

SpectroMagic Parade

Arguably better than anything else in the park, the SpectroMagic parade floats down Main Street once or twice during selected seasons of the year, though it's scheduled every night during 1997 in celebration of Disney's 25th anniversary. Its predecessor, the Electric Light Parade, contained float after float of Disney movie scenes made of small, Christmas-tree type lights against a black background. SpectroMagic goes one step further. It kept the lights but added additional special effects like giant holographs and fiber-optics. Also themed to Disney movies, high-tech sensors imbedded in the street recognize each passing float and cue overhead speakers to play music that complements the theme. An exciting presentation.

Viewing can be difficult. Crowds form at least a half hour before the performance and many times earlier, especially on Main Street. If you're a night owl and two performances are scheduled, ignore the first parade. By the second parade, worn-out parents have returned to their hotel with exhausted children in tow. Decent seating can be found until right before showtime.

While there are no bad viewing areas for parades, Liberty Square is a personal favorite. With your back facing the Liberty Square Riverboats, you get a forward view of floats as they leave the Hub, and a sideways view as they turn toward Frontierland. For those in wheelchairs, there is a reserved area across the street near the Liberty Tree. Main Street tends to fill earlier.

To bring out these self-lighted floats, the usual Magic Kingdom lighting must be reduced. With limited walking space and dimmer lights, many people have trouble navigating the crowds. Those in wheelchairs or the visually impaired may find it impossible. If you do not want to watch the parade, tour Tomorrowland or Fantasyland to avoid problems.

MAGIC KINGDOM RESTAURANTS

There are three ways to buy food in the Magic Kingdom: at a sit-down restaurant, at a fast-food restaurant, or from a food cart. For simplicity, the food carts are not listed here, but they sell a wide range of products and are found everywhere. Traditional amusement park food is abundant: popcorn, cookies, ice cream bars (shaped like Mickey of course), and soda, but a number of vendors also serve healthier fare, such as fresh fruit or juice. In Frontierland, a food cart vendor sells massive turkey legs, slow-roasted and juicy.

It's possible to tour the Magic Kingdom — and many people recommend it — without ever sitting down to eat. Grab some turkey and wait in line; grab a soda and wait in line; grab some ice cream and wait in line. It may not be relaxing, but it does save time.

Most MK visitors dine at one of the many fast food restaurants. The selection in each is similar, yet different. Pecos Bills in Frontierland has a Tex-Mex flavor; the Columbia Harbour House in Liberty Square offers New England-style fare. Behind the themed facades, most serve burgers, fries, and something healthy for the diet conscious. The fast-food places are listed here along with a brief list of food sold. In general, it's not worth crossing half the park if you're interested in fast food. If you get hungry in Fantasyland, eat at Pinocchio Village Haus. If your stomach growls in Tomorrowland, stop at Cosmic Ray's Starlight Café. All serve decent food.

At press time, priority seating for full-service restaurants could be arranged sixty days in advance by calling (407) WDW-DINE. ("Priority seating" means that a table is not immediately ready but your name goes to the top of the waiting list when you arrive.) Reservation policies have changed more than once, so check before leaving home.

Here are two suggestions for dining on your Magic Kingdom day:

• **Eat a late lunch.** Since most full-service restaurants are centrally located, they're easy to reach. You get an unhurried hour in air-conditioned comfort during the day's most crowded times. And, in addition to smaller crowds, lunch prices are better. Portions — almost the same size as those for dinner — can cost as much as 1/3 less.

• **Leave the park**. Eat at the Contemporary, the Polynesian, or the Grand Floridian. By monorail, the trip is part of the fun and, outside the park, you don't feel like part of a production line. Buffets served at the resorts can save money and time but not at the expense of good nutrition.

For more information, refer to the chapter on Park Touring Tips. In the following descriptions, B (breakfast), L (lunch), and D (dinner) indicate the meals served.

FULL SERVICE RESTAURANTS

Tony's Town Square Restaurant

Remember the Disney movie Lady and the Tramp? Remember the romantic scene where the dogs eat a piece of spaghetti, meet in the middle, and accidentally kiss? That all happened at Tony's, or rather, in the alley outside Tony's, recreated in the Magic Kingdom and located on Town Square, across from City Hall. The decor fits both an Italian restaurant and the Victorian architecture of Main Street, with lots of ornate woodwork and polished brass.

For lunch, the menu has light entrees and traditional Italian fare. One person can enjoy a burger while another has pizza. Other offerings include seafood and steaks. For dinner, heavier entrees include chicken, steaks, and, of course, spaghetti with meatballs. Tony's Town Square Restaurant is also the only restaurant inside the Magic Kingdom that offers a full-service breakfast. Moderate to expensive. Priority seating available. B, L, D.

The Crystal Palace

Offering a full buffet — the only one in the Magic Kingdom — the Crystal Palace is not a sit-down restaurant yet not fast food. Not knowing how to categorize it, it ends up here.

Very Victorian with ornate windows, a raised ceiling, trees, and even birds, the Crystal Palace satisfies guests who want a good meal fast. While large, it has an intimate atmosphere thanks to towering tropical plants and a divided room lay-out. Tables at either end of the restaurant have a relaxed, outside-the-crowds feel. Transformed from a previous life as a cafeteria, The Crystal Palace now features Winnie the Pooh all day long. That's great for kids but it negates a bit of the building's original elegance. Open all day, the Crystal Palace serves American meals that include fish, spit-roasted chicken, and prime rib. Pasta dishes are offered along with healthy salads, desserts, and plenty of side dishes. First thing in the morning, it's the best place to get a full breakfast without wasting time. Moderate to expensive. Priority seating available. B, L, D.

The Plaza Restaurant

While the decor of Tony's Town Square and the Crystal Palace have a traditional Victorian look, the Plaza Restaurant relies on mirrors and an art nouveau decor, reminiscent of French restaurants.

Located between Main Street and the Plaza Pavilion (en route to Tomorrowland), this out-of-the-way spot is easily missed by the crowds. Serving traditional American cuisine, those looking for healthy food can find it here, as well as those looking for the kind of ice cream sundaes that lower your body temperature a few degrees. Moderate. Priority seating available. L, D.

The Liberty Tree Tavern

Guests from Boston and Philadelphia will feel like they've returned home. The Liberty Tree Tavern's hardwood floors, Williamsburg walls, pewter table settings, and English-styled china recreate the taverns of 1776. Servers wear traditional dresses or vests. Even the windows have the bubbles and swirls found in old glass.

Food is traditional. For lunch, they serve sandwiches and salads along with heavier entrees. In the evening, they now host a character dinner featuring Disney favorites with food served family style. Served by a waitress, food options include fish, shrimp, prime rib, chicken, and lobster. New England clam chowder is served all day.

Reservations are recommended. Those visiting from New England may not find it as unique as travelers from other parts of the country. Expensive. Priority seating available. L, D.

King Stefan's Banquet Hall

As the centerpiece of the Magic Kingdom, first-time guests expect a ride or some kind of attraction inside Cinderella's Castle. Well, this is it. It's not exactly what kids want, but it gives the castle substance for those willing to eat a full-course meal and relax for an hour. For the record, King Stefan is Sleeping Beauty's father.

Of the sit-down restaurants in the Magic Kingdom, King Stefan's ranks number one in fantasy value. Good Italian and New England restaurants exist in other parts of the United States, but there are few medieval restaurants, much less ones that exist inside a real castle. (Not to mention Cinderella's occasional appearance.) Everything fits, from the vaulted ceiling to the towering windows. Pewter place settings add to the theme. You expect to see King Henry chewing on a turkey leg, then throwing it to the dogs.

During lunch, Roast Beef sandwiches, salads, and lighter fare are served. For dinner, prime rib is the specialty, but they also serve chicken and seafood. In the morning, guests enjoy the "Once Upon a Time" character breakfast. Expensive. B, L, D.

Fast Food Restaurants and Specialty Snacks

Main Street
• *Main Street Bake Shop*. Cookies, pastries, and great stuff to add inches to your waist.
• *Plaza Ice Cream Parlor*. There's almost always a line at this place.
• *Casey's Corner*. Featuring an occasional piano player, they specialize in hot dogs and sweets.

Adventureland
• *El Pirata y el Perico*. Mexican fare including tacos, taco salads, and nachos. Open seasonally.
• *Aloha Isle*. Juice, Dole whips, and fresh fruit.
• *Sunshine Tree Terrace*. Citrus drinks and non-fat yogurt.

Frontierland
• *Pecos Bill Café*. Western styled fast food with either indoor or outdoor seating. Serving burgers, barbecued chicken, salads, and hot dogs.
• *Aunt Polly's Landing*. Located on Tom Sawyer's Island, it's a bit inconvenient to get to, but if you like picnic fare, it's worth the trip. Outdoor dining on the verandah gives a great view of Liberty Square across the water and the riverboat as it cruises down the Rivers of America. Food includes sandwiches, cold chicken, ice cream, and apple pie.
• *Diamond Horseshoe Saloon Revue*. Sandwiches, chips, and dessert.

Liberty Square
• *Sleepy Hollow*. Light food including vegetarian entrees and sandwiches served on pita bread. The brick courtyard provides a great place to escape the crowds.
• *Columbia Harbour House*. Fast food with atmosphere a cut above the rest, serving fish, salads, chicken, and sandwiches. Open seasonally.

Fantasyland
• *The Pinocchio Village Haus*. Standard hot dog, hamburger, and salad

fare. The decor is intriguing with plenty of small rooms rather than one large dining hall. Decorated in a storybook way, the tale of Pinocchio is painted on the walls. One room looks down into the Small World ride.

• *Lumière's Kitchen*. Named after the candlestick in Beauty and the Beast, the selections appeal mostly to kids.

• *The Little Big Top*. Beverages. Open seasonally.

• *Enchanted Grove*. Lemonade and lemonade slush. Tucked between Fantasyland and Tomorrowland, this is easy to miss, but refreshing on a hot day.

• *Mrs. Pott's Cupboard*. Also named for a Beauty and the Beast character. Ice cream specialties.

• *Hook's Tavern*. Soft drinks and chips.

Tomorrowland

• *Cosmic Ray's Starlight Café*. A huge fast food place — the largest in the Magic Kingdom — it's definitely not the place to escape the crowds. There is, however, some dining outdoors on the Hub side that can be pleasant. Serving burgers, chicken, sandwiches, soups, and salads.

• *The Plaza Pavilion*. Located to the right of Tomorrowland's main entrance, it has quiet, outdoor seating that overlooks the Hub. It specializes in deli sandwiches, pizza, and salads.

• *Auntie Gravity's Galactic Goodies*. Natural foods, frozen yogurt, soft drinks.

• *Lunching Pad*. Light food including smoked turkey legs and desserts.

MAGIC KINGDOM SHOPPING

Few people go to the Magic Kingdom to shop, yet most end up shopping anyway. With over 50 different stores, half the joy lies in discovering them. Each land has places that sell not only Disney merchandise but also items appropriate to their area's theme. Adventureland, for example, stocks African merchandise, straw hats, ecology T-shirts, and native jewelry. Frontierland stores sell leather goods, silver and jade jewelry, and ten-gallon hats. Liberty Square shops have pewter and china. On-site guests can have purchases delivered to their hotel room. Off-site guests may have them shipped to the front of the park, to be picked up just prior to departure.

A side note: many stores stock life's necessities such as aspirin and raincoats but do not display them. If you find you need something, stop in a store and ask. If they do not have the item behind the counter, they will direct you to the nearest store that does. If you still can't locate your product, call the merchandise hotline at (407) 824-5566 for further information.

Select Magic Kingdom shops worth mentioning include:

• *The Main Street Emporium.* While many stores offer Disney themed merchandise, the Emporium, located on Town Square, is souvenir headquarters. Take a minute to enjoy the Emporium's windows, recreations of Disney movies that, if viewed in sequence, follow the movie's plot. When shopping Main Street, you can actually walk indoors from one end to the other, going outside only at the cross street. It appears that there are many shops; in reality, it's more like one store that's been creatively divided.

• *Disneyana Collectibles.* Found beside Tony's Town Square Restaurant, this store features artistic renditions of Disney classics, like Mickey etched glass end tables that retail for $2000. Movie cels — once given away to Disneyland patrons — sell for thousands of dollars. While you might not buy anything, it's certainly the most fun store for browsing. In addition to shopping, Disney memorabilia is displayed in a small museum-like setting.

• *Kodak Camera Center.* Located on the right side of Main Street as you enter — across the street from the Emporium — the Kodak Camera Center sells not only film and instant cameras, but also offers two-hour film developing. For those who do not want to carry a camcorder around, they can be rented here.

• *Ye Olde Christmas Shoppe.* Located in Liberty Square, the entire shop sells Christmas decorations, an anomaly in the heat of a Florida summer.

• *Sir Mickey's.* Stocking character clothing, the shop is interesting not for what it sells but for how it looks. A magical beanstalk has begun to take over the store, eating through windows and raising the inside ceiling. Located behind the castle in Fantasyland.

• *Merchant of Venus.* You may not buy anything, but it's certainly worth a stop. After seeing all the Disney special effects — and not knowing how they did it — here's your chance to purchase some technological magic to take home. Located behind the ExtraTERRORestrial Alien Encounter in Tomorrowland.

DON'T MISS...

Here's a quick reference list of attractions you should see before leaving the Magic Kingdom. Items with a bullet indicate a roller coaster-type ride.

Adventureland
Tropical Serenade (The Enchanted Tiki Birds)
Jungle Cruise
Pirates of the Caribbean

Frontierland
• Splash Mountain
• Big Thunder Mountain Railroad
Country Bear Jamboree
Diamond Horseshoe Saloon Revue

Liberty Square
The Hall of Presidents
The Haunted Mansion

Fantasyland
It's a Small World

Tomorrowland
• Space Mountain
The Carousel of Progress
The Timekeeper
The ExtraTERRORestrial Alien Encounter

Parades
"Remember the Magic" parade
SpectroMagic (evenings during high season)

EPCOT CENTER

146 Getting to Epcot

147 First Things First

149 Touring Tips

151 Guidelines For Those Who Don't Mind
       a Lot of Walking

152 Lands and Rides

172 Shows

174 Restaurants

182 Shopping

183 Don't Miss...

Chapter Ten

EPCOT CENTER

Often thought of as "Disney's second park," Epcot Center uses Disney's story-telling talent and technological showmanship to convert dry educational topics into intriguing entertainment. While fun for all ages, Epcot appeals to adults more than kids.

"Epcot" is an acronym for **E**xperimental **P**rototype **C**ommunity **O**f **T**omorrow, not **E**very **P**arent **C**arries **O**ne **T**oddler, though the latter may be truer than the former. As originally conceived by Walt Disney, it was to be a town always on the forefront of technology, where the homes and community lay-out promote interaction and involvement — a concept more like the Disney-created town of Celebration located just west of Walt Disney World. After Walt's death, the Epcot concept changed. When you scrape away the educational facade, Epcot is still a theme park, but without all the thrill rides. In its two themed lands, Future World and World Showcase, only two rides even resemble a roller coaster.

Future World is a science center, bigger and better than those found anywhere else. Future World takes abstract ideas — like how blood flows through the body or how solar energy works — and makes them real. On one level, it's an effective teaching tool for young folks, clearly demonstrating key concepts of anthropology, history, biology, etc. On a second level, adults well beyond high school and college find it an adventure for the mind. While traveling through the Spaceship Earth ride, for example, guests marvel at the AudioAnimatronic figures, the way scenes sound and even smell. But they also marvel at the history of man, how we've changed over the centuries, how we've stayed the same, and how science and the arts shaped our current existence.

Epcot Center

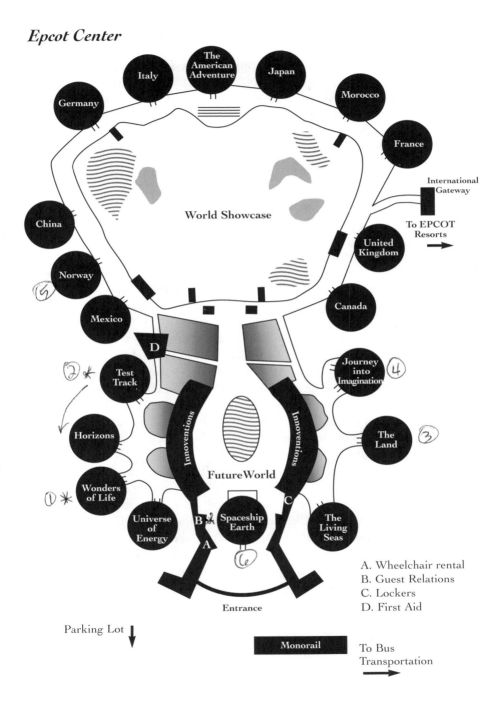

A. Wheelchair rental
B. Guest Relations
C. Lockers
D. First Aid

Entrance

Parking Lot ↓

Monorail   To Bus
Transportation

World Showcase presents the flavor of other lands and cultures. Most nations cannot be reproduced in a small exhibit, but Disney Imagineers present the feel of a country. Dine in Japan and, for a short while, experience the Japanese spirit. Stroll through Morocco's open air markets and get a brief glimpse of arid, dessert life. Price a piñata in Mexico's open air (but indoor) market and imagine what it's like in a small town south of the border.

Epcot does not offer the same physical thrills as the Magic Kingdom, but it has things the Magic Kingdom does not. Epcot has roller coasters for the mind.

GETTING TO EPCOT

Off-site guests can get to Epcot two different ways. Exit 26B off I-4 is fast and direct. Just follow the signs. Those people staying west of the maingate on US 192 can us the main entrance onto World Drive, again following the signs for Epcot. There will be a turn-off on your right.

On-site guests can reach Epcot a number of ways. Most take a bus from their resort which drops them off to the right of Epcot's main entrance. Guests staying at Monorail hotels — the Polynesian, Contemporary, or the Grand Floridian — can board the monorail and transfer to a second monorail at the Transportation and Ticket Center (TTC). Guests at the Polynesian can walk to the TTC and avoid the transfer. The Epcot monorail stops near the front entrance of Epcot after circling Future World.

On-site guests staying at one of the Epcot resorts — Yacht and Beach Club, Boardwalk, Swan, or Dolphin — may walk or take watercraft. Unlike other transfer methods, Epcot resort guests enter Epcot by way of World Showcase at the International Gateway. More relaxing and less grand than the main entrance, International Gateway feels like the back door. If visiting for a second or third time, it's perfect. If visiting for the first time, try to use the main entrance where Spaceship Earth (the giant golf ball thing) stands as a grand entryway. You lose part of the show by entering the back of the park.

At presstime, parking was $5 per day, free to resort guests. Save your parking ticket if traveling to other Disney parks since a single payment is valid at all three. Once parked, memorize your car's location. If forgotten, tell a parking lot employee the time you arrived and they'll tell you approximately where you parked. A tram connects all parking areas to the front entrance, but many people walk rather than ride.

FIRST THINGS FIRST

First time guests pass through the Epcot Center turnstiles, marvel at the gardens, funnel towards Spaceship Earth, and line up to ride. But to get the most from Epcot, skip Spaceship Earth first thing in the morning. Lines dwindle down to nothing later in the day. After entry, bear left, go under Spaceship Earth and look for Guest Relations, a very short distance on your left. Stop in. Ask for a map and entertainment guide if you did not already receive one. Also make a dinner reservation if you have not already done so. Consider a late lunch to save money.

You probably will not be close to your chosen restaurant at dinner time. It's difficult to estimate your location, say, six hours from arrival and, when it's time to eat, you may find that where-you-are and where-you're-supposed-to-be are a formidable distance apart. Never-the-less, try to guess. If you think you'll be in World Showcase around dinner-time, pick a restaurant there. If in Future World, choose the Coral Reef or The Garden Grill Restaurant. At the worst, you can cancel your reservation later.

Plenty of fast food restaurants serve food all day, generally without a long wait except over the meal hours. In Future World, the fast food fare remains similar to that in the Magic Kingdom: pizza, burgers, hot dogs, and salads, with a wider selection in The Land. But in World Showcase, fast food mirrors the host country. The American Adventure still serves hamburgers, but you can enjoy Chinese dinners, French pastries, German Bratwurst, and Mexican tacos — all from fast food vendors.

In Epcot, dining is part of the total experience. Customs and attributes of a culture are reflected in the food they create, the way they serve it, and the surrounding decor. In Germany, for example, you can view their unique architectural style and hear the town clock ring in the hours. But the Bavarian food, costumes, and instruments inside the Biergarten restaurant make Germany real. When you count to three in German, raise a mug of beer, and toast with fellow revelers, you're there.

Future World relies heavily on AudioAnimatronic figures and special effects while World Showcase is more sedate with only one major attraction, two small rides, and a handful of movies. But each country has live shows highlighting their nation's culture including Mexican dancers, American singers, Chinese acrobats, and Japanese entertainers.

You need a map to navigate but it's helpful to visualize Epcot as a figure eight entered at the bottom. The top half of the figure eight, World Showcase, circles a large lake, World Showcase Lagoon. The bottom half of the figure eight surrounds two buildings that house Innoventions and the Fountain of Nations. All Future World rides sit on the outside of the figure eight. Outer walkways connect outside attractions in Future World, though when you first arrive, you must cross through Innoventions to reach either side.

On a practical level, guests don't always know that they're in Future World. In conversation, "Epcot" is usually used to refer to both the entire theme park and, more specifically, to Future World. (As in "We rode Spaceship Earth at Epcot.") When referring to the countries, however, guests correctly identify World Showcase. (As in "We visited Morocco when we were in World Showcase.")

Today, Epcot plays second fiddle to the Magic Kingdom. Repeat visitors — the majority of guests now that WDW is 25 years old — can revisit the Magic Kingdom over and over again, just as they can see a favorite motion picture more than once. But Epcot, to some, is like those Oscar-winning movies with a message — wonderful but less relaxing. To bolster Epcot attendance, Disney continues to warm it up with new entertainers, kid-friendly programs, and faster rides like Test Track. They also revamp old stories to make them livelier, such as the new Universe of Energy storyline that features Ellen DeGeneres.

The following services are offered at Epcot:

• **Wheelchair and Stroller Rental.** Located on your left before Spaceship Earth. There's also a location at the International Gateway. Keep your receipt. Should anyone take your wheelchair, the receipt guarantees a replacement and is also good the same day at other Disney parks.

• **Money.** SunTrust operates an ATM machine on the left just inside the main entrance and along the walkway between Future World and World Showcase. Currency exchange is handled at Guest Relations or the American Express Travel Office.

• **First Aid.** On the left near the Odyssey Center where Future World and World Showcase meet behind Test Track.

• **Baby Care.** Also at Odyssey Center, on the left just before World Showcase.

• **Lost and Found.** Located at the Gift Stop by the front entrance. To check on items after you leave, all (407) 824-4245.

• **Storage Lockers.** Located on the right side of Spaceship Earth shortly after passing under it. They're also found outside near the Epcot bus stop.

• **Information.** For directions or general questions, ask any cast member or stop by a World Key kiosk where, by touching a computer screen, guests can walk their way through a storehouse of Epcot information. For educational questions about Disney World itself or to any Epcot exhibit, stop at The Discovery Center, on the right shortly after passing under Spaceship Earth.

• **Package Services.** Guests staying at a Disney resort can have purchases delivered directly to their room. Off-site guests may request a similar service that delivers all goods to a central location near the Entrance Plaza where they can be picked up at the end of the day.

• **Pets.** Except for service animals, pets are not allowed in Disney parks. It is also against Florida law to leave them unattended in a vehicle. The Epcot Pet Care Center is located outside the entrance and charges about $6 per day.

• **Disabled Guests.** Sight impaired guests may request complimentary tour cassettes at Guest Relations. At the same location, hearing impaired guests can rent Assistive Listening Devices which amplify selected attractions. TDD's may also be rented. In addition, written scripts are available at each attraction.

TOURING TIPS

Unlike the Magic Kingdom, most Epcot attractions accommodate a lot of people at the same time. Some rides are continuous motion, meaning a string of connected vehicles carries a set number of people per hour no matter the time, day, or season of the year. Lines for these tend to move fast. Other attractions, such as Wonders of Life and The Living Seas, have more than one activity housed inside a single building. Wonders of Life not only has one major and one minor ride, but it also has short movies, hands-on exhibits, and food — all under one air-conditioned roof.

Epcot is also big. Very big. Just as a marathon runner must pace himself, reserving enough energy to make it to the finish line, so must Epcot visitors understand the task at hand. If you're not sure you can handle the physical workout, rent a wheelchair. If you think you can handle it but find you're mistaken around 2 p.m., there's a second rental location at the International Gateway.

The following tips should make your day a little more pleasant:

• Arrive early. The doors open at least a half hour before the scheduled time, though not everything opens at once. If you like to sleep in, don't despair. Lines can be reasonable all day long in the off season.

• Guests staying off-site should avoid Epcot Center on days when on-site guests are allowed to enter the park one hour earlier than the general public. (See Chapter 8: Park Touring Tips).

• Make dinner reservations up to 60 days in advance by calling WDW-DINE. If trying to get a group consensus from traveling companions however, note that World Showcase restaurants recreate a country's heritage through authentic cuisine, representative architecture, and native servers. As such, they do not offer one or two "American" selections for members of a group who do not like the choices. You cannot, for example, get prime rib in Morocco or a hot dog in China.

• If visiting on more than one day, see IllumiNations one evening and, on the other, make late dinner reservations at one of the World Showcase restaurants. Have a bottle of wine with the meal. By the time you leave an hour after IllumiNations, it will seem as if you're the only people still inside Epcot. It's one of the best times to appreciate the park's beauty.

• Boats navigate across the World Showcase Lagoon and buses circle on the walkway. Use them for transportation if you can, but since they do not stop at each country, they rarely save you from extra walking.

• A Tip Board near Innoventions details the wait time for every attraction in Epcot.

• Remember that anytime you plan to "skip this attraction now and return later," you must do a lot more walking. Because Epcot covers a vast territory, you're rarely close to the same place more than once. If you visit all countries in World Showcase, for example, you've walked 1.3 miles. If you go back to "see the things we missed the first time," that becomes 2.6 miles — and that doesn't include your hike through Future World.

• Currently, World Showcase opens two hours after Future World. At the end of the day, Future World — with the exception of Spaceship Earth, shops, and Innoventions — closes two hours before World Showcase. Plan to visit one or two Future World attractions early in the day, but then move to World Showcase as soon as it opens. To confirm operating times before you arrive, call (407) 824-4321.

• IllumiNations is held at the same time Epcot closes. Expect crowds. At the show's conclusion, you might want to relax in a World Showcase garden or shop in Innoventions while the elbow-to-elbow crowds fight their way to the parking lot or monorail.

• Ask to view the restaurants in World Showcase. You can't eat in all of them, even if you stay for a week, but there's nothing wrong with taking a look. Unique ones such as Morocco and Germany should not be missed. Generally, a Disney host or hostess will be happy to let you in. Ask at the door.

GUIDELINES FOR THOSE WHO DON'T MIND A LOT OF WALKING

If you think you can handle a hectic pace and you've walked four miles each day to prepare for this marathon, try the following itinerary:

Arrive early, at least half an hour before the scheduled opening. After you pass through the entrance turnstiles, make a left under Spaceship Earth (skip it for now unless you're first inside and/or they have not opened the rest of the park yet) and stop at Guest Relations for your map/entertainment guide and dinner reservations.

Next, if you like roller coaster attractions, head left (through Innoventions) to Wonders of Life. Ride Body Wars. Exit Wonders of Life, pass Horizons, and ride Test Track. Next, cut through

Innoventions to The Land. Ride Living With The Land but ignore everything else in the pavilion. Once you leave the land, make an immediate right to Journey Into Imagination. Ride the Journey Into Imagination ride. Afterward, enjoy Honey, I Shrunk the Kids, located in the same building.

If still on your feet with a traceable pulse, leave Journey Into Imagination, bear right, and follow the path to World Showcase. At World Showcase Lagoon, make a left. Pass Mexico and enter Norway. Ride the Maelstrom. Backtrack and enjoy Mexico, then reverse again and see the rest of World Showcase and Future World. Unseen Future World attractions should have reasonable lines by the time you get there. (If you get there.)

For those who hate roller coasters: Epcot has no true roller coasters, but two rides throw you around. Follow the above itinerary, but avoid Body Wars and Test Track.

For those who only want to know where to start: Universe of Energy. Hug the left side of the figure eight, touring each attraction as you come to it.

For those who plan their own itinerary but want a list of the rides with the most uncomfortable waits:
Body Wars (inside Wonders of Life)
Spaceship Earth (early in the day)
Living With the Land (inside The Land)
Journey Into Imagination ride
Maelstrom (Norway)

LANDS AND RIDES

How to Read the Attraction Descriptions

Each attraction is followed by a letter from "A" to "E", based on the early Magic Kingdom days when each ride required a separate ticket for admission. An "A" ticket worked for simple attractions such as the buses that circle World Showcase Lagoon. "E" attractions were top-of-the-line, with "B", "C", and "D" falling inbetween. Since individual ride tickets were never used at Epcot, judgments are subjective.

Note — Includes background information on the ride. For example, if the ride is an "E" ticket in substance but not entertainment value, it's noted here.

Movement — Describes all motion on the ride, along with anything else, that might make adults uncomfortable. Disney "surprises" en route are not described unless they move you fast, throw you around, or jump in your face.

Line — Describes the queue line, whether it's inside or outside, air-conditioned or not, long or short.

Wait time — Attempts to judge the wait in relation to other attractions. For example, a long wait time does not necessarily mean hours in line. Body Wars has a long wait time. That means that, when the park is very busy, expect to wait up to an hour. On a less-crowded day when you can get on some rides with no wait at all, expect ten or fifteen minutes. In other words, "long" is a relative term based on the day of your visit — not actual time. Remember that other things affect your wait including the time of day and whether or not a near-by attraction just spilled 2000 people onto the sidewalk.

Wheelchair Access — Notes any special problems encountered by those in wheelchairs. Remember that WDW cast members will not help a guest transfer from wheelchair to ride. If you cannot transfer yourself alone or with the help of a companion, sigh and move on to a ride that accommodates you. If you can ride, look for a cast member at each attraction's entrance. Most times, they'll find you.

The following descriptions start at Spaceship Earth and circle Future World clockwise, then move to World Showcase and circle the lagoon in the same direction. Innoventions and other attractions in the central plaza of Future World are described just before World Showcase.

FUTURE WORLD

When the Magic Kingdom's Tomorrowland grew up, it became Future World. This land sizes up our present and our past, and offers suggestions for the future. Innoventions showcases new technology that we'll use in the not-too-distant future. Horizons goes a step further. So does Spaceship Earth. In Epcot's first year of operation, nary a Disney character could be found. Today, that's changed, and Epcot continues to soften its atmosphere in an attempt to attract new crowds.

Escape Spots: Gardens, shrubbery, waterways, and benches separate Innoventions from the surrounding attractions. Most people pass by these quickly on their way to the big stuff, but these gardens harbor great get-away spots — some so secluded that you have to look around a bend to find them. With nearby vendors selling everything from ice cream to fresh fruit to sodas, they're an ideal place to relax amid the well-manicured Epcot greenery.

Spaceship Earth

TICKET: E

NOTE: Perhaps the most enterprising ride in Epcot, Spaceship Earth traces the history of communication. The subject sounds limiting, but it's not. Communication is the backbone of civilization, the key ingredient that man uses to operate a society, to solve problems and fight a common enemy. Tracing communication's history from the Stone Ages, this fifteen-minute ride passes through every major civilization and continues into the future, noting all the changes pioneered by computer and space technology.

A must-see.

MOVEMENT: Smooth. Hard plastic cars lead slowly upward within the giant ball as scenes unfold. At the top, the cars turn backwards and take riders down a steep incline, almost lying on their backs. It's slightly uncomfortable with no neck support, but the discomfort is minor and should deter no one.

LINE: Outdoors. Mostly shaded but not air-conditioned. The entire line is visible from the walkway.

WAIT TIME: Medium to long in the morning; short in the afternoon.

WHEELCHAIR ACCESS: Fair. Guests must transfer from their wheelchair into the ride vehicle. Guests scared of dark or enclosed places are advised not to ride.

Universe of Energy

TICKET: E

NOTE: The home of the Epcot dinosaurs, this exhibit tackles issues concerning our historical use of power and where the energy of tomorrow might come from. While a major part of the attraction, the dinosaurs are really a footnote to history, an example of the time when our fossil fuels were created. The story — and this is a 45-minute ride — was dry until 1996 when "Ellen's Energy Adventure" debuted, a comedy spiel starring Ellen DeGeneres. While the dinosaurs-died-and-became-gasoline explanation remains the same, it now comes seasoned with humor. Putting money where its mouth is, the Universe of Energy ride vehicles are powered by solar cells located on the roof.

MOVEMENT: Smooth. Anyone may ride.

LINE: Most of the time, the wait is indoors and air-conditioned. If busy, the line may wind outdoors. Once in the cars (only it looks like an auditorium), guests remain seated throughout the attraction.

WAIT TIME: Medium to long.

WHEELCHAIR ACCESS: Good. Wheelchair guests may remain seated throughout the performance.

Rather than a single attraction, **Wonders of Life** offers one major attraction, Body Wars; one moderate attraction, Cranium Command; and a number of smaller presentations that explore the human body. Essentially a study in Biology, each exhibit focuses on some facet of what it means to be human. Hands-on exhibits include stationary bikes that analyze energy consumption, hot and cold contraptions that demonstrate how the sense of touch works, and an area that analyzes a golf or tennis swing. Small but worthwhile exhibits include:

• *AnaComical Players.* Improvisational theater stressing the human body.
• *Goofy About Health.* Cartoon stressing the importance of exercise.
• *The Making of Me.* A short film exploring human reproduction.
Carrying a warning, the film includes an actual human birth. Walking a fine line of acceptability, the film is not as graphic as it could be, yet not as tame as many other Disney attractions.

Body Wars

TICKET: E

NOTE: For roller coaster lovers only. This is a flight simulator, meaning that the entire audience of about 40 people is thrown around while a movie plays in front of them. The plot makes the ride worthwhile: Your spaceship is the size of a blood cell. You enter a person. You travel to the site of a splinter but something goes wrong and you're forced on a wild ride through the human body. Intense, educational, and fun, it is none-the-less not for the faint-hearted.

MOVEMENT: In point of fact, you actually go nowhere. Your vehicle sits on machinery that can lift the front, the rear, or the sides, although you see only the interior. A computer makes sure the movements coincide with a movie playing in front of the car. If the movie shows you coursing out of control through the blood system, for example, the cart moves the front up and the rear down. Feeling the pressure of your back against the seat, you attribute it to the high speed of travel rather than the fact that the vehicle is leaning up hill.

While you're seated securely and belted in, the danger lies in the jerky movements the car sometimes makes. If the ship hits something in the movie, the effect is simulated by jerking the entire vehicle. A second danger is motion sickness. If you can't ride in the back seat of a car and hate to fly because turbulence upsets you, avoid Body Wars. If you rarely suffer from motion sickness, you should be fine. The ride is identical to Star Tours at Disney-MGM Studios, but Body Wars is rougher.

Guests with "heart conditions, motion sickness, back or neck problems, or other conditions that may be aggravated" are advised not to ride. Guests must be 40 inches tall.

LINE: Indoors but it winds behind walls. Check the sign at the entrance for wait times and assume a few minutes less.

WAIT TIME: Medium to long.

WHEELCHAIR ACCESS: Fair. Guests must be able to transfer from wheelchair to auditorium style seating.

Cranium Command

TICKET: D

NOTE: See this. More show than ride, it incorporates the one element that makes a Disney attraction stand out — good writing. Centering on the nervous system and the brain, the show demonstrates how stress and diet affect thinking. A cartoon preshow establishes the plot and should not be missed.

MOVEMENT: None. Guests stand for the preshow then sit in a theater for the main performance.

LINE: Indoors and air-conditioned. Most is visible before entering.

WAIT TIME: Medium.

WHEELCHAIR ACCESS: Complete. Guests may remain in their wheelchair throughout.

Horizons
TICKET: E
NOTE: Dedicated to the future, Horizons takes a look human life in the years to come: where we will live, what we will eat, and how we will communicate. While the ride paints a rosy picture of science and how it will shape our destiny, Horizons' own future is less optimistic. Soon it will be shut down for major reworking. It's not Epcot's best right now, but selected special effects — along with a relatively short wait — make the attraction worth enjoying.
MOVEMENT: Smooth. Anyone may ride.
LINE: Indoors most of the time. On busy days, it extends outside.
WAIT TIME: Short to medium.
WHEELCHAIR ACCESS: Fair. Riders must transfer from wheelchair to vehicle.

Test Track
TICKET: E
NOTE: The World of Motion closed in January of 1996 and, funded with GM money, became Test Track in spring of 1997. The original ride that traced the history of transportation was completely scrubbed for this new venture which transforms riders into crash test dummies who undergo the development tests — wind, cold, heat, and even crashes — that new cars endure.
MOVEMENT: Scheduled to be more active than anything else at Epcot, the actual movement compares to riding in a convertible with the top down, albeit over rocky terrain. Vehicles use real seatbelts and travel on real tires, scaring riders with speed and special effects more than roller-coaster-type hills. Anyone who has avoided a car accident by slamming on the brakes can imagine the type of thrills that await. Here, however, you can relax in the certain knowledge that Disney would never slam guests into a wall at 25 miles per hour.

Guests with "heart conditions, motion sickness, back or neck problems, or other conditions that may be aggravated" are advised not to ride.
LINE: Mostly indoors and shaded.
WAIT TIME: Long.
WHEELCHAIR ACCESS: Fair. Guests must be able to transfer to car.

Journey Into Imagination has two attractions, a playground of sorts, and some intriguing outdoor fountains. The Image Works, a hands-on playground of computers, special effects, and games, uses technical tricks to entertain. Guests color images onto a computer screen, step on colored lights that make sounds, and create music by increasing or decreasing the length of a beam of light. To kids, this is a play area. To adults, it's a marvel of modern technology.

Journey Into Imagination: The Ride
TICKET: E

NOTE: Of all Epcot attractions, this one has the greatest diversity of reactions. Some love it; others think it silly. Most Epcot rides explore a process, such as farming or history or energy production. But Journey Into Imagination explores a concept — that moment of inspiration when a painter takes a vase full of lilies and turns it into a masterpiece, or when a writer strings common words together and makes a story leap off the page. It explores science, asking what factors come together when a person suddenly hits on the cure for polio? What moment of inspiration split the atom?

The ride does not explain the process of invention; it celebrates the moment. It looks at the way humans relate words to ideas, paintings to feelings, and known facts to theories. Much of it is whimsical, filled with colors and special effects. You may love it or not, but it's certainly one that should not be missed.

MOVEMENT: Smooth. Anyone may ride.

LINE: Indoors and air-conditioned on slow days, extending outside and into the sun on busier ones. Riders board from a stationary floor while the vehicle continues to move slowly. Cast members will stop the ride for a few seconds if necessary.

WAIT TIME: Medium to long.

WHEELCHAIR ACCESS: Fair. Riders must transfer themselves from wheelchair to ride. Cast members will stop the ride.

Honey, I Shrunk The Audience
TICKET: D

NOTE: Along with Cranium Command at Wonders of Life, this exhibit is one of Epcot's best, though not one of the most expensive. Again, good writing makes it stand out. It helps if you saw the movie this is drawn from, but it's not necessary. In a nutshell, the man being honored in the show shrunk his kids to the size of ants in his first movie. In the sequel, he "blew up" the youngest, making him a few stories taller than the casinos in Las Vegas. In this show, the ride's name explains it all.

MOVEMENT: None. A 3-D theater presentation. There are a few physical surprises best discovered inside. One, for example, involves a few drops of water in your face. Only people who truly hate surprises should avoid the show.

LINE: Air-conditioned and indoors. A clock above the main entrance marks the time until admission. There is a preshow that explains the background of the main presentation along with a few commercials for Kodak.

WAIT TIME: Medium.

WHEELCHAIR ACCESS: Good. Guests may remain in their wheelchair throughout.

The Land, another exhibit housing multiple attractions, explores man's delicate link to nature. People living in developed countries take food for granted, forgetting that what we need is not always wrapped in cellophane and stocked in the local supermarket. While one exhibit explores farming, another talks about nutrition, and a third discusses the ecology.

Living With The Land

TICKET: E

NOTE: Distinctly educational, Living With The Land looks at growth conditions around the world and then shows — through live plants and animals — steps that can be taken to ensure a constant food supply for the future. The 15-minute tour includes a few Disney-style scenes of farm communities and rain forests, but most of the tour deals with agriculture.

MOVEMENT: Smooth. Trip is by boat, but movement is limited to a thin canal.

LINE: Indoors and air-conditioned.

WAIT TIME: Medium to long. Since The Land is a popular spot for lunch and dinner, the line tends to be longer at those times. If possible, schedule your ride for the middle of the afternoon or, preferably, early in the morning.

WHEELCHAIR ACCESS: Good. Riders may remain in their wheelchair throughout, boarding selected wheelchair-accessible boats.

Greenhouse Tour
TICKET: D
NOTE: The tour covers the same territory as the boat tour, but lasts 45 minutes. There's a lot more time for questions and, of course, more information is included — perfect for those people that find their curiosity peaked. Once free, the tour now costs $6 for adults and $4 for children.
MOVEMENT: Walking tour.
LINE: Reservations are required and must be made in person, on the day of the tour, at the Green Thumb Emporium.
WAIT TIME: Varies. If you plan to eat lunch at The Land (and many do, so it's busy over the meal hours), make a tour reservation first. Because tours are reserved, it sometimes requires a return later in the day, adding a lot of extra walking to an itinerary.
WHEELCHAIR ACCESS: Good. Completely accessible.

Food Rocks
TICKET: D
NOTE: The message — to eat balanced, nutritional meals — may get lost behind the foot-tapping entertainment. Famous songs enjoy a turn of phrase and become advocates for good nutrition. Little Richard, for example, belts out a unique version of Tutti Frutti. You don't need to listen to the radio to recognize the melodies. Most have made it to Muzak systems by now. The show is fun and fast-paced.
MOVEMENT: None. Theater presentation
LINE: Indoors and air-conditioned.
WAIT TIME: Short.
WHEELCHAIR ACCESS: Good. Guests may remain in their wheelchairs throughout.

Circle of Life Theater
TICKET: C
NOTE: Featuring Pumbaa and Timon, characters from the Disney movie, *The Lion King*, this movie looks at the delicate balance between man's progress and the preservation of nature. Shown on a huge screen, the movie goes beyond the technology found in your local cinema. Well done and taking a moderate ecological stance, it's a good choice on a hot afternoon.
MOVEMENT: None. Theater presentation.

LINE: Indoors and air-conditioned
WAIT TIME: Short
WHEELCHAIR ACCESS: Good. Completely accessible.

The Living Seas
TICKET: E
NOTE: This attraction includes different hands-on exhibits, a very short ride, and a 27-foot deep, 200-foot diameter fish tank. According to the Disney story-line, guests, after boarding elevators that take them deep into the ocean, explore marine life in the underwater colony of Sea Base Alpha. The exhibits explain a wide range of oceanic concepts, from tides to oceanography. A separate tank hosts Florida manatees, an endangered species.

The Living Seas schedules two tours for those with extra cash, extra interest, and extra time. A behind-the-scenes exploration of dolphin behavior, called D.E.E.P., takes about three hours, costs $45, and is open to anyone over 16. A second tour, called DiveQuest, allows certified scuba divers to explore the aquarium. The cost of $145 includes 30 to 40 minutes in the water. To reserve either tour, call (407) WDW-TOUR.
MOVEMENT: Smooth. There's a very short ride under the large aquarium, but once in Sea Base Alpha, large windows allow visitors to study the tank's inhabitants at their leisure. All other exhibits are reached by walking.
LINE: Indoors and air-conditioned unless very long.
WAIT TIME: Medium.
WHEELCHAIR ACCESS: Good. The short ride under the tank is inaccessible, but the same scenery can be viewed — albeit at a slightly different angle — from Sea Base Alpha.

Innoventions
Much of Future World showcases the past or talks about the distant future, but Innoventions doesn't talk about the next century or the next decade. It talks about today and tomorrow. Walking a fine line between informative exhibits and blatant advertising, Innoventions is worth exploring. Most people find something they're interested in and other things they choose to pass by. It's also electric. At times, the facts, figures, lights, music, and details are almost too much for the mind to handle.

But it's a good place to spend time on a hot afternoon.

161

The Discovery Center

Located on your right after passing under Spaceship Earth, the Discovery Center looks like a teaching area reserved for students, instructors, and academia. But it's not.

The Discovery Center is not only the intellectual heart of Epcot, but it's the fact-finding nucleus for all of Walt Disney World. The first floor specializes in school supplies and computer software, but the second floor holds an archive of Disney memorabilia. In theory, the Discovery Center handles only topics covered in Epcot and Walt Disney World, but since Epcot's mission is nothing less than the study of mankind, it's a powerful information source overlooked by most people.

In The Land, for example, guests learn about hydroponics, a method of growing plants. On a 15-minute ride, only a limited amount can be said about hydroponics; only a few questions can be answered. The Discovery Center is the human element that completes the learning process. They stock a 28-page brochure on hydroponics. In fact, they stock brochures or pamphlets for all the most-frequently asked questions.

Ask them what songs play during IllumiNations. How many stones in Cinderella's Castle? What plants are indigenous to their native countries in World Showcase gardens and what plants are actually "faking it"? Where are the hidden Mickeys? (All over Walt Disney World, Imagineers hid Mickey's image in buildings, fences, and gardens. The Discovery Center is the only place to find the "official unofficial list" of locations.)

If cast members cannot answer a question, they'll research it, sometimes mailing it to guests' homes after their return.

WORLD SHOWCASE

In the Magic Kingdom, Small World is more than a bunch of dolls with moving lips and a catchy song. It graphically displays the similarities shared by people the world over. The underlying message: we are one world, one people.

On a larger scale, World Showcase attempts the same thing. A short century or so ago, the world's cultures lived somewhat isolated lives. Groups of people shared common songs, customs, and even genetic traits. That, of course, is gone. Today, it's just as easy to e-mail Japan as it is to call a neighbor. The world grew smaller. Today, not everyone in Scotland wears a kilt and not everyone in Japan wears a kimono. But in World Showcase, the cultural differences are not only highlighted, they're celebrated. The architectural colors and details in China stand in stark contrast to German buildings that rely on pictures as much as design. Governments come and go, but the human race — excitingly different from culture to culture — is essentially good.

World Showcase commemorates that goodness.

For those in wheelchairs, most attractions and restaurants in World Showcase are completely accessible. Even the countries with sidewalks and curbs have numerous ramps for the handicapped, unlike some of their host countries.

World Showcase Transportation
TICKET: A
NOTE: Two forms of transportation connect points in World Showcase: British double-decker busses and French-style boats. Bus transportation circles the lagoon with designated stops along the way. Boat transportation crosses the lake. Two separate docks near the main entrance host boats, each connecting to opposite corners of the World Showcase lagoon.

While World Showcase transportation adds atmosphere to the park, it's almost always faster to walk. The number of steps saved by riding must be balanced against the inconvenience of waiting in yet another line. If you've always wanted to ride a double-decker bus, do it. Or if you've already toured World Showcase but have dinner reservations in one of the countries on the far side of the lagoon, hop on and enjoy the ride. Or if waiting in line sounds infinitely better than additional pressure on aching feet, enjoy the break. Otherwise, walk.
MOVEMENT: Smooth. Anyone may ride.
LINE: Outdoors, some shaded and some not.
WAIT TIME: Mixed. It depends on direction and time of day.
WHEELCHAIR ACCESS: Good for the boats, but wheelchairs can-not access the double-decker busses.

Mexico

Perhaps the most unusual pavilion, Mexico appears small from the outside, little more than a great pyramid constructed by Aztec Indians centuries ago. The only country completely enclosed, Mexico unfolds once you step inside. Themed with 24-hour darkness, the interior recreates a small street in old Mexico. In the center, an open-air market stocks souvenirs, piñatas, and puppets, while along the exterior, stores with tiled roofs sell Mexico's more expensive treasures. Behind the shops, a boat ride, El Río Del Tiempo, provides riders a festive look at Mexico's history.

To the rear, the San Angel Inn serves gourmet Mexican food in an outdoor cantina that borders the blackened waters of an ancient river. Boats traveling El Río Del Tiempo sail silently by, framed by lush foliage, mysterious mists, and Aztec pyramids. From hidden speakers, a Mariachi band plays. Using candlelight to complete the atmosphere, this outdoor-yet-indoor eatery has a style found nowhere else in Walt Disney World and it's considered by many to be WDW's most romantic restaurant.

While most people do not think of Disney World as a museum-type experience, a number of pre-Columbian — and priceless — artifacts directly inside the pyramid give visitors a look at early Mexican history.

El Río Del Tiempo: The River of Time
TICKET: D
NOTE: A relaxing tour of Mexico history and customs. It's lightly entertaining.
MOVEMENT: Smooth. A boat ride, but without hills or rocking.
LINE: A short part of the line cannot be seen. On busy days, it winds through the open air market and, on very busy days, outside. In general, it's air-conditioned and comfortable.
WAIT TIME: Medium to short.
WHEELCHAIR ACCESS: Look for an attendant and access through the exit. Modified boats make riding easy without the need to transfer out of a wheelchair. To enter the Mexico pavilion itself, wheelchair guests use a ramp to the right of the pyramid.

Norway

One of the world's oldest countries, the Norwegian people have a symbiotic alliance with nature, building homes on rugged countryside and relying on the sea for both food and recreation. Rugged and cold, this Norwegian homeland looks out of place in warm, humid Florida. From the intricate, natural wood architecture of the buildings to the Norwegian-made sweaters and crafts found inside, everything reflects harsh weather and rustic lifestyles. And they have trolls, of course. Norway is famous for trolls. They're sold in the gift shop and they play a part in The Maelstrom, a Norwegian sea adventure and the only action ride in World Showcase.

Akershus, Norway's gourmet restaurant, serves food buffet style. While many people prefer a traditional sit-down dinner, the buffet allows diners to sample a wide range of Norwegian cuisine, unfamiliar to many Americans. Servers not only describe ingredients and preparation techniques, but will also explain an entree's place in Norwegian culture.

The Maelstrom
TICKET: D

NOTE: A boat ride with a small amount of action, the Maelstrom gives riders a feel for Norwegian life; what it's like to be married to the sea and to have nature as both partner and enemy. At the end of the ride, passengers disembark indoors in a small replica of a Norwegian town. When theater doors open, guests enter and view a short film. While the ride recreates Norway's lifestyle, the movie recounts its history.

MOVEMENT: At one point, the boat moves rapidly backwards where you fear you will fall, but do not. Immediately following that, the boat drops down a hill (forward) comparable to a tall sliding board. While scary to those unaccustomed to action rides, it's nothing at all to roller coaster enthusiasts. Riders may get hit with a drop or two of water but there is no real chance to get wet. If the hill scares you, don't go. It's not worth the worry. Most people enjoy it, however, regardless of their age. Guests are warned to "be in good health and free from heart conditions, motion sickness, back or neck problems, or other conditions that may be aggravated by this ride."

LINE: Most is air-conditioned and out of sight. Since the length of the indoor line can be adjusted, it can't be pre-judged even if the line spills outdoors into the Norwegian town square. Inside, the line may make a beeline for the boats or it might wind round and round. On the bright side, it moves fairly fast.

WAIT TIME: Medium to long.

WHEELCHAIR ACCESS: Fair. Guests must be able to transfer to the boats and, in case the ride breaks down (unlikely), walk short distances to reach the exits.

China

How do you take a country the size of China and squeeze it down into a few buildings and a garden? You don't. But designers concentrated on the traditional stately grace of China and reproduced the feel of the country. Chinese gardens, beautiful and unique, complement intricately detailed and vibrantly colored buildings. Traditional Chinese music plays from hidden speakers.

One of the most recognizable ethnic foods for Americans, two separate restaurants prepare Chinese cuisine — one for those who want a top-of-the-line dinner with cocktails and one for those hunting fast food. Gift shops sell traditional items like silk robes and Chinese prints along with high-priced antiques.

Wonders of China: Land of Beauty, Land of Time
TICKET: D
NOTE: What the pavilion cannot do — i.e., explore the far corners of this huge and culturally diverse land — the movie can. Using Circle-Vision 360, the movie surrounds the audience as the Disney film crew takes visitors to Beijing's Forbidden city, the Great Wall of China, Shanghai, and other seldom seen areas. But China is more than architecture and geography. This vast country known for food and Communism has depth, substance, and heart. China's controversial government takes a back seat in this film that focuses more on people than politics.
MOVEMENT: None. Theater presentation. Because of the nature of the 360° movie, guests stand to watch.
LINE: Air-conditioned and indoors.
WAIT TIME: Short.
WHEELCHAIR ACCESS: Complete. Guests may remain in wheelchairs.

Germany

Specializing in the "wurst" food in Epcot (that's "wurst" as in Brat"wurst" and Knock"wurst"), the German pavilion celebrates both the diversity of German style as well as its people's festive nature.

Indeed, the symbol of Germany seems to be a laden mug of beer with suds flowing down the side, held erect by a German who then counts to three, drinks, and laughs. Internationally famous Oktoberfest is celebrated every day of the year in World Showcase.

Germany has no movies or rides, but the Biergarten restaurant, serving food buffet style, offers entertainment in a unique setting. Disney designers created the nighttime atmosphere of an outdoor German garden (though actually indoors) where restaurant patrons sit in a semi-circular configuration at long tables. In front, amidst the German buildings and waterwheel of an old mill, a stage showcases a company of entertainers. Lederhosen-clad Germans play everything from accordions to saws and cowbells. The half-hour show performs only at night. For those who wish to see the show but eat elsewhere, ask the host or hostess if you may watch from the entranceway.

Italy

For many countries, cooking is part of the culture, but nowhere is food as important as in Italy. Conjure up a quick mental image of Italy, and most people picture a gray-haired woman piling up plate after plate of pasta. Italy cannot be reproduced in a small amount of space. Artifacts from the time of the great Roman Empire deserve their own area; the canal of Venice another; distinctive religious shrines another. Unable to include everything, Disney created a smaller Italy with just a few of the things that make it unique, including antiquities, music, and food.

The restaurant, L'Originale Alfredo di Roma Ristorante, serves pasta made on site. While the architecture and music recreate Italy, the smell of tomato sauce mixed with garlic, oregano, and olive oil makes you believe you're really there.

The American Adventure

Walt Disney World is, and always has been, extremely patriotic. From the daily flag ceremony in the Magic Kingdom to the red, white, and blue finale of the Electrical Water Pageant, Walt Disney World honors the United States.

Nowhere, however, is Disney patriotism more evident than at the American Adventure. Architecturally, it's more subdued than any other country. The lone building's style recreates structures built immediately after the American Revolution, reminiscent of

Philadelphia or Boston around the early 1800's. One small store sells souvenirs; a fast food restaurant pushes burgers. There is no sit-down restaurant. Along the Lagoon, a large outdoor theater — The American Gardens Theatre — hosts special events and shows throughout the year.

The main attraction is the American Adventure show, an AudioAnimatronic theater presentation that lasts a full half-hour. The show's design and technological innovations leave most other shows in the dust, even by Disney standards. Hosted by Ben Franklin and Mark Twain, a revolving carousel below the stage allows figures to rotate unseen, rising on cue to explain their piece of history. Behind the figures, a movie screen (the largest rear-projection screen in the world) runs in synchronization with the story, supplying an appropriate background. This show should not be missed.

Try also to catch the Voices of Liberty performing inside the American Adventure. This cadre of six male and female performers sing in harmony in the first floor waiting area — one of the best live performances in Walt Disney World.

The American Adventure Show

TICKET: E

NOTE: Told through the actual words of many famous Americans, the show captures moments of U.S. history. But more importantly, it captures the spirit of the people, from the driving need for independence in 1776 to the hard-fought battles of the Civil War and the 1960 confrontations to establish equality among all races. While interesting to foreign visitors, it should be required viewing for all Americans.

MOVEMENT: None. Theater presentation.

LINE: Indoors and air-conditioned. When the gates open, guests ride up escalators to the second floor, then walk across the building to the theater's entrance.

WAIT TIME: Medium. While everyone waiting is usually admitted to the large theater, the wait can be half an hour if a performance just began.

WHEELCHAIR ACCESS: Good. Completely accessible. Guests use an elevator and may remain in their wheelchairs throughout. Ask a cast member for directions once inside.

Japan

Without a major attraction, Japan relies on traditional architecture, gardening, and crafts to recreate the atmosphere of the country. Today, downtown Tokyo is not much different from New York City. But World Showcase's Japan is far more conventional, recreating the Japan of a hundred years ago. Traditional music floats across walkways that span Japanese gardens, where mostly native Florida plants imitate those grown in Japan's countryside. Ponds and streams, a traditional part of Japanese gardens, are abundant. For a short rest, relax on one of the benches.

The Mitsukoshi Department Store is a transplant — an actual store famous in Japan. Known as "Japan's Sears," the department store stocks traditional cultural treats — Bonsai trees, kimonos, and dolls.

Morocco

The only country representing the continent of Africa, Morocco is also the least familiar to Americans. Even without the Florida heat to back up the fantasy, the outdoor market and architectural style highlight a country used to a hot climate. Brass and copper souvenirs spill out into the street, sold from open air markets. Alleyways with twists and turns reflect the area's ancient construction. A small museum, the Gallery of Arts and History, hosts changing exhibits. A second area, part store and part display, sells handmade Berber carpets and other floor coverings. Centrally located, a fountain reflects the tile-based architecture of Morocco.

Marrakesh, the Moroccan restaurant, serves traditional fare, heavy on the lamb and chicken. High ceilings and ornate styling make it one of the most unusual places to eat. Belly dancers, native to Morocco and definitely G-rated here, perform daily.

France

In movies, scenes of Paris always have the light sound of a small accordion playing in the background, something not actually heard in Paris but existing in World Showcase. Small shops, three restaurants, a movie, and even the Eiffel Tower faithfully reproduce the spirit of France. The shops sell all things French, from Impressionist paintings to perfumes. One shop, La Maison Du Vin, serves wine ranging in price from a few dollars to a few hundred dollars.

In France, food is an art form and two top-flight restaurants specialize in the cuisine. A third restaurant, found outdoors like the famous cafés along Paris streets, features light meals. If nothing else, stop in Boulangerie Pâtisserie, a small French pastry shop located in a back street, for one of their sugary delicacies. But expect a crowd. A relaxing garden sits to the right of France. Because the area is a dead end, no one is going anywhere in a hurry. With benches and flowers in abundance, it's a good place to relax. Buy a pastry or a glass of wine and take a break.

Impressions de France
TICKET: D
NOTE: A moving presentation, Impressions de France is projected onto five different screens, though not surrounding the audience. Like other movies in World Showcase, the presentation shows viewers things that the pavilion cannot: the simple life of a French farmer, the magnificence of landmarks such as Versailles, and the breathtaking wonder of the Swiss Alps. Like all Disney movies, this one's high quality.
MOVEMENT: None. Theater presentation.
LINE: Indoors and air-conditioned.
WAIT TIME: Short to medium, depending on season and time of day.
WHEELCHAIR ACCESS: Good. Guests may remain in their wheelchairs.

United Kingdom
Another land without a major attraction, the United Kingdom attempts the gargantuan task of representing a country with a diverse history, geography, and style. For much of its existence, the United Kingdom was not even "united." Populated since recorded history began, towns and cities in the United Kingdom have modern homes sitting next to 400-year-old houses, creating an eclectic mix of styles.

Epcot's United Kingdom uses eight different architectural styles, from Georgian to English Tudor to English Victorian. Gardens are lovingly recreated using selected British plants and other "look-alikes" native to Florida. In the back of Great Britain, a garden area offers an out-of-the-way escape from the crowd.

English pubs represent the everyday world in Great Britain and

The Rose & Crown recreates the atmosphere along with the ale, though at prices higher than those charged at a small shire in the English countryside. The menu in the dining room is full of artery-clogging English standards: fish and chips, lamb, and steak-and-kidney pie. Selected tables have a good view of the World Showcase Lagoon for those who wish to dine and enjoy IllumiNations during dessert. Take note of the Rose & Crown's exterior which changes from side to side. Depending on your perspective, it's a rustic country pub, a hundred year old urban pub, or a big-city pub.

Canada

Geographically diverse, Canada has cities that rival Chicago and New York along with mountains and vistas more like Alaska. From French-speaking Quebec to the backwoods communities of the Northwest Territories, World Showcase's Canada takes samples from the massive country and encapsulates them. Built on a hill, the Hôtel du Canada rises above other buildings, its height less than it seems thanks to forced perspective, a movie-making trick of the eye accomplished by building the top of the building smaller than the bottom. Below the hotel and built into the hillside, a crag of rock has both a waterfall and stream, a small taste of the Canadian Rockies.

Canada is not known for its food like many of the other countries, and a cafeteria-service restaurant, Le Cellier, enjoys smaller crowds. Sometimes closed in the off-season, it offers Canadian fare, heavy on the beef, salmon and turkey.

O Canada!

TICKET: D

NOTE: Surrounding the audience completely using the Circle-Vision 360 technology, this movie vividly displays the expansive beauty of Canada. Towering mountains and miles of grassy plains are given equal weight with the people and customs. The movie awes audiences.

MOVEMENT: None. Theater presentation. Because the movie surrounds the audience, there are no seats and everyone stands for the 18-minute performance.

LINE: Indoors and air-conditioned.

WAIT TIME: Short to Medium.

WHEELCHAIR ACCESS: Good. Guests may remain in their wheelchairs.

SHOWS

Unlike the Magic Kingdom, Epcot schedules few permanent shows on a grand scale. On the other hand, Epcot has more intimate live performances than any other park. World Showcase artists entertain everywhere, adding yet another dimension to their home country. Visitors can enjoy native dancing in Japan and Mexico, singing in Germany and the United States, or a comic troop in Great Britain — plus much more. Since showtimes change daily based on crowds and hours of operation, keep one eye on the lay of the lands and the other on the daily entertainment schedule. If the country you're visiting has a show scheduled in half an hour, browse in the gift shops, buy a cup of coffee and sit in a garden, or stroll to the lakefront area. At once educational and entertaining, the shows give World Showcase its human dimension.

In addition to the World Showcase entertainment, Epcot schedules events throughout the year, some educational and some entertaining. Big name performers such as Nell Carter and Rosemary Cloony sing at the American Gardens Theatre in the summer. At times, famous artisans create new artwork on site, such as Hummel creators located in Germany. At Christmas, Holidays Around the World highlights the differences — and similarities — from culture to culture. In the past, Epcot has hosted the World Festival of Kites, the National Inventor's Expo, and a monthly "festival" for kids. As Imagineers continue to warm up the Epcot ambiance, expect more in the future.

In other words, Epcot is not a static place. Anything can happen during your visit. Enjoy the discovery.

The few permanent shows and tours of note are as follows:

IllumiNations

Arguably the greatest attraction in Epcot, IllumiNations ties the lands of World Showcase together in a magnificent grand finale. Classical music, laser lights, fireworks, fountains, and Disney special effects combine and do things that go beyond most people's expectations. Like the ending to a great movie, it's unfair to describe it here in detail, but look forward to it. Through 1997, a special 25th anniversary presentation replaces the traditional show.

IllumiNations takes place in the middle of World Showcase Lagoon, but not every spot around the lagoon has a perfect view. To throw one more problem into the mix, IllumiNations is the final event scheduled at Epcot. At its conclusion, everything but for a gift shop or two is closed down. That means you not only want a good view of the show, you also want a convenient area to fight (or avoid) the departing crowds. No spot is perfect for both viewing and park exiting, but some are better than others.

Consider the following:

• *Rose & Crown Pub's verandah.* IllumiNations can be viewed from the Rose & Crown's verandah, but you must 1) make a dinner reservation for at least one hour earlier than IllumiNations showtime and 2) you must stop by during the day and inform the host or hostess that you wish to have lake front dining. They're very accommodating but won't guarantee a lake front table. There is also a small lakeside park, not easily seen from the main walkway, on the right side of the pub as you walk toward France.

• *Matsu No Ma Lounge.* On the second floor of the Mitsukoshi Building, the front windows offer a magnificent view of Epcot. Though the view of IllumiNations is partially blocked, the trade-off in comfort (it's air-conditioned) may be worth it. Because it's inside, music is also less pronounced.

• *Cantina de San Angel.* On the waterfront across from Mexico's main building, you can relax in comfort with a drink and a snack at this fast food Mexican restaurant. Plan to arrive anywhere from 45 minutes to 1 1/2 hours before the show, depending on the season of the year. Competition for a good seat is stiff. On the positive side, this is the best location of all if you're willing to put in the time.

• *The back of World Showcase.* Germany, Italy, America, and Japan have relatively unrestricted views. Because crowds have an eye to leaving as soon as IllumiNations concludes, fewer opt for these spots that are farther from the front exit. If you're one of those people planning to hurry out, this is a bad idea. If you plan to rest and watch the throngs depart, consider it.

Gardens of the World

A three-hour tour of Epcot gardens, the Gardens of the World tour is hosted by a Disney horticulturist who discusses design and the differences between World Showcase gardens. Not offered every day of the week, those interested in this tour can reserve space ahead of time by calling (407) WDW-TOUR. The cost is $25.

Hidden Treasures of World Showcase

For those constantly asking the question, "How does Disney do it?", here's the answer. A tour guide spills Disney secrets and points out things usually missed by first time visitors and even most repeat guests. How does Disney age their buildings? Where did they get the idea for World Showcase? Guests even get to go behind the scenes. Cost is $25 per person. Call (407) WDW-TOUR for more information.

Fountain of Nations Water Ballet Show

Many times overlooked as just another pretty sight when walking from one place to another, this massive fountain, located in the center of Future World, dances to music. Visually fun, the fountain performs regularly during the day. Check the daily guide for times. Outside tables at the Electric Umbrella are a good spot to drink a Coke, enjoy a light snack, relax, and watch the production.

Character Meals

Aimed at the elementary school crowd, Disney offers an array of meals where the characters show up, socialize, and spend quality time with youngsters. While adults can certainly attend without kids, the main draw is food, Mickey Mouse, and friends. Check the daily schedule for meals and times. Reservations can be made by calling (407) 939-3463.

EPCOT FULL SERVICE RESTAURANTS

No Disney theme park offers greater selection — and diversity — than Epcot Center when it comes to elegant, unusual dining. Future World has two good restaurants but they're out-numbered by the twelve in World Showcase. Most are relatively expensive with entrees starting as low as $12, but ranging up to $25 and more. Most full service restaurants serve alcoholic beverages.

If money is a concern, skimp on meals in the Magic Kingdom and even Disney-MGM Studios. If you plan only one great meal, make it an Epcot one. At the two other parks, food is not an integral part of the experience. No one goes to Hollywood to eat and, except for the apple in Snow White's mouth, no one reads fairy tales for the culinary information. But Epcot is different. Food is part of culture. If trying to save money, consider a late lunch where food is less expensive.

Reservations for most restaurants can be made 60 days in advance by calling (407) WDW-DINE, though it's now called "priority seating." Simply put, a reservation means a table is waiting; priority seating means that you get the first one to open up after you arrive. The difference is small given the size of Disney restaurants, but it allows Disney to serve more guests (and yes, make more money).

Even if you're unsure where you'll be at dinnertime, try to make a reservation. You can always cancel it. Also, if you're hungry and passing an intriguing restaurant, don't be afraid to ask a host or hostess if you can dine right away without a reservation. People can and do make reservations they don't keep. This works better in the off-season and at the less popular restaurants. Italy, for example, books up early. Morocco does not. Canada, the least popular dining spot, has cafeteria service and does not take reservations, making it a good fall-back choice (busier seasons only) for those who don't like to plan too far ahead.

The following descriptions start with the two restaurants in Future World and continue clockwise around World Showcase Lagoon. The same pattern is followed for the fast food restaurants.

FUTURE WORLD

The Coral Reef

Located to the right of the Living Seas' main entrance, the Coral Reef has one wall that fronts the gigantic aquarium. Lighting in the restaurant is subdued, with much of it coming from the tank itself. Six-foot sharks swim slowly by, their sleek bodies only a few feet away as they slide through crystal clear water. While aquarium-front tables are preferred — and be sure to request one — the restaurant is tiered so that all diners can view the aquarium without obstructions.

Specializing in seafood both in the tank and on the table, the Coral Reef's green/blue decor matches the ocean theme. Beyond the zoological enjoyment of watching fish swim by, there's something calming and serene about an "underwater" restaurant, and blood pressure drops a few notches by the time you eat dessert. Entrees include Maine lobster, swordfish, and other tastes of the sea. L, D. Expensive.

Garden Grill

Located on the top level in The Land, the Garden Grill turns slowly, allowing patrons to view three scenes from the Living With The Land boat ride below. Because tour boats pass below unseen, diners can enjoy the scenery without distraction. Since the restaurant turns constantly, each table faces the main lobby of The Land for a short while, giving diners a less-than-scenic view of the crowds outside.

With the American farm and plain scenes, almost any food from the heartland goes well here, but they also throw in some seafood to round out the menu. Once the venue of adults, the restaurant now has Disney characters all day long and, for breakfast, serves an all-you-can-eat buffet. B, L, D. Moderate.

WORLD SHOWCASE

Thanks to an exchange program with other countries and an employee search in the Orlando area, servers and hosts in World Showcase restaurants and shops can trace their lineage to the featured country. While it helps theme the country, it also gives visitors a chance to meet people with first hand knowledge of "their days on a farm in France," or "what is was like growing up in Japan."

Mexico — San Angel Inn

While all World Showcase restaurants faithfully recreate the food and atmosphere of their home country, the San Angel Inn uniquely offers outside dining — indoors. Outside the restaurant, tourists shop in the town square. In back, the River of Time meanders slowly by, backed by an ancient pyramid, mists, and tropical fauna. The sky is dark, the tables lit only by candlelight. Fine china and linens carve out a semi-formal oasis in the midst of a Mexican evening. If you're celebrating a special anniversary, few other Walt Disney World restaurants are as romantic.

The San Angel Inn serves a gourmet mix of Mexican cuisine along with wine and beer. While some Mexican standards are served, they also offer less well-known entrees and desserts.. Expensive. L, D

Norway — Restaurant Akershus

Tapping into the Norway of medieval times, the Restaurant Akershus is located inside a castle. Served buffet style — koldtbord in Norwegian — a diner may sample a little bit of everything. If you want to be waited on, skip the Restaurant Akershus. But don't avoid it simply because it's a buffet. Serving hot and cold meats, cheeses, salads, and bread, it's a cultural treat served in an elegant atmosphere. Because a buffet encourages questions, diners in Norway learn more about the host country than those eating in other World Showcase restaurants. Moderate. L, D.

China — Nine Dragons Restaurant

An elegant building, the Nine Dragons is more ornate than most Chinese restaurants found outside Disney World. It serves food both familiar and unique. Attempting the gargantuan task of preparing different Chinese cuisines, the menu lists Cantonese, Kiangche, Hunan, Mandarin, and Szechuan dishes, with pastries or red bean ice cream for dessert. One of the most popular restaurants in World Showcase; reservations are necessary. Expensive. L, D.

Germany — Biergarten

Huge mugs of beer and a party atmosphere make this German restaurant a stand-out — definitely the place to quaff a few brews and laugh with neighbors from across the country. If you want romance, go to France or Mexico. If you want a good time, visit Germany.

Long tables face rails in a tiered dining room that faces a stage. During lunch, the atmosphere is calm, but during dinner, a half hour program repeats itself every hour, ensuring that everyone sees it at least once. The restaurant itself recreates a German town nestled in the mountains. A mill sits to the side with a mountain stream turning a giant wheel. Geraniums decorate surrounding houses while overhead, the night time sky (a fake Disney one) promises no chance of showers, ever. Female servers look a little bit like the St. Pauli girl, only not as provocative. The restaurant recently changed from table service to buffet style, giving diners less service, but a better sampling of German food. Moderate. L, D.

Italy — L'Originale Alfredo di Roma Ristorante

Another extremely popular restaurant, reservations are almost always necessary here. Chefs prepare pasta on site and in full view of the public. All the traditional Italian fare is served — spaghetti for instance — but also a number of less famous gourmet items. The specialty is fettucine Alfredo, but other dishes incorporate seafood, chicken, and sausage.

The decor is unique. Painted to resemble Italian scenes, it's difficult to tell which waiters are real and which are nothing more than a flat rendition on the wall. Not all doors are real and not all windows are glass. A design found in Italy, it makes the atmosphere unusual, even though Italian restaurants are an American staple. At dinner, strolling singers complete the Italian transformation. Expensive. L, D.

Japan — Teppanyaki Dining Rooms

Diners sit around a grill with other patrons while the chef prepares the meal, grilling and mixing with style and art. Dining with other Epcot guests adds to the atmosphere, making the visit more than just a place to eat. Some people enjoy meeting kindred spirits while on vacation; others prefer to keep to themselves. The former will love the Teppanyaki Dining Rooms; the latter might prefer to eat elsewhere.

The Japanese Chef becomes an ambassador, both humorous and interesting. Because the meal is also a show, there is ample opportunity to hear stories about Japan and have questions answered. Decorated in simple, tasteful style, the Teppanyaki Dining Rooms are a unique experience for those who have not visited Japan or Benihana's, the Americanized restaurant that serves the same cuisine. Expensive. L, D.

Japan — Tempura Kiku

This second — and much smaller — Japanese restaurant features tempura dining. Like the Teppanyaki Dining Rooms, the atmosphere encourages diners to talk with each other. The tempura cooking style — meaning different foods are batter-dipped and then fried — gives shrimp, scallops, lobster, beef, and chicken a unique flavor. Not for those watching their intake of fat. Expensive. L, D.

Morocco — Restaurant Marrakesh

Many foreign foods made inroads into American culture. Indeed, some food — Italian, for example — can be found in Cleveland as easily as Rome. Moroccan food, however, is not an American staple. The selections here reflect the meat, plants, and spices traditional to Morocco. Lamb and chicken form the backbone of most dishes. Almonds, saffron, and cinnamon spice it up; wheat and pastry hold it together.

The restaurant has a dinner-for-two that includes different

Moroccan foods, a good choice if you like to experiment. Served by people in traditional Moroccan dress, the high ceiling of the restaurant includes intricate inlaid tiles. A belly dancer performs during dinner, but the sensual style is toned down and children are sometimes offered a free dance lesson. While reservations are recommended, it is sometimes possible to walk in, since many Epcot visitors lean toward the well-known cuisines. Expensive. L, D.

France — Chefs de France

This World Showcase country has no less than three different restaurants, all supervised by true French chefs. Chefs de France relies on crystal chandeliers, etched glass, framed French art, and brass accents to imitate the styles of the home country. Linen table-cloths make this one of the top choices for those guests who wish to live the good life.

Chefs de France's nouvelle cuisine does not rely on the heavy butter and cream concoctions found elsewhere. Sauces are lighter. Still, the dishes contain more than a few calories. Expensive. L, D.

France — Bistro de Paris

Located on the second floor, the Bistro de Paris recreates the Paris of a hundred years ago. Those seeking traditional French cuisine should make their reservations here. From the food to the music, diners are no longer in Epcot. They're dining in France. The French decor includes lots of wood, brass lights, heavy leaded glass, and simple elegance with ornate accents. The setting is intimate, with tables nestled by windows or walls. It's expensive, but the heavy food will stick with you all day. It's not unusual to leave, wondering where you're going to find the strength to keep touring but, of course, you do. Expensive. L, D.

France — Au Petit Café

Not fast food yet not elegant dining, Au Petit Café is perfect for a light meal. Most of the restaurant is outdoors, adding the French ambiance of a sidewalk café to this World Showcase country. For diners, it's a wonderful way to enjoy the Florida warmth and understand why the sidewalk café is so popular in France.

Diners sit under an awning. While plastic walls are rolled down in foul weather, it's not made for rain. Also, they do not accept reservations, seating diners on a first-come, first-served basis. If you wish to register for a table when it's busy, plan to wait. Moderate. L, D.

Great Britain — Rose & Crown Dining Room

Part of the pub by the same name, the Rose & Crown Dining Room serves hearty meats and side dishes, cooked in traditional styles for people who like meat and potatoes. Among other things, they serve roast lamb, steak-and-kidney pie, and fish and chips. The Rose & Crown feels earthy and natural, a result of the wood, glass, and brass decor, and magnified by the server's friendly working-class attitudes. Traditional prints line the walls.

Guests looking for a good view of IllumiNations can make a late reservation and request outside dining, offered seasonally. For those who want to soak up a little British atmosphere without dining — along with a pint of ale — no reservations are needed to stop at the pub and quaff a cold one. Bowing to American tastes, the beer is served cold, not room temperature as in Great Britain. Expensive. L, D.

Le Cellier

Unlike other World Showcase restaurants, Le Cellier is a cafeteria rather than a full-service restaurant. And, unlike other World Showcase restaurants, it sometimes closes during slow seasons. It also does not accept reservations.

Perhaps the greatest strike against Canada is the lack of uniquely Canadian cuisine. While a distinct geographic line divides the United States and Canada, the same hearty pioneers settled both wildernesses and the same raw ingredients go into the food. In other words, the offerings in Canada look suspiciously American. If you want good food fast, Le Cellier is a satisfying choice.

The restaurant recreates the rocks and low ceilings of a wine cellar, serving hearty food like stew, salmon, and pork-and-potato pie. Lighter meals are also served. If you choose to eat two full meals during the day, this is an ideal stop for lunch. Moderate. L, D.

EPCOT FAST-FOOD RESTAURANTS AND SPECIALTY SNACKS
FUTURE WORLD

• **Pure and Simple.** Located inside Wonders of Life, this healthy food stand serves salads, yogurt, waffles, and sandwiches.

• *Sunshine Season Food Fair.* Located on the first floor of The Land, this food court imitates a country fair with different booths including: The Beverage House, The Bakery Shop, The Barbecue, Cheese and Pasta, Sandwich Shop, Ice Cream, The Potato Store, and Soup & Salad. A great place to eat for those who like different things, it gets crowded at meal times. In addition, each store has a separate queue, so people choosing different items must enter different lines and hope they're served at approximately the same time. Otherwise, someone eats alone.

• *Electric Umbrella Restaurant.* Located in Innoventions with standard fast food fare: burgers, chicken sandwiches, and salads.

• *Fountain View Espresso and Bakery.* Pleasant coffee shop offerings include espresso, cappuccino, and pastries. Located in Innoventions.

• *Pasta Piazza Ristorante.* Fast food Italian serving pizza, pasta, and salads. Breakfast is also served. Located in Innoventions.

WORLD SHOWCASE

• *Cantina de San Angel.* Located on World Showcase Lagoon and directly across the walkway from Mexico, Cantina de San Angel serves fast Mexican food — tacos, enchiladas, and tortillas.

• *Kringla Bakeri og Kafé.* Located in Norway, Kringla Bakeri og Kafé serves open faced sandwiches along with unusual Norwegian desserts.

• *Lotus Blossom Café.* In China, the Lotus Blossom Café serves eggrolls and stir-fried entrees. While indoors, the street-side walls are open and the restaurant is not air-conditioned.

• *Refreshment Outpost.* Between China and Germany, this foreign legion refreshment stand serves sodas and ice cream

• *Sommerfest.* Located in Germany, Sommerfest serves many of the foods associated with Germany: bratwurst sandwiches, pretzels, Black Forest cake, and, of course, Beck's beer.

• *Liberty Inn.* As American as apple pie — or here, an apple pastry — the Liberty Inn specializes in hot dogs, hamburgers, and french fries.

• *Yakitori House.* Serving traditional Japanese food in an oriental atmosphere, this fast food restaurant features broiled chicken and beef.

• *Matsu No Ma Lounge.* Serving both appetizers and alcoholic specialty drinks, the Matsu No Ma Lounge also has a great view of World

Showcase and, across the lagoon, Spaceship Earth. It's not a fast food restaurant, but a lounge that serves light snacks.

• *Boulangerie Pâtisserie.* Serving those wonderful French pastries along with quiche and coffee, the crowds form early for those interested in a true continental breakfast.

• *Rose & Crown Pub.* Part of the pub is a sit down restaurant, the other part a pub offering light snacks and beer.

• *Refreshment Port.* This new snack bar located near Canada serves sodas, frozen yogurt, and cookies.

SHOPPING IN EPCOT CENTER

In Future World, shopping is a sideshow, something guests do if they happen to find an interesting store. In World Showcase, however, shopping is part of the experience. The style of the merchandise and the decor of the store reflect the people and customs of the host country. Even if you've traveled from Ecuador and never owned a sweater, you can still marvel at the style and quality of a Scottish cardigan. Even if you never drink alcohol, you can marvel at the selection of French wines. On-site guests can have purchases delivered to their hotel room. Off-site guests may have them shipped to the front of the park, to be picked up just prior to departure.

Not all of the shops are listed here, only those with unique goods or interesting features. You'll discover the rest as you explore Epcot. A side note: many stores stock life's necessities such as aspirin and raincoats but they do not display them. If you need something, stop in a store and ask. If they do not stock the item behind the counter, they will direct you to the nearest store that does.

• **Camera Center.** Located almost under Spaceship Earth, the Camera Center handles all film needs including same day photo processing and camcorder rentals.

• **Centorium.** The main store for memorabilia and mementos, this Innoventions-located store usually stays open later than the rest of the park. While crowds are elbow-to-elbow at closing, it's also a good time for last minute souvenirs while the other 30,000 guests fight to get to their cars.

• **The Art of Disney Epcot.** Near Innoventions, this shop features expensive lithographs and artwork based on Disney characters and concepts.

• **Glas und Porzellan.** This German shop sells porcelain produced by the Goebel company, including the famous M.I. Hummel figurines. But in addition to sales, the process of creation is described with examples of production.

• **Mitsukoshi Department Store.** While not as specialized as other World Showcase stores, Mitsukoshi is an old Japanese name. The specialty items inside must be sought, just as they would if actually visiting Japan.

DON'T MISS...

Here's a quick reference list of those attractions worth waiting in a long line to see, though hopefully you'll visit on a slow day. Those marked with a bullet indicate an action ride not suitable for all.

Future World

Spaceship Earth

• Body Wars (in Wonders of Life)

Cranium Command (in Wonders of Life)

Horizons

• Test Track

Honey, I Shrunk the Audience (in Journey Into Imagination)

Journey Into Imagination (a must-see for some while
    others don't care for it)

Living With the Land (inside The Land)

World Showcase

The American Adventure

IllumiNations

DISNEY-MGM STUDIOS

187 Should You Visit Universal Studios or Disney-MGM Studios?

188 Getting to MGM-Disney Studios

189 First Things First

191 Touring Tips

192 Guidelines For Those Who Don't Mind a Lot of Walking

193 Attractions

202 Parades and Shows

203 Restaurants

207 Shopping

208 Don't Miss...

Chapter Eleven

THE DISNEY-MGM STUDIOS

The Disney-MGM Studios, Disney's third theme park, is also the smallest. While it takes almost two days to fully explore Epcot or the Magic Kingdom, first time guests can enjoy Disney-MGM Studios in less than a day. In other words, you can explore leisurely and walk less. Don't hurry and don't panic. In the busy season, thick crowds and lengthy lines make the small park feel even smaller. But in the off-season, when crowds are reasonable, mature travelers find the restaurants and attractions adult-friendly.

Disney-MGM Studios is an actual working movie studio, but only marginally. The original movie theme park — Universal Studios, Hollywood — began accidentally. As the movie business grew, the public fell in love with the glamour of Tinseltown, the stars, and everything else that smacked of Hollywood. As a result of demand, Universal Studios added a backstage tour to its on-going movie business. The tour grew, real movie special effects led to recreations, and suddenly they had a theme park and a movie studio. Sensing success, Disney and Universal both built movie parks in Orlando.

Disney-MGM Studios is first and foremost a theme park. Movies can be filmed there as can TV shows and radio programs. Some are. Ed McMahon's Star Search filmed on one sound stage as do Disney Channel favorites such as the now defunct Mickey Mouse Club. You will probably not, however, see filming for major shows when you visit. The outside shot of the home from The Golden Girls sits on the Disney-MGM Studios' back lot, but all interior shots were filmed in California. The Studio Showcase displays props from recent movies, but ones also made elsewhere.

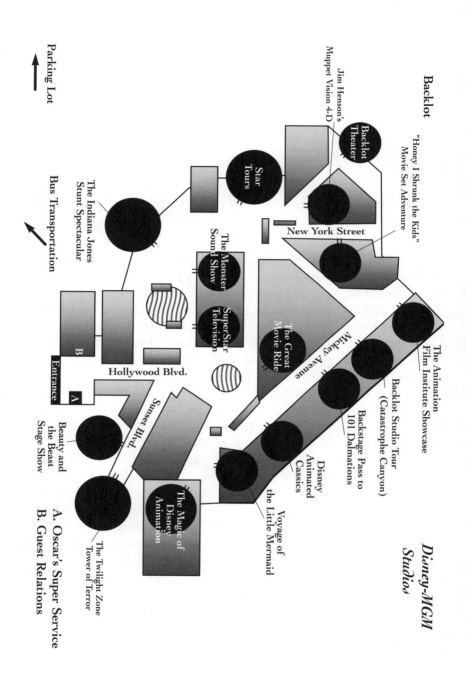

Disney-MGM Studios

Backlot

"Honey I Shrunk the Kids" Movie Set Adventure

Jim Henson's Muppet Vision 4-D

Backlot Theater

Star Tours

New York Street

The Indiana Jones Stunt Spectacular

The Monster Sound Show

SuperStar Television

The Great Movie Ride

Mickey Avenue

The Animation Film Institute Showcase

Backlot Studio Tour (Catastrophe Canyon)

Backstage Pass to 101 Dalmations

Disney Animated Classics

Voyage of the Little Mermaid

Hollywood Blvd.

B

Entrance

A

Sunset Blvd.

Beauty and the Beast Stage Show

The Magic of Disney Animation

The Twilight Zone Tower of Terror

A. Oscar's Super Service
B. Guest Relations

Parking Lot

Bus Transportation

One exception to that rule is within the Disney animation department. Historically, the on-site animation studio produced short pieces like McDonald's commercials that feature Disney characters. But today, the number of Orlando animators continues to grow as they shift production from California to Central Florida. They're currently working on the first feature length film to be entirely produced on-site.

SHOULD YOU VISIT UNIVERSAL STUDIOS OR DISNEY-MGM STUDIOS?

It depends. Both have strengths and weaknesses.

If you purchased one of Disney's multiple park passes, you'll probably opt for Disney-MGM for financial reasons, especially if visiting for the first time. You paid for it; you go. If not visiting for the first time, many people buy one-day passes to Epcot and/or Magic Kingdom and then, rather than seeing Disney-MGM a second time, drive to Universal Studios.

If you have large reserves of energy, you can visit both on one trip without seeing the same things twice. A small amount of similar movie-making information is presented at both parks, but overall, they're two different experiences. For one thing, Disney-MGM has rides and shows based on the Disney classics and the MGM musicals. Universal Studios relies on its own movies, such as Jaws and E.T., as well as the Hanna-Barbera cartoon characters.

They also aim for different audiences. Like all things Disney, the Disney-MGM attractions are G-rated. They reflect adventure films, love stories, and musicals. Universal, while appropriate for all ages, slants many rides to an older crowd, with heavier doses of science fiction, horror, and action.

Assuming you can visit only one park, however, consider the following:

• If you want a Hollywood fantasy, visit Disney-MGM. If you want to visit a real (looking) movie studio, go to Universal. Disney-MGM Studios looks and feels less authentic. Billed as "the Hollywood that never was and always will be," the shops and restaurants are bigger-than-life, the art deco touches grander, and the campy restaurant themes less realistic. Disney Imagineers took the public's perception of Hollywood and made it tangible, much as they did with the wild west in the Magic Kingdom's Frontierland. It's the Hollywood that exists in the public's mind rather than the Hollywood that sits in California. On the other hand, Universal Studios comes closer to portraying a real motion picture studio.

• If you're in the mood for action, choose Universal Studios. If you prefer to be entertained, choose Disney-MGM. Universal Studios has more rides but Disney-MGM Studios has more shows. Disney has two rides that jostle you around; Universal has five. In addition, Universal Studios' rides recreate famous movies and rely on action and audience excitement. Even a ride for children — The Funtastic World of Hanna Barbera, for example — is a motion simulator, meaning the audience sits in a compartment that jerks back and forth in synchronization to a cartoon. The difference in style is subtle and most people like both, just as a person who loves a good action/adventure film sometimes enjoys a tear-jerker.

• If you want to understand the secrets of movie-making, visit Disney-MGM Studios. If you want entertainment with a small helping of movie-education, visit Universal Studios. Ironically, even though Universal Studios makes more movies than Disney-MGM, the back-stage tour at Disney is more informative and includes sound stages, costume departments, special effects studios, backlots, and a sample film with props and sets that show how it all comes together. Universal Studios presents information in an attraction format, generally theater style, where entertaining stage shows explain make-up, special effects, or post-production work. At Disney, the stages could actually be used in a production. At Universal, they're there only to entertain guests.

• The bigger size of Universal Studios makes it feel less claustro-phobic. But if concerned with the amount of walking required, choose Disney.

GETTING TO THE DISNEY-MGM STUDIOS

For guests staying off-site, the most direct and easiest route is to take exit #25 off I-4 to Disney's maingate. A short distance after exiting onto U.S. 192, turn north onto Disney property. (It's well marked.) Disney-MGM Studios sits on the right, directly after Earful Tower. It's also possible to take the main exit for Epcot Center, exit #26B, and follow the signs to Disney-MGM Studios though it's more confusing and sends guests to a secondary parking lot entrance.

Most guests staying on-site take buses to get to the park, but those staying in Epcot area resorts — Disney's Yacht and Beach Club, Disney's Boardwalk Resort, The Swan, and The Dolphin — can take watercraft. Buses drop passengers close to the main turnstiles; watercraft dock off to one side.

At presstime, parking was $5 per day, free to resort guests. Save your parking ticket if traveling to other Disney parks since a single day's payment is valid at all three. Once parked, memorize your car's location. A tram connects all parking areas to the front entrance, but many people walk rather than ride.

FIRST THINGS FIRST

Once you pass through the park turnstiles, Hollywood Boulevard beats a direct path to Mann's (formerly Graumann's) Chinese Theater, the home of The Great Movie Ride. The stores along the way are fun, a throw-back to the 1920's, and Disney actors mingle with guests, adding another dimension to the "Hollywood that never was." Dubbed "Streetmosphere," these actors recreate stereotypical actors seen in a hundred movies. In other words, it's fun. But before you get sucked into the action, stop by Guest Relations located on your immediate left after passing through the turnstiles and ask for a park map/entertainment schedule if you do not already have one.

Once armed, continue down Hollywood Boulevard. Halfway down and on your right, Sunset Boulevard intersects the street. On the corner, a large board provides a continually updated schedule of the park's activities. Make dinner reservations here if you have not already done so.

Unlike Epcot and the Magic Kingdom, the Disney-MGM Studios does not have clear-cut lands to explore. Hollywood Boulevard (the main entrance) and Sunset Boulevard (that first street on the right) replicate different eras of Hollywood. The remainder of the park is a movie studio production lot. If you're lost in the Magic Kingdom and all the buildings look like jungle huts, you can pretty much guess that you're in Adventureland. But if lost in Disney-MGM Studios, you're either in the Hollywood section — or you're not.

The lay-out of Disney-MGM is similar to the Magic Kingdom, with Hollywood Boulevard designed like Main Street. One notable difference, however, is Sunset Boulevard, a street halfway down and home to the Tower of Terror and the Beauty and the Beast stage show. The far end of Hollywood Boulevard circles a garden in front of Mann's Chinese Theater. Different sections of the park can be reached from this central Hub.

Surrounding the Hub is the true movie-making section of the park. To the right, guests can see the Little Mermaid or the Magic of Disney Animation. While this area is not strictly a dead end (you can take a short-cut down Mickey Avenue to New York Street), it's generally faster to return to the Hub and explore the rest of the park from there.

A walkway just left of Mann's Chinese Theater leads to New York Street, Jim Henson's Muppet Vision 4-D, and the Hunchback of Notre Dame stage show. A hard left at the Hub connects to Star Tours, the Indiana Jones Stunt Spectacular and two movie-making presentations.

The following services are offered at Disney-MGM Studios:

• **Wheelchair and Stroller Rental.** Located at Oscar's Super Service, the gas station immediately to your right when first entering the park.

• **Money.** SunTrust operates an ATM outside and to the right of the front gate.

• **First Aid.** By Guests Relations, on the left after passing through the entrance turnstiles.

• **Baby Care.** By Guest Relations, on the left after passing through the entrance turnstiles.

• **Lost and Found.** Located past the entrance turnstiles on your right. For information after you've left Disney-MGM Studios, call (407) 824-4245.

• **Storage Lockers.** Located next to Oscar's Super Service on the right immediately after the entrance turnstiles.

• **Information.** For directions or even general questions, ask any cast member. For more specific information, stop at Guest Relations.

• **Pets.** Except for service animals, pets are not allowed in any Disney parks. It is also against Florida law to leave them unattended in a vehicle. The Disney-MGM Studios Pet Care Center is located outside the main entrance and charges $5 per day.

• **Disabled Guests.** Sight impaired guests receive complimentary tour cassettes at Guest Relations. At the same location, hearing impaired guests can rent Assistive Listening Devices which amplify selected attractions. TDD's may also be rented. In addition, written scripts are available at each attraction.

TOURING TIPS

While the Disney-MGM Studios has two thrill rides, it is mainly a theatrical park. For most attractions, guests sit and watch.

Because of the large number of live shows, it's important to read the entertainment guide before you tour. Shows are scattered throughout the park and many do not run back-to-back. Without referring to the entertainment schedule, you could end up walking miles from show-to-show after touring the other attractions, not getting a good seat, or worse — missing a show altogether.

The following tips should help plan your day:

• Arrive early if you can, at least a half hour before the park officially opens. If you wish to sleep in, plan on staying until the park closes. Since the Disney-MGM Studios can be seen in less than one full day, those who arrive early tend to depart before closing. If arriving around 11:00, save attractions with long lines for late afternoon.

• Guests staying off-site should try to avoid the Disney-MGM Studios on days when on-site guests are allowed to enter the park one hour earlier than the general public. (See Chapter 8: Park Touring Tips).

• Postpone shopping on Hollywood Boulevard until the afternoon or at closing. After rides shut down, shops remain open. While this is the busiest shopping time and you'll fight elbow-to-elbow crowds, it gives you more park time on a one-day admission.

• Even on a day with no lines, guests can wait half an hour for an attraction if a show just started. A short line may indicate a short wait time, but it may also indicate that a 30-minute show just accepted an audience and it is now building up for the next feature.

• The Tip Board at Sunset Boulevard will give you a wait-time overview for the entire park.

• Don't avoid a show or ride because it's based on a movie you're unfamiliar with or a "kid's movie." Disney's stage productions translate well to all generations.

• For repeat visitors: In past years, outdoor sets and warehouses were explored by tram in The Backlot Tour and everything inside on a walking tour called Inside the Magic. Together, the two attractions thoroughly explained movie-making technology. Today, that's changed. Inside the Magic is gone, its assets divided among three other attractions. The study of filming miniatures (where guests learned how to film navel scenes) is now part of the Backlot Tour, viewed before boarding the trams. Post-production facilities are now part of Disney Animation Classics (or The Making Of…). All sound stages and special effects areas, are now part of Backstage Pass to 101 Dalmatians.

GUIDELINES FOR THOSE WHO DON'T MIND A LOT OF WALKING

Arrive at least a half hour early. On the entertainment schedule, check the times for Voyage of The Little Mermaid and plan on seeing the first show. If you have at least twenty minutes before the show, and you enjoy a good morning scare, make a beeline to Tower of Terror. Ride. If less than twenty minutes to showtime, ride Tower of Terror after The Little Mermaid.

After Voyage of the Little Mermaid and Tower of Terror, make a left at the Hub and ride Star Tours, another high-motion ride. Next, check your entertainment schedule. You might want to return to the same area where you saw Voyage of the Little Mermaid and see The Magic of Disney Animation followed by the Backstage Studio Tour. Also consider the Great Movie Ride. But you might want to begin touring the park in a more orderly fashion.

After the animation tour and the backstage tour, lines should be forming at most attractions and there's no advantage to racing any-where. Slow down and enjoy the rest of the day.

For Those Who Wish To Know Which Rides Have Lengthy Waits But Want To Plan Their Own Itinerary:

Tower of Terror
Voyage of the Little Mermaid
The Great Movie Ride
Star Tours

ATTRACTIONS

How to Read the Attraction Descriptions

Each attraction is followed by a letter ranging from "A" to "E". Before Walt Disney World switched to a one-price admission policy, each ride required a ticket. "E" tickets were the best, required for all top-of-the-line attractions. "A" tickets worked only on the simplest rides. "B", "C", and "D" fell somewhere inbetween.

Note — Information to help you enjoy the ride is included. For example, if the ride is an "E" ticket in substance, but not entertainment value, it will be noted. Also, if an attraction is based on a movie which some may not have seen, it is explained.

Movement — Describes all motion on the ride, along with anything else that might make adults uncomfortable. Entertainment "surprises" are not described, only those things that move you fast, throw you around, or jump in your face.

Line — Describes the queue line, whether it's inside or outside, air-conditioned, or visible from the street.

Wait time — Attempts to judge the wait in relation to other attractions. For example, a long wait time does not necessarily mean hours in line. Star Wars has a long wait time. That means that, when the park is very busy, expect upwards to an hour in line. On a less-crowded day when you can get on some rides immediately, expect ten or fifteen minutes. In other words, "long" is a relative term based on the day of your visit — not necessarily exact time. Remember that other things also affect your wait, including the time of day and whether or not a nearby attraction just spilled 2000 people onto the sidewalk.

Wheelchair Access — Notes any special problems encountered by those in wheelchairs. Remember that WDW cast members will not help in a transfer from wheelchair to ride. If you cannot transfer yourself alone or with the help of a companion, sigh and move on to a ride that can accommodate you. If you feel you can ride, look for a cast member at the entrance to the attraction. Most times, they'll find you.

The ride descriptions assume you make a right at Sunset Boulevard and then return to Hollywood Boulevard. From there, the descriptions start on the right of the Hub, return across the Hub, and then proceed clock-wise around the park.

Twilight Zone Tower of Terror
TICKET: E

NOTE: This is an updated version of the Magic Kingdom's Haunted House, only now it's a hotel, the special effects reflect 20 extra years of technology, and the ride actually scares you. According to the Disney story line, around 1939, a hotel wing, elevator, and group of passengers disappeared in a storm. That disappearance has never been adequately explained.

Like a good movie, the ride has a plot. Once you enter the elevator and start moving, however, the plot evaporates and you're left to enjoy the special effects and wait for the fall.

MOVEMENT: The good news: 95% of the ride is a gentle interesting journey. The bad news: 5% involves a two-second drop straight down an elevator shaft — twice. Or maybe three times. The fall, controlled by computer, may be changed by Imagineers at will. The elevator may hover for a minute at the top, drop a foot, then hesitate. When it finally does fall, it feels worse than it is because the elevator is not just dropped — it's thrown. More than gravity gets it started.

But by the time you inhale sharply, it's over. Your brain barely recognizes the danger before the elevator slows. Guests with "heart conditions, motion sickness, back or neck problems, or other conditions that may be aggravated" are advised not to ride. Must be 40 inches tall.

LINE: Most of the initial queue winds up to the hotel, around the porch, and in the front door, partially shaded and outdoors. Once inside where it's air-conditioned, a short line leads to the hotel's library where guests view a pre-show that establishes the plot. After the preshow, a second line winds through the hotel's antiquated (yet air-conditioned) boiler room. For the main ride, guests board an elevator with seats and lap bars.

Note: For those who wish to experience this with a companion who chooses not to ride, both may wait together until they reach the ill-fated elevator. A Disney cast member will then direct the non-rider to a real elevator where, a few minutes later, they can meet their companion at the ride exit.

WAIT TIME: Long.

WHEELCHAIR ACCESS: Poor. Riders must be able to transfer from wheelchair to elevator seating.

Beauty and the Beast Stage Show
TICKET: E
NOTE: With notable Disney twists, the show follows the story line of the child's fable and can be enjoyed whether you've seen the Disney movie or not. The idea for the currently running Broadway play actually began with this production. It should not be missed.
MOVEMENT: None. Theater presentation.
LINE: Entire production is shaded but outdoors and can get very hot on a summer afternoon. In the off-season, early arrivals get better seats but even last minute guests should find something in the rear.
WAIT TIME: Short.
WHEELCHAIR ACCESS: Good. Completely accessible.

The Magic of Disney Animation
TICKET: E
NOTE: More than anything else, The Magic of Disney Animation is entertaining. With the talents of Walter Cronkite and Robin Williams — an unlikely duo — Disney created a walk-through attraction that amuses both seniors and preschoolers. On the tour, guests sit for a theater presentation that explains how animation works. Next, they walk through a working animation department where overhead televisions clearly explain the creation process. Finally, guests sit in a second theater that highlights the finished product — those famous Disney films.

Like all top-flight Disney attractions, the key here is the writing, for which a lot of credit goes to Robin Williams. For the walk-through portion, the televisions lead visitors through the tour with a continuing monologue, but you can stay as long as you wish to watch the artists work. One important note: animators work fairly regular hours though a few will also be present on evenings and weekends. For the best tour, try to visit Monday through Friday before 6 p.m.
MOVEMENT: None. Theater or walk-through presentation.
LINE: There is an air-conditioned waiting area before the doors open to the first theater presentation. The pre-counted guests mill about looking at replicas of Disney's Oscars and other artifacts from films. If full, other guests wait outside.
WAIT TIME: Medium to long.
WHEELCHAIR ACCESS: Good. Completely accessible.

Voyage of the Little Mermaid

TICKET: E

NOTE: At first glance, Voyage of the Little Mermaid sounds like a kids-only production. But see it. Like many movie-based shows, it loosely follows the original plot but award-winning songs carry the production. If you haven't seen the movie, it's a bit confusing, but still top-notch Disney entertainment. Because it's produced indoors, the Disney people have free rein with special effects. Even those who don't enjoy Caribbean-style music are awed by the technology and inventiveness of the show.

MOVEMENT: None. Theater presentation.

LINE: The line is outdoors but shaded. Entire length is visible from the street.

WAIT TIME: Long.

WHEELCHAIR ACCESS: Good. Completely accessible.

The Great Movie Ride

TICKET: E

NOTE: Possibly the grandest ride at Disney-MGM Studios, The Great Movie Ride transports guests through famous movie scenes. Large cars carry many people at one time, meaning the line moves rapidly and then stops for a while. A unique feature of The Great Movie Ride is that the guests traveling in the last half of the ride caravan enjoy a slightly different show than those traveling in the front. If you decide to ride twice, try to change locations the second time. (The line splits at one point. If you went left the first time, go right the second.)

MOVEMENT: Smooth. While the cars move through the attraction, nothing shakes, rattles, or rolls.

LINE: Line is inside and air-conditioned, winding past movie memorabilia housed in display cases, including such famous props as Dorothy's ruby slippers from *The Wizard of Oz*. The final wait zone before boarding looks like a theater and movie trailers play on the screen. Each on-screen clip advertises a movie recreated on the ride.

WAIT TIME: Medium, but if extending outside, expect a long wait.

WHEELCHAIR ACCESS: Good. Guests may remain in their wheelchairs throughout the ride. Look to a cast member for directions.

SuperStar Television
TICKET: E
NOTE: SuperStar Television uses movie-making technology to paste park guests' images into well-known television shows. In the wait area, Disney cast members select people to "star" in the production, meaning you may see your spouse interviewed by Howard Cosell or talking to Norm, Cliff, and Sam on the set of Cheers. If you wish to be in the production, arrive early and stand near the front of the line.
MOVEMENT: None. Theater presentation.
LINE: Outdoors but shaded.
WAIT TIME: Medium. The show lasts over half an hour so even with little or no line, you could be waiting up to 30 minutes.
WHEELCHAIR ACCESS: Good. Completely accessible.

The Monster Sound Show
TICKET: E
NOTE: The name notwithstanding, the show is more "sound" than "monster." In any good movie, a large number of the sounds — lightning, wind, rain, etc. — are not part of the original shoot, but added afterward by special effects people. At The Monster Sound Show, this process is explained with the help of audience volunteers. (If they ask you to help, go ahead and try it. They don't allow camcording in the theater, so your family can't embarrass you later.)

At the conclusion of the show, guests exit through SoundWorks, an audio playground where hands-on activities demonstrate other movie-making sound tricks. Don't miss the small sound booths located across from the main exit doors, where guests enjoy one of the best — yet often overlooked — illusions in all of Walt Disney World. Advanced recording technology creates a sound so realistic that when you hear rain, you involuntarily put a hand out to make sure the roof isn't leaking.
MOVEMENT: None. Theater presentation.
LINE: Outdoors and partially shaded. A short preshow prepares you for the main presentation.
WAIT TIME: Medium.
WHEELCHAIR ACCESS: Good. Completely accessible.

Indiana Jones Epic Stunt Spectacular
TICKET: E
NOTE: Everything's big in the Indiana Jones Epic Stunt Spectacular

— the theater, the stage, the special effects, and even the jokes. Very loosely based on the original Indiana Jones movie, Raiders of the Lost Ark, the show's premise is just an excuse to recreate some death-defying movie stunts. For those who have not seen the movie, the action is a bit disjointed, but that in no way affects the thrill. A massive production, it's well worth seeing. Rumors say it will be revamped in the future.

MOVEMENT: None. Theater presentation. While covered, the theater is outdoors and may be hot in summer or early fall afternoons.

LINE: Outdoors and partially shaded.

WAIT TIME: Short. The theater holds 2,000 people. But by arriving early and waiting until cast members allow you to enter, you're assured a seat down front.

WHEELCHAIR ACCESS: Good, though located at the highest tier of seats and far from the stage.

Star Tours

TICKET: E

NOTE: Derived from the Star Wars' movie trilogy, robots take guests on a brand new flight across the universe. Outside of not knowing the main characters, you don't have to be familiar with the original movie.

MOVEMENT: You actually go nowhere. Your vehicle sits on machinery that can lift the front, the rear, or the sides, although you see only the interior. A computer makes sure the movements coincide with a movie shown in the front of the ride vehicle. If the movie shows you coursing out of control through the universe, for example, the cart moves the front up and the rear down. Feeling the increased pressure of your back against the seat, you attribute it to the speed of travel rather than the fact that the vehicle just tilted upward.

While you're seated securely and belted in, the danger lies in the jerky movements the car sometimes makes. If the ship hits something in the movie, the effect is simulated by jerking the entire vehicle. If you hold securely to the arm rests, you should be fine. A second danger, however, is motion sickness. If you don't ride in the back seat of cars and hate to fly because turbulence upsets you, avoid Star Tours. Guests with "heart conditions, motion sickness, back or neck problems, or other conditions that may be aggravated" are advised not to ride. Must be 40 inches tall.

LINE: Indoors and air-conditioned unless long.

WAIT TIME: Long.

WHEELCHAIR ACCESS: Fair. Guests must be able to transfer

themselves from wheelchair to auditorium-style seat inside the Star Wars vehicle.

Jim Henson's Muppet Vision 4-D

TICKET: E

NOTE: This show's fun, but decidedly better if you're familiar with the Muppet characters. The humor entertains the younger set, but like most Muppet productions, an occasional joke takes aim at adults. Because of Disney special effects, it's difficult at times to distinguish between things happening in the movie and those actually taking place in the theater. Unless you take the 3-D glasses off, you don't know whether to duck or stay seated. Light, entertaining, and air-conditioned, it's a good show for all ages.

MOVEMENT: None. Theater presentation.

LINE: Inside and air-conditioned if short, outside and partially shaded if long.

WAIT TIME: Medium

WHEELCHAIR ACCESS: Good. Guests may remain in their wheelchairs throughout the performance.

"Honey, I Shrunk the Kids" Movie Set Adventure

TICKET: C

NOTE: Billed as a "movie set," this playground is really rough and tough, built for the demanding play of the elementary school generation. Most real movie sets only have to fool the camera. The critics for this one are far more demanding.

While not constructed with mature travelers in mind, it's fun to walk through if the crowds aren't too thick. The play elements — a giant ant, monstrous Cheerios, and towering blades of grass — come directly from the movie of the same name. You don't have to understand the plot, however, to enjoy feeling very, very small. If visiting, walk to the top of the stairs and stand in front of the giant dog's nose for a minute. You'll understand once you get there.

MOVEMENT: None. A walk-through attraction.

LINE: The entire line and attraction are outdoors. Though shaded, it gets stuffy during the summer.

WAIT TIME: Varies. In the busy season, it's medium to long. When kids are in school, there is generally no wait.

WHEELCHAIR ACCESS: Fair. Wheelchairs may enter but cannot enjoy most of the slides and playthings.

The Hunchback of Notre Dame — Backlot Theater
TICKET: E
NOTE: Taken from the 1996 Disney animated film, this live action, stage production relies heavily on the movie's songs. A thinned-out story-line ties the popular showstoppers together. Staging, costumes, and entertainment are first-rate, making this one of those better-than-expected attractions. For good seating, arrive at least 20 minutes before showtime.
MOVEMENT: None. Theater presentation.
LINE: Outdoors though shaded.
WAIT TIME: Medium. For the best seats, arrive early, though even last minute arrivals may find something in slower seasons.
WHEELCHAIR ACCESS: Good. Guests may remain in wheelchairs throughout.

The American Film Institute Showcase
TICKET: C
NOTE: This walk-through exhibit features props and sets from TV shows and movies. A changing exhibit, most costumes and props come from works appearing currently or within the past two years.
MOVEMENT: None. A self-guided tour.
LINE: None.
WAIT TIME: None.
WHEELCHAIR ACCESS: Good. Completely accessible.

Backlot Studio Tour
TICKET: E
NOTE: The first film studio tour — Universal Studios, Hollywood — took guests through all exhibits by way of a tram. Imitating that initial success, the Disney-MGM Backlot Studio Tour also uses a tram that winds through the backlot as well as the huge wardrobe and lighting department. For those who wish to see actual movie props and garner some inside information on the movie-making business, the Backlot Studio Tour (along with Backstage Pass to 101 Dalmatians) provides facts, figures, and sets.

Worth mentioning: Most of the wardrobe and lighting employees work normal hours, i.e., daytime, Monday through Friday. While a few people work off-times, a visit during weekday work hours is much more interesting. One final note for those who have visited before:

Once upon a time, the Backlot Tour was experienced exclusively by tram. Today, the tram tour no longer boards beside The Magic of Disney Animation. Rather, it boards near the old drop-off point in the rear of the park.

MOVEMENT: A tram ride after a walking/standing preshow. The most exciting part of the ride occurs when the tram stops inside Catastrophe Canyon that is, according to the tram guides, a working movie set. But it's not. During the show, the tram rocks back and forth — not enough to harm anyone — as it simulates an earthquake. Next, tons of water cascade around the tram getting a few guests wet but not soaked. If you don't want to get wet, sit on the right side of the tram. (Putting it differently: the first people to board the tram get the wettest.)

LINE: Outdoors but shaded.

WAIT TIME: Medium. It's generally short in the morning and late afternoon, though waits are reasonable any time during the off-season.

WHEELCHAIR ACCESS: Good. Wheelchairs may be folded and taken along for guests capable of sitting on regular tram seats. For those who cannot transfer easily, they may remain in their wheelchairs. Look for a cast member to get directions to the handicapped boarding area.

Backstage Pass to 101 Dalmatians

TICKET: E

NOTE: Backstage Pass is one of three attractions focusing on how-to-make-movies. Backstage Pass takes visitors onto sound stages and to areas that explain special effects. Contrary to the name, the attraction is not just for fans of 101 Dalmatians, but for anyone who wants insight into the magic of movies. Two things of note: One, the tour does not end where it started, but closer to the Voyage of The Little Mermaid. Two, the tour takes 35 minutes. There are exits along the way, but if you wish to see the show uninterrupted, visit the rest room before you go.

MOVEMENT: None. A walking tour.

LINE: Outdoors. The attraction itself is air-conditioned.

WAIT TIME: Short.

WHEELCHAIR ACCESS: Good. Guests may remain in wheelchairs throughout.

Disney Animated Classics (or The Making Of…)
TICKET: D
NOTE: The name changes. If focusing on a new Disney Release, the title is The Making Of (fill in a movie's name). In the future, expect The Making of Hercules or The Making of The Legend of Mulan. Otherwise, it includes the post-production studios (once part of the Inside the Magic tour) and ends with a theater presentation with information specific to Disney movies, such as how they voice their characters, write their music, and conceive their plots.
MOVEMENT: None. Walking and theater presentation.
LINE: Outdoors

PARADES AND SHOWS

Hollywood Boulevard's Streetmosphere

Disney coined the term "Streetmosphere" to describe the entertainment on Hollywood Boulevard. Just as the buildings are bigger than life, so too are the inhabitants. Everyone knows the naive young girl from Small Town, Middle America, who casts off the comfort of family and roots, travels to California, and throws open her arms as she steps off the bus, prepared to take Hollywood by storm. That woman lives on Hollywood Boulevard at Disney-MGM Studios. Her agent is here too, that charlatan promising untold wealth, fame, and glory while trying to swindle her out of her last dollar.

The movie director — the artistic guy who demands everyone follow directions — also calls Hollywood Boulevard home. In other words, everything fits the Tinseltown fantasy. But unlike other shows, these performers converse with park guests. Expect the director to ask you to star in his next movie. Or rehearse what you'll say when the gossip columnist asks who you're dating now. Or just smile when the talent scout swears he'll "make you an overnight star."

Toy Story Parade

Premiering in late 1995, the parade mirrors the Disney movie. Without a show to explain the action, those who missed the movie may be a bit confused, but still enjoy the march of familiar playthings.

Toy Story was the first film to be completely animated by computer. In the plot, toys come to life when people leave the room. Woody, a pull-string cowboy doll, is a young child's favorite plaything, but on the child's birthday, he gets a Buzz Lightyear action figure. Woody finds himself displaced in the child's heart and jealous of the new toy who, with the voice of Tim Allen, doesn't seem to realize he's a toy. Buzz and Woody are joined in the parade by other familiar toys, most at least thirty years old, including Mr. Potato Head, Etch-A-Sketch, and the Slinky Dog.

The parade marches up Hollywood Boulevard, circles the Hub in front of Mann's Chinese Theatre, crosses in front of SuperStar Television and the Monster Sound Show, then exits near Star Tours. Check the entertainment schedule for specific times which vary.

Sorcery In The Sky Fireworks

Scheduled seasonally (meaning only during busier times), this fireworks display fills the sky while a towering Mickey Mouse, dressed in his Sorcerer's Apprentice attire, presides over the festivities. Try to watch from anywhere along Hollywood Boulevard, as long as trees do not block the view of Mann's Chinese Theater.

Character Meals

Aimed at the elementary school crowd, Disney offers an array of meals where the characters show up, socialize, and spend a bit of quality time with youngsters. While adults can certainly attend without kids, it's not usually the number one draw for mature travelers. As we went to press, the Soundstage Restaurant had Disney characters in attendance all day long. Check the daily schedule for changes. Reservations can be made ahead of time by calling (407) 939-3463.

DISNEY-MGM STUDIOS' RESTAURANTS

Forget the educational restaurants of Epcot or the realistic fantasy restaurants of the Magic Kingdom. At the Disney-MGM Studios, dining choices range from historic Hollywood eateries to campy recreations of a life "that never was." The Prime Time Café and the Sci-Fi Dine-In Theater not only recreate an era, they make it better. Dinner can be pure, unadulterated fun. Since you can't eat in each restaurant, ask the host or hostess if you can look inside, then feel free to wander around, checking out the decor.

Plenty of fast food options exist and they're listed after the sit-down restaurants. In addition, food vendor carts throughout the park sell everything from healthy fruit to not-so-healthy-but-great-on-a-hot-afternoon ice cream and popsicles. With a good breakfast under your belt, you can snack your way through the day, saving room for a dinner at one of the nicer restaurants.

If possible, eat meals at non-normal times. Eating a late lunch guarantees a needed break after six hours of touring, an escape from the day's thickest crowds, and prices cheaper than those charged for identical entrees ordered after 4:00. If you want a meal served fast, but a grade above counter-service, try the Hollywood and Vine "Cafeteria of the Stars."

If you don't have a dinner reservation before the day of your visit, walk half-way down Hollywood Boulevard to the Studios' Tip Board where a cast member will set up a reservation. If you prefer to check out the restaurant first, reservations may also be made in person.

DISNEY-MGM STUDIOS FULL SERVICE RESTAURANTS

Reservations for most restaurants can be made 60 days in advance by calling (407) WDW-DINE, though it's now called "priority seating." A reservation means a table is waiting; priority seating means that you get the first one to open up after you arrive. An additional 30,000-square foot, sit-down themed restaurant, slated to open in 1998, will be accessible to both park visitors and those who only wish to eat. Owned in part by David Copperfield, the Magic Underground will include — in addition to food — magic both on stage and in the audience. Expect guests to disappear, tables to levitate, waiters to know slight-of-hand, and other acts of legerdemain.

Hollywood Brown Derby

Located on the right side of the Hub, this Tinseltown landmark faithfully recreates the California original. While the menu includes standard fare appealing to every taste, it also has items unique to the Brown Derby, most notably Cobb Salad (named after owner Bob Cobb) and Grapefruit Cake. The decor is somewhat formal, especially for a theme park. Elegant chandeliers, wood accents, brass, embossed China, and row after row of movie star pictures create an upscale atmosphere. As an added touch, it's not unusual to find Louella

Parsons and Hedda Hopper at their reserved tables, still feuding after all these years.

As the most formal restaurant at Disney-MGM Studios, the Brown Derby attracts fewer children and is a good choice for those who want to avoid the younger generation. Expensive. L, D.

50's Prime Time Café and Tune In Lounge

The 50's Prime Time Cafe does more than recreate the look and feel of the 50's — it white-washes the decade. In early television sit-coms, June Cleaver kept the house immaculate while wearing a frilly dress and neat-as-a-pin apron. So did Donna Reed. And so, too, do the efficient "Mom" waitresses at the Prime Time Café. Each and every table can watch television shows from that era, with classic routines spliced together into a continuous show.

While the atmosphere exaggerates the time (Mom tells you to clean your plate before you get dessert and punishes you if you don't), the cluttered decor is created by knick-knacks from the 1950's. People who remember that era get a warm feeling from meatloaf served on Fiestaware, water pitchers identical to ones used 40 years earlier, or vinyl kitchen chairs similar to ones purchased when they first got married. In addition to comfort foods, they serve a smattering of health-conscious favorites camouflaged in 1950's wording. It's a fun restaurant and a good choice for stick-to-your-ribs food served in a nowhere-else-in-the-world atmosphere.

Connected to the Prime Time Café, the Tune In Lounge has a bar and living room area. It's perfect for a cold beer on a hot day, or for those who want to enjoy the Prime Time atmosphere without eating there. You miss the thrill of the "Mom" waitresses, but still get a taste of the '50's. Moderate. L, D.

Sci-Fi Dine-In Theater

Like the 50's Prime Time Café, atmosphere plays a larger role in this restaurant than food. Well worth a look even if you choose to eat elsewhere, the entire restaurant sits under one of the special Disney indoors-but-it-feels-like-outdoors skies. In the front, a massive movie screen plays clips from the camp science fiction classics — all grade B flicks — where alien monsters preyed on helpless victims. The tables sit inside the "cars" facing the screen.

Locked into a drive-in movie theme, chefs must serve fast food favorites like burgers, hot dogs, french fries, and shakes. But they also offer nicer selections to please non-drive-in palates. Never the less, it's not a place for the discriminating gourmet. Think of it as fun and you'll have a great time. Better yet, make reservations and order only dessert. Moderate. L, D.

Mama Melrose's Ristorante Italiano

Depending on what you want from your dinner, Mama Melrose's Ristorante Italiano is either the best restaurant choice at Disney-MGM Studios or the worst. If you love pasta served in an Italian restaurant, eat here. The atmosphere recreates big city restaurants owned by Italian immigrants, and has a lived-in look. The food is traditional; the garlic smell heavy and welcome.

The theme is not unique, even though the exact style is not found outside New York City. If you want to spend a day enjoying the "Hollywood" fantasy of Disney-MGM, the Brown Derby or Prime Time Café do a better job. If you want the most relaxing restaurant, eat at Mama Melrose's. Because it's harder to find (behind Muppet Vision 4-D), it's also easier to get a reservation. Many times, you can walk right in. Expensive. L, D.

Soundstage Restaurant

If cartoons were made using real actors and props, they'd be filmed on a soundstage that looked like this. Giant sets recreate recent Disney features in this buffet restaurant. Complemented by movie music, the restaurant appeals to families with children. Expensive. L, D.

DISNEY-MGM FAST FOOD AND SNACKS

Fast food at Disney-MGM Studios has all the pluses (fast, somewhat inexpensive, and fairly good) and the minuses (served in cardboard with a factory-produced feel) that it has at the other Disney parks. If you prefer fast food, consider the following:

• **Hollywood and Vine.** Cafeteria service. The food selection is diversified and filling with a better atmosphere than other fast-food places. Sticking with the 50's theme, the cafeteria looks and feels like a diner, but with accents and decor that's better-than-it-actually-was. Open for breakfast, lunch, and dinner.

• **Sunset Ranch Market.** Actually three separate food stands, this

open-air market offers healthy favorites like fruit and vegetables along with American standards like hot dogs, chili, ice cream, and fries.
• **Starring Rolls Bakery**. If you like baked goods, you'll find them here, featuring cookies, pies, cakes, and coffee.
• **Min and Bill's Dockside Diner.** Open during busy season only, this snack stand looks like a boat floating in the water. Serves sandwiches, fruit, and soft-serve yogurt.
• **Dinosaur Gertie's Ice Cream of Extinction.** On the opposite side of the lake from Min and Bill's Dockside Diner, this building-that-looks-like-a-dinosaur serves frozen slush drinks.
• **Commissary.** Fast food, but with an accent on healthy fare.
• **Backlot Express.** Large restaurant featuring burgers, chili, and salads.
• **Toy Story Pizza Planet.** An annex to an arcade, it features (what else) pizza and salad.
• **Studio Catering Company.** Snack food including churros, ice cream, and popcorn.

SHOPPING

Mickey and the other Disney characters are never far away, no matter where you are in the park. A number of shops stock character merchandise, many specializing in a specific movie. Under the Sea, for example, sells Little Mermaid merchandise and is located beside the exit from Voyage of the Little Mermaid. On-site guests can have purchases delivered to their hotel room. Off-site guests may have them shipped to the front of the park, to be picked up just prior to departure.
The following stores offer something a little different:
• **The Darkroom.** Located at the beginning of Hollywood Boulevard on the right, The Darkroom sells film and cameras, offers two-hour photo processing, and rents cameras or camcorders.
• **Sid Cahuenga's One-Of-A-Kind.** Located on Hollywood Boulevard directly across from Oscar's Super Service, Sid Cahuenga's One-Of-A-Kind's decor is off-the-wall. Most things sold were originally owned by one movie star or another and are now for sale to the general public. Also sold are autographed pictures of recent and not-so-recent stars, the only place in all of WDW where, once in a while,

you can purchase Walt Disney's autograph. It's worth a look even if you don't plan on buying.

• **Animation Gallery.** Located beside the animation tour, this shop sells only things associated with Disney animation, including cels from movies.

• **Buy the Book.** A replica of the bookstore in the ABC (now owned by Disney) sit-com Ellen, this store features books, coffee, and props from the show.

• **It's a Wonderful Shop.** Located near Muppet Vision 4-D, this shop sells nothing but Christmas decorations, 365 days per year.

DON'T MISS...

Here's a quick reference list of those attractions worth seeing, even on a busy day. Those marked with a bullet indicate an action ride not suitable for all.

• Twilight Zone Tower of Terror

Beauty and the Beast Stage Show

Voyage of the Little Mermaid

The Magic of Disney Animation

Backlot Studio Tour

The Great Movie Ride

Indiana Jones Epic Stunt Spectacular

• Star Tours

The Hunchback of Notre Dame Stage Show

OTHER DISNEY ATTRACTIONS

211 Water Parks

213 The Disney Institute

217 Discovery Island

218 Disney's Boardwalk Resort

219 Downtown Disney

Chapter Twelve

OTHER DISNEY ATTRACTIONS

A wise man once said that you can't be "all things to all people." But Disney tries. And, if not totally successful, has "more things for more people" than any other place on the face of this planet. To its credit, the Disney corporation listens to guests both from formal surveys and informal comments. They also study the market and view client satisfaction as an on-going process, not a goal already achieved. Some things will never be found in Central Florida. While Blizzard Beach recreates the feel of a ski lodge, Walt Disney World will never host the Winter Olympics. Outside of that, anything is possible.

Four areas — The Boardwalk Resort, The Disney Institute, Discovery Island, and the Disney Village Marketplace (extended to Disney's West Side) — cater to the needs of mature travelers. Three water parks — Blizzard Beach, Typhoon Lagoon, and River Country — attract the pre-adult set. Pleasure Island, a kind-of Magic Kingdom for grown-ups, appeals mainly to younger adults.

As with everything Disney, each attraction is better than you expect. If you brought a World Hopper pass, for example, you may decide to visit Typhoon Lagoon for a few hours rather than swim in your hotel's pool. You go knowing you will never get on a water slide and expecting nothing more than a few adult-friendly swimming pools with nicely landscaped bushes. But upon arrival, you discover that the atmosphere is as intriguing as any land of the Magic Kingdom. Building designs, landscaping, and scenery fit the theme. Music from invisible sources adds to the fantasy. Out-going employees complete the magic.

Most people don't have time to visit everything and, for most mature travelers, that means foregoing the water parks. But don't assume that nothing will please you. Almost everyone finds something they enjoy.

WATER PARKS

Water parks are a relatively new phenomena and Disney's original water park, River Country, was one of the nation's first. While still fun, its meager slides and play toys were quickly eclipsed by larger parks outside WDW. Today, River Country is still the area's smallest water park but also a good choice for mature travelers who don't care to slide 60 mph down a fiberglass ramp with their bathing suit wrapped somewhere around their neck.

After River Country, Disney created Typhoon Lagoon and, most recently, Blizzard Beach, which opened in 1994. There are also two non-Disney water parks nearby, Wet 'n Wild located on International Drive and Water Mania off US 192 near Kissimmee. In general, Wet 'n Wild — the biggest water park in the world — has more slides and rides; Water Mania offers cheaper rates. If your main goal is to ride as much as possible, consider Wet 'n Wild. If vacationing on a shoestring budget, consider Water Mania. Otherwise, swim with Disney.

The key difference between Disney water parks and off-site water parks lies in the atmosphere. Wet 'n Wild looks like other water parks found near most major cities, only bigger. Slides are fiberglass and plastic configurations, some enjoyed by inner tube and some with nothing more than your bathing suit. (And those don't always stay on.) Gardens are attractive and the park sponsors special events with live bands and contests, notably in the summer. But there's nothing inherently different about Wet 'n Wild other than its size. The same is true for Water Mania. At Disney, everything adheres to the park's motif, just as it does in the theme parks. Both Typhoon Lagoon and Blizzard Beach have man-made mountains. Slides are not chunks of suspended fiberglass supported by huge girders — they're part of the landscape. Even without the slides though, the Disney parks *feel* more fun.

If you consider a good water park the key to a successful vacation, remember that one or more are closed during winter months. In addition, Central Florida weather from November through April is erratic. It might be 80° and sunny or it might be 55° with clouds.

Typhoon Lagoon

The Disney people say that a typhoon blew through Central Florida, flooded Walt Disney World, stranded boats and, in its wake, accidentally built a water playground. It's not true, of course. But Typhoon Lagoon looks tropical. It sounds tropical. That's enough.

211

Typhoon Lagoon is marginally better than Blizzard Beach for mature travelers. Home of the "world's largest wave pool," there's a lot of water activity for those who don't like sliding boards. The wave pool itself ends in a sandy, beach-like area where the final wave remnants lap against the shore. In addition, Castaway Creek — essentially a swimming pool that circles the park with constantly flowing water — is perfect for sitting in an inner tube and watching the scenery change, floating along at about one foot per second. Typhoon Lagoon has fewer slides than Blizzard Beach, making it less attractive to the young adult set. Also, demand is higher for Blizzard Beach right now since many repeat guests want to try Disney's newest creation.

A one-day admission costs $24.95 plus tax for an adult; $19.50 for a child (3-9); free for guests with a Five-Day World Hopper Pass or a Length-of-Stay Pass.

Blizzard Beach

The Disney people keep building water parks and the public keeps filling them. To keep up with demand — and the competition — their newest park has more slides than either Typhoon Lagoon or River Country. The most demanding slide, Summit Plummet, sends riders on a 120-foot free-fall at speeds of 60 mph (It's not too bad if you close your eyes, clamp your nose shut, tense your rear end, and hold your breath for the entire six seconds — but why?) The slide resembles a ski jump. Like Typhoon Lagoon, Blizzard Beach has a "river" that circles the park, including a short sojourn through an icy cave where frigid water drops from the underside of icebergs. There's also a wave pool, though smaller than the one found at Typhoon Lagoon.

For scenery and Disney special effects, nothing beats Blizzard Beach. According to a Disney cast member with an imagination set on hyper-drive, a winter storm blew through Central Florida and they hurriedly built a ski resort, only to be confused once the weather warmed up again. Left with unused ski lifts, slalom courses, and chalets, they quickly converted it into a water park.

Okay, the story's weak, but they had to come up with something to explain the strange set-up. A ski lift (with skis under each seat) transports passengers to the top of the mountain. White hills of snow border water slides. Buildings look like ski chalets, though carved with trees and animals native to Florida. In the background, they play Christmas music. (Yes, Christmas music — year 'round.)

It's fun.

Again, crowds will be thick for at least a few more seasons thanks to the newness of the park and the greater number of slides. For relaxation and more mature activities, consider Typhoon Lagoon or, better yet, River Country. But for the most outrageous design, visit Blizzard Beach. It's located in the southeast portion of Walt Disney World near the All-Star Resorts.

A one-day admission costs $24.95 plus tax for an adult; $19.50 for a child (3-9); free for guests with a Five-Day World Hopper Pass or a Length-of-Stay Pass.

River Country

The smallest, most difficult to reach, and oldest Disney water park is also most appealing to adult visitors. River Country has no wave pool or sliding boards that propel the human body at warp speed, shielded only by the thin fabric of a bathing suit. But River Country does have a huge swimming pool with two slides. Also, a large section of Bay Lake has been sectioned off and transformed into an "old-time swimming hole" with rides that Tom Sawyer might have enjoyed. Even River Country's few slides are milder than those at the other parks. White Water Rapids, for example, is a leisurely raft ride where you slide a bit, bounce against fellow inner-tubers, slide a bit more, and continue to bounce your way to the bottom. Not too wild, it can be enjoyed by almost everyone.

River Country can be reached by bus from the TTC or by boat from the Magic Kingdom. Guests arriving by car should follow signs that direct them to the main parking lot for Fort Wilderness. From there, catch a Fort Wilderness bus that will eventually drop you off close to River Country.

Admission for one day runs $15.95 plus tax for adults and $12.50 for children (3 to 9); free for guests with a Five-Day World Hopper Pass or a Length-of-Stay Pass. It's also possible to buy a combination ticket for River Country and Discovery Island, a zoological park just a short boat ride away. Combination tickets cost $19.95 for adults and $14.50 for children.

THE DISNEY INSTITUTE

While part of Walt Disney World, think of The Disney Institute as a different type of vacation altogether. Even though Institute guests can enjoy the other activities within Disney World, the Institute does not mesh easily with the theme park atmosphere. Guests cannot participate in the daily Institute programs (which they've paid for in advance) and visit the parks. There's just not enough hours in the day.

Opened in February of 1996, The Disney Institute has had trouble finding an audience, perhaps because they over-extended, advertising to every niche market that had previously avoided Central Florida. In their first year of operation, they adjusted to low demand and eliminated almost half the programs offered. Then, in the fall of 1996, Disney combined the Institute with Disney University, a corporate off-shoot that helps private businesses improve employee relations. Currently, both corporate clients and independent vacationers live side-by-side. A special $49 per day rate, initially offered for three months and only to Florida residents, was extended, but expect more changes as the University and Institute merge.

Even with the downsizing, low-demand, and mixing-of-Institute-and-University guests, mature travelers should consider the Disney Institute.

The Institute appeals to three types of guests. First, it attracts people looking for a specific type of get-away each year. Spa vacations, for example, are big business world-wide. Now, Disney can offer a spa vacation that includes therapeutic massage, exercise, and body pampering. Other guests may take a yearly golf vacation that includes professional instruction — people who might otherwise go to Bermuda or Scotland. Now they can have a golf vacation in Central Florida, learning and playing with recognized pros.

A second group of people enjoys conversation and intellectual stimulation. These folks just like learning and sharing ideas. They might take classes in aerobics, cooking, animation techniques, and gourmet cooking, all in one day — an eclectic blend of subjects. They meet new people in each program and, because the small class size encourages discussion, touch base with other people and other cultures. To them, the learning is a bridge to conversation, a tool to expand the mind.

A third group of people love all things Disney and want to know as much as they can about the company and its founder. (Affectionately referred to as "DIS's," for Disney Information Sponges) How does Disney do animation? How does Disney create the beautiful topiaries? How does Disney "antique" buildings or create signs or generate new ideas? At The Disney Institute, these guests learn the secrets from Imagineers who built and designed major attractions.

In other words, The Disney Institute attracts all those people who, before its opening, spent their money somewhere else. That very trait — trying to be all things to all people — might be the Institute's problem. For many niche vacationers, part of a destination's appeal is that they'll be surrounded by people who think like they do. But at the Institute, two women on a spa vacation may be housed next door to a golf-nut. Those seeking intellectual stimulation may, after seeing an Institute ad for gardening or rock-climbing, believe that Disney isn't catering to their needs.

So should you go? Definitely probably. Few couples share all the same hobbies and few individuals care about only one thing. For these vacationers, the Disney Institute is the perfect compromise. While the husband's chipping, putting, and driving, the wife can be cooking, pruning, and animating. Or while both primp, swim, and sauna during the day, they can shop just before dinner and enjoy jazz at 10:00. In other words, the diversity is an advantage.

Unlike other resorts, The Disney Institute is a fixed-stay vacation, meaning guests choose either a three- or four-day package plan, arrive on the same day as all other participants, choose from the same classes, and leave at the same time. Think of it as a trip to summer camp. While cumbersome, the fixed-stay format encourages discussion among members. Contrary to images pulled up by the word "institute," the learning is not boring. Instructors emphasize enjoyment. For example, students studying animation make their own cartoon. They do not sit for three days taking notes. And there are no tests at The Disney Institute. It's fun. After all, it's Disney.

To top everything off, celebrities may show up at any time. In addition to Walter Cronkite, Institute speakers have included Billy Dee Williams, Francis Ford Coppola, blues artist James Cotton, and other celebrities, all sharing information about their particular specialty.

Disney Institute facilities are state-of-the art, with an acoustically balanced performance center, outdoor amphitheater, 28 program studios, movie theater, closed-circuit television and radio station, 38,000-square foot sports and fitness center, full-service spa, clay tennis courts, five swimming pools, and an 18-hole championship golf course. Located a short distance from Downtown Disney, The Institute looks like a small New England town. Institute hotel rooms, located within walking distance, were once part of the Village Resort. All facilities are accessible to the handicapped, but some programs may not be suitable for everyone.

For those interested in The Disney Institute, ignore the rest of Disney World during your stay. If taking a one-week vacation, stay at the Institute, then move to a different hotel for the remaining days. It's awkward, but you'll get maximum enjoyment from both parts of your vacation if they're physically separated.

The Institute offers the following programs, but expect to find others added and even dropped since the Institute reacts to market demands. In addition to the listed topics, a number of youth programs also appeal to young adults, ages 10 to 17. They've also introduced a Day Camp facility to entertain youngsters.

Entertainment Arts
Animation — Subjects include computer animation, creating your own cartoon, Stop-Motion and Clay Animation, and the Voices of Disney.
Photography — Guests learn the secrets of portrait, outdoor, and candid photography
Radio and Audio — Classes study how radio works.
Showbiz — Topics cover make-up and improvisational acting.
TV and Video — Guests learn how to improve home videos and receive insights on television production.

Sports And Fitness
General — Topics cover everything from Aerobics to Weight-Training and Self-Defense. One class covers Cardiointensive workouts.
Golf — Classes study the game, analyze technique, and suggest ways to improve your play.
Rock Climbing — They had to build a fake mountain.
Tennis — Learn defensive moves, offensive moves, and winning moves.

Lifestyles
Family Focus — Workshops show how to preserve family history; includes genealogy
The Changing Society — Learn to use the computer.
Visiting Instructor Programs — Study the art of dance, fashion, or investing.

Story Arts
Classes offer insight into Disney technology, design, and story-telling techniques.

Culinary Arts
Includes everything from romantic dinners to a study of eating. In separate classes, guests learn to turn food into creative artworks, bake sweet treats, and taste wine. One class focuses on healthy eating.

Design Arts
Participants study Disney architecture and interiors, as well as how to decorate their own house using everything from antiques to dried flowers.

Gardening and the Great Outdoors
Gardening — Topics cover topiary creation (those sculpted animals found all over Disney World), as well as organic and home gardening. *The Great Outdoors* — A study of birds, gators, and other Florida wildlife by canoe.

The Disney Institute's booking procedure is different from that of the other resorts. To make reservations or to request information, you must call The Disney Institute directly at (800) 496-6337. Reservations may also be made through a travel agent.

DISCOVERY ISLAND

In the middle of Bay Lake — near Fort Wilderness and Wilderness Lodge — a small island existed pre-Disney. After the mouse's arrival, it was planted with twenty types of palm trees, populated with exotic animals, and transformed into a tropical paradise. In the beginning, they named it Treasure Island and Magic Kingdom guests paid an extra fee to catch a boat to Bay Lake and explore it. But over the years, that romantic theme fell by the wayside and today, it's just your average beautiful island with wondrous plants and beautiful birds. Unfortunately, with competition coming from Disney's Animal Kingdom, its days are numbered.

As a garden, it's too small to compete with nearby Cypress Gardens or even Harry P. Leu Gardens in Orlando. As a zoo, it's too small to compete even with the Central Florida Zoo. Nothing on the island attracts thousands of tourists, but therein lies the beauty. Many mature travelers fit it into their itinerary as a welcome escape from frenzied touring. They offer a few shows — a parrot show, for example — but they're all small productions that take place along the side of the walkway. Many animals roam freely, including Patagonian cavies, which look like gigantic bunnies with cosmetic alterations. At one point, trees and elevated walkways take guests through a giant aviary. While completely enclosed, the aviary screens blend into the trees and guests don't feel cut off from nature. You may not be in the pristine wilderness of Florida but you feel like you are. Sometimes that's all that matters.

Discovery Island is accessible for wheelchairs, with enough hills and ramps to make it somewhat challenging. Because the entire island is outdoors, it can be hot and miserable in the dog days of summer. While a canopy of trees shades the walkway, it's usually not enough to make a midsummer's visit enjoyable for Northerners. In hot parts of the year, visit in the morning. Note that Discovery Island closes as dusk.

Accessible only by boat, Discovery Island can be reached from the Magic Kingdom, the Contemporary Resort, or Fort Wilderness. Guests arriving from off-site should follow signs to the Fort Wilderness parking lot. From there, bus service connects to Pioneer Hall where tickets can be purchased prior to departure. Tickets cost $11.95 for adults and $6.50 for children; Discovery Island/River Country combination tickets cost $19.95 for adults and $14.50 for children.

DISNEY'S BOARDWALK RESORT

The Boardwalk Resort attracts mature travelers the way Pleasure Island attracts twenty-somethings, though there is no cover charge (that's the good news) and only four bars (that's the bad). The New England ambiance of a seaside boardwalk (located an hour from a real ocean) provides the architectural background.

• **The Atlantic Ballroom.** Those who enjoy dancing to a live orchestra can dust off a seat and call this place home. The 10-piece dance band — appropriately called The Atlantic Ballroom Orchestra — plays not only the sounds of the '40's, but also contemporary favorites. The club looks like a dance hall built during the roaring twenties. Admission costs $5 per person.

• **Big River Grille & Brewing Works.** A pub with a difference, guests can actually see their beer being brewed. Includes range of light dinner fare.

218

• **Jellyrolls.** A "a rip roarin' foot stompin'" club, Jellyrolls is a piano bar with a comedic difference. Two pianos entertain in a relaxed club atmosphere. It's similar to Blazing Pianos, another nightclub/piano bar on International Drive, but with the quality touches incorporated into all Disney shows.

• **ESPN Sports Bar.** Planned before Disney took over the ABC television network, the ESPN Sports Bar is an ironic accompaniment to the Disney/ABC merger. Sports bars are part of the American landscape, most with beer-sponsored decor and big-screen TV's. The ESPN Sports Bar holds the same appeal, but like all things Disney, is better, bigger, and cleaner, with a total of 70 television monitors.

In addition to the clubs, the Boardwalk has two full-service restaurants (Spoodle's and Flying Fish Café — see Chapter 13), and two snack shops.

DOWNTOWN DISNEY

At one time, the Disney Village Marketplace stood alone. Then they built Pleasure Island beside it. Now they're building yet another new area, called Disney's West Side, behind Pleasure Island. Like the Energizer Bunny, they keep going and going... But with all that expansion, Disney decided it needed a new name for the entire complex, one that referred to all three areas at one time. As a result, Downtown Disney came into existence, a massive playground of bars, restaurants, and shopping.

Disney Village Marketplace and Disney's West Side

The Disney Village Marketplace allows guests to enjoy the charm of Disney without paying fees to enter a theme park. While decidedly commercial and existing to make-a-buck, the area is relaxing, clean, and offers an escape from the intense work-out of active vacationing. This should continue to be true in the future. Like so many other things at Walt Disney World, however, growth is the operational word. By the end of the century, a majority of the Village and West Side restaurants will not be Disney owned.

With that in mind, the following list highlights unusual stores and all sit-down restaurants considered part of the Village Marketplace or Disney's West Side. But expect changes. It's the only thing you can be sure of at Walt Disney World.

Marketplace and West Side Shops
- **AMC 24-Screen Theatre Complex.** The biggest movie theater in Florida.
- **The Art of Disney.** For those rich folks seeking mementos of their trip to Walt Disney World, this is the place to buy. Worth a trip even if you can't afford anything, The Art of Disney sells high-priced art that relates in some way to Disney. Leather chairs look like Mickey Mouse and engraved scenes from classic Disney films decorate crystal tables. The Walt Disney Company commissioned talented artists to create pieces in a variety of mediums. Wall decor includes original Walt Disney World artwork along with animation cels from movies.
- **Authentic All-Star.** Sports gear featuring team logos.
- **Captain's Tower**. An open-air shop, the Captain's Tower features specialty items.
- **Christmas Chalet.** Enormously successful, the Village found that many people buy Christmas decorations year-round. Disney oriented products dominate but they also stock other quality pieces.
- **Discover**. What Discover sells is less important than what it says. Everything fits an ecology theme, reminiscent of surf shops. T-shirts, plants, stuffed animals, and games all center on Mother Nature and her preservation.
- **Eurospain.** Fine glassware, including crystal and on-site engravings.
- **The Gourmet Pantry.** A two-part store, one half is a kitchen shop with a special area of Gourmet Mickey cookware. The second part functions as a convenience store, stocking food items used by people camping or cooking meals on their own. There's also a small bakery section selling cookies and candy.
- **Great Southern Craft Co**. Americana featuring country-styled items.
- **Harrington Bay Clothiers.** Upscale men's fashions from noted designers.
- **Resortwear Unlimited.** Sportswear and swimwear for women.
- **2R's Reading & Writing.** A bookstore reminiscent of Mom and Pop operations.
- **Team Mickey's Athletic Club.** Mickey Mouse is a real jock. Judging by the merchandise sold in Team Mickey's Athletic Club, the famous mouse plays everything from soccer to tennis, though he appears to specialize in golf. Non-Mickey things are also sold.
- **Toys Fantastic.** This store features an incredible array of Hot Wheels, Barbies, and Disney toys.

• **Summer Sands.** Bathing suits and Florida souvenirs.
• **World of Disney.** Souvenir shoppers who don't want to waste theme park time rummaging through stores can find (almost) everything under one roof at World of Disney, a huge building with connected rooms. Stuffed animals, T-shirts, kids' clothes, watches, knick-knacks — it's all here. Opened in 1996 with 38,000 feet of retail space, it's so large that many people have trouble locating an item. Ceiling decorations and displays make it a must-see even for those who don't plan to buy anything.

Note: Prices for an item are the same whether you buy it inside a theme park or in World of Disney, but Magic Kingdom Club members receive a 10% discount at the Village and West Side. Expect most — but not all — things sold in the parks to be available in World of Disney.

With so many changes on the horizon, it's difficult to paint an accurate picture of Village Marketplace restaurants. New deals are being announced regularly and the following have a 1997 opening planned: Dan Akroyd's House of Blues themed with a country rhythm and blues format; Wolfgang Puck's Cafe that serves California cuisine; and Lario's, Gloria Estefan's eatery that serves up Latin food and music. In the winter of 1998, a new theatrical presentation, Cirque du Soleil, premiers in the West Side. It's a high-energy performance to be staged in a theater that looks like a European performance hall and circus tent.

Full-Service Restaurants
• **Rainforest Cafe.** Opened in 1996, the Rainforest Cafe looks as if it belongs in the Magic Kingdom's Adventureland. Inside, everything is bigger-than-life, from the stools with animal legs to the greenery and forest ambiance. Rain falls, animals move, and kids scream. Consider Rainforest Cafe for a fun meal but not a quiet get-away. Expect a long wait for a table over lunch and dinner hours. Moderate. L, D.
• **Planet Hollywood.** Another visually thrilling restaurant, Planet Hollywood capitalizes on the public's fascination with movies. Owned in part by Demi Moore, Bruce Willis, Sylvester Stallone, and Arnold Schwarzenegger, this spherical building creates an out-of-this-world restaurant. You don't need to order a meal to visit if you want to sight-see and quaff a cold one. A small lounge on the second floor is general-

ly less crowded than the bar area on the first floor. Order a beer and explore.

Because of the Disney location, most movie items come from Disney films, including Herbie the Love Bug, an actual Volkswagen suspended from the ceiling. Because of its popularity, expect to wait for a table. Moderate. L, D.

• **Fulton's Crab House.** One of the focal points of the Disney Village Marketplace and formerly the Empress Lily (named for Walt Disney's wife), Fulton's Crab House looks like a three-story paddle-boat anchored in Lake Buena Vista. In reality, it's a building and not a ship. Managed by the Levy Organization who also operate the Fireworks Factory and the Portobello Yacht Club, it specializes in seafood. The menu changes daily, due to the changing "catch of the day." They specialize in fresh seafood. Expensive. B, L, D.

• **Cap'n Jack's Oyster Bar.** The big draw at Cap'n Jack's is the location — in the middle of Lake Buena Vista (the lake, not the town). Reached by a hallway, it sits at the end of an enclosed pier. Cap'n Jack Guests sitting on the restaurant's Marketplace side see the Village shops that circle the lake; guests on the opposite side view Pleasure Island and shores draped with trees. Specializing in Strawberry Margaritas, seafood and shellfish, it's fine for a meal, but preferred for an appetizer or cocktail before dining elsewhere. It's also perfect in the middle of a strenuous day of shopping. Moderate. L, D.

Fast-Food Restaurants

• **Minnie Mia's Italian Eatery.** The name says it all. Pizza, pasta, and salad specialties.

• **Goofy's Grill.** Specializing in burgers, hot dogs, and french fries.

• **Donald's Dairy Dip.** Ice cream concoctions.

Pleasure Island

Located next to the Disney Village Marketplace and part of Downtown Disney, Pleasure Island does for drinkers what the Magic Kingdom does for kids. Instead of Frontierland, Pleasure Island has the Neon Armadillo Music Saloon. Instead of Adventureland, they have the Adventurer's Club. Instead of Tomorrowland, they have Mannequins Dance Palace. Each of the seven bars has a unique theme and separate architectural front. A central street party celebrates New Year's Eve every night.

Most Pleasure Island guests have not strayed too far past their twenty-first birthday, though a few clubs might appeal to mature travelers, notably the Comedy Warehouse, the Pleasure Island Jazz Company, the Neon Armadillo, and/or the Adventurer's Club. The dress code is upscale casual and the parking free. Depending on your age and style, you may prefer Disney's Boardwalk Resort. But, if Pleasure Island is included in your pass, stop by one evening to see Disney technology in action.

The bars are:

• **Pleasure Island Jazz Company.** The newest of the Pleasure Island Clubs, the Pleasure Island Jazz Company has a 1930's feel and looks like an old warehouse. Conjuring up all styles of jazz played quietly enough that you can still hold down a conversation, jazz aficionados will find this single club worth the entire price of a Pleasure Island admission.

• **Rock and Roll Beach Club.** If Elvis played at Pleasure Island, he'd perform here. The Rock and Roll Beach Club's relaxed style features (what else) a sand and surf theme, a couple floors for dancing and drinking, and a live band playing music from the 50's to the 90's.

• **Mannequin's Dance Palace.** Finish any conversation before entering Mannequin's. High-tech lights, a rotating dance floor, and special effects dominate the interior of the club. Even if you hate it, you'll be mesmerized as you grope your way toward the exit. If you linger long enough, you might get to see the dancers bombarded with soap bubbles, confetti, and even snow.

• **8Trax.** The seventies live again, from the groovy lighting and funky waitress outfits to the music. For those not particularly fond of the 70's, 8Trax holds no appeal. For those who came of age during the era, it brings back memories.

• **Adventurer's Club.** Part comedy club, part museum, part fantasy, the Adventurer's Club is the most Disneyesque bar in Pleasure Island. It's like boarding a ride in the Magic Kingdom where, in addition to AudioAnimatronic entertainment, a waitress serves extra dry martinis. African memorabilia lines the walls. In the main lounge, the entertainment changes as different figures come to life. Some action takes place in alcoves where puppets tell stories, masks talk, and actors interact with guests. The library, a separate room, periodically opens and guests file in. After a short comedic presentation, guests file back out. Humor is light yet fulfilling — well worth a visit.

• **Comedy Warehouse.** Occasionally, a big-name comedian performs at the Comedy Warehouse, generally requiring an additional fee to enter. Most times, however, a comedy troupe performs improvisational comedy, meaning that audience members suggest topics and cast members perform skits and make jokes based on those suggestions. The fact that it's all improvised — and still funny — makes the show worth seeing.

• **Neon Armadillo Music Saloon.** A classy Country and Western bar, the Neon Armadillo is usually filled with fans and even city folks like the urban cowboy style. Featuring a live band, it has a warmer atmosphere than other Pleasure Island Clubs. While most guests visit different bars, the Neon Armadillo attracts a select crowd that stays for the entire night. Rumors say it may close soon.

In addition to the clubs, a number of unusual stores are found on Pleasure Island. While in restricted territory at night, they're freely accessible during the day. Pleasure Island has five restaurants. The two sit-down restaurants — The Fireworks Factory and the Portobello Yacht Club — physically sit on Pleasure Island but do not require admission. They're accessible from the Disney Village Marketplace. The fast food places — D-Zertz, and Hill Street Diner — are accessible during the day but require a Pleasure Island admission after 7:00 p.m.

• **The Fireworks Factory.** Built like a bombed-out factory, the Fireworks Factory serves Southern barbecue favorites. It's tough to make a barbecue place upscale, but The Fireworks Factory pushes the theme about as high as it can go. It's a great choice if you're looking for Southern style vittles. Moderate to expensive. L, D.

• **The Portobello Yacht Club.** The atmosphere is nautical, an upscale Yacht Club for the rich and elite. The food is mainly Italian featuring pasta and even pizza, though other entrees are offered. A bit more formal than the Fireworks Factory, the Portobello Yacht Club also has outdoor dining on Lake Buena Vista. Expensive. L, D.

• **Missing Link Sausage Co.** Fast food featuring sausage, hot dogs, and kielbasa. Inexpensive. L, D.

Prior to 7:00 p.m., you may wander freely around Pleasure Island, sampling the shops and the atmosphere. After 7:00 p.m., the entertainment kicks on and all people over the age of three must pay $16.95 plus tax. Those already inside Pleasure Island at 7:00 p.m. may stay, but without the wrist band worn by paying guests, they will not be admitted to the clubs. Drinking age is 21; you must be 18 to enter alone. Children under 18 must be accompanied by an adult.

OTHER DISNEY DINING AND SHOWS

13

226 Dinner Shows

228 Resort Restaurants

Chapter Thirteen

OTHER DISNEY DINING AND SHOWS

If considering a nice dinner, refer to the Disney Village Marketplace restaurants listed at the end of Chapter 12 and, if you have a length-of-stay pass, also think about restaurants inside Epcot. But don't ignore the restaurants inside Disney resorts, even if staying off Disney property.

Guests staying at any single hotel must be able to eat numerous meals in one location without growing tired of the food or decor. For these folks, each resort has a coffee shop, buffet and/or fast food spot, as well as one restaurant worth discovering. From the upscale style of the Grand Floridian's Victoria and Albert's to the relaxing elegance of the Contemporary's California Grill, visitors find that many hotel restaurants offer the same type of themed adventures found within the parks, only more adult-oriented and relaxing.

DINNER SHOWS

At present, Walt Disney World has two dinners shows, the Polynesian Review and the Hoop-Dee-Doo Musical Review. (Repeat guests: Note that Broadway at the Top, a popular dinner show that played in the Contemporary Hotel, closed in 1994.) Reservations to all shows can be made up to two years in advance (subject to change) by calling (407) WDW-DINE, which translates to (407) 939-3463.

Hoop-Dee-Doo Musical Review. Chow down at an authentic Western hoe-down that serves traditional vittles like fried chicken, barbecued ribs, corn on the cob, and strawberry shortcake. It's not one of them citified shows where the audience sits back and watches the action on stage. At the Hoop-Dee-Doo Review, the food is part of the performance, as are the waiters and waitresses. The singin', dancin', and eatin' are all definitely G-rated, but still fun. Given the theme, you'd expect a lot of children, but a significant number of mature travelers consider it one of Disney's best attractions. Entertainers put on three shows each night in air-conditioned comfort.

While distinctly unsophisticated (food is served in buckets), it's not inexpensive. Adult admission is $36, kids (3-11) $18. If visiting during busy season, plan to make a reservation at least several months ahead of time. If you did not have the foresight to reserve seating, try calling them directly at (407) 939-3463 on the day you wish to attend. If you still can't get a reservation and don't mind giving up an entire evening trying, show up at the door, add your name to the waiting list, and hope they have some no-shows.

The Hoop-Dee-Doo Review is located in Pioneer Hall in Fort Wilderness. Guests staying on-site can reach it by boat from the front of the Magic Kingdom or the Contemporary Hotel. Off-site guests must park in the Fort Wilderness main parking lot and wait for a bus to transfer them to the show area.

Polynesian Luau and Mickey's Tropical Revue. Presenting three Polynesian shows per night, the first dinner show at 4:30 is called Mickey's Tropical Revue and features Disney characters. The next two performances are simply called the Polynesian Luau and operate without the famous mouse's luau-ing capabilities. It goes without saying that more families with children attend the early show.

Located in Luau Cove on the west side of the Polynesian Resort, the key Disney element in the Polynesian Luau is quality of service and attention to detail. Given the decor and food service, it's easy to imagine that you're on a small Pacific island watching a traditional native dance. While the Hoop-Dee-Doo Review has a Disney feel, the Polynesian Luau makes guests forget they're in Central Florida.

Luau Cove can be reached by monorail or by walking (fairly far) from the TTC. Mickey's Tropical Revue costs $30 for adults and $14.00 for children (3-11). For the Polynesian Luau, adults are $34.00 and children $18.00. The price for all shows includes entertainment and an all-you-can-eat buffet. The show is performed outdoors.

RESORT RESTAURANTS

Each resort, with the exception of the All Star Resorts, has at least one sit-down restaurant and one fast food restaurant. While the decor of the fast food restaurants differ from resort to resort (many are food courts), the advantage of fast food is obvious — it's fast, it's cheap, and you don't tip anyone. But traveling to another resort takes time and Disney veterans know that a hamburger served at the Polynesian closely resembles one served at the Grand Floridian. For that reason, fast food restaurants are not listed here.

The full-service resort restaurants are like a culinary Magic Kingdom. Think of each resort as a different land, themed to a different idea, with every detail conforming to that concept. Expect Cajun food at Port Orleans, southern cooking at Dixie Landings, and steaks at Wilderness Lodge. Sometimes, Disney chefs must force food to fit the menu. You can enjoy Trail Dust Shortcake at Wilderness Lodge, for example, though in real life it's made with strawberries, ice cream, and whipped cream, commodities in short supply in the old West. But since it sounds western, it's added to the menu.

The same is true for low fat/healthy foods. It's difficult to imagine a cowboy concerned about his waistline or a Polynesian warrior fretting about cholesterol, but specialized entrees are available at both the Polynesian and Wilderness Lodge resorts. In addition, Disney chefs honor special requests. If your diet calls for difficult changes, ask if they're available when you make a reservation. Minor menu modifications — salad dressing on the side, no butter in the broiling, etc. — can be requested when you place your order.

When deciding where to eat, don't forget that this is Walt Disney World. You don't have to remain in one place. If you're staying at Dixie Landings, take the river cruise down to Port Orleans and have a cocktail. Reboard and continue to the Disney Village Marketplace for an appetizer at Cap'n Jack's Oyster Bar. Then take a bus to the Grand Floridian for dinner. Afterward, hop on the monorail and enjoy an after-dinner drink at the top of the Contemporary.

Some mature travelers feel that Disney servers present dinner courses too fast, rushing diners through their meals. Others appreciate the fast service. Remember that many Disney guests spent the entire day at a theme park; some have small children with an attention span of 30 seconds; others may be eating in the same restaurant for the third time. As a result, servers do tend to rush the meals because most patrons prefer it that way. If you want to dine leisurely, request slower service at the beginning of the meal or, as an alternate plan, don't order everything at once, choosing each course as you come to it. If problems are encountered along the way, complain politely. WDW food service managers take great pains to correct their mistakes.

At lunch time, not all restaurants are open. Because most people go to the theme parks during the day, restaurants both within Disney World and off property serve breakfast and dinner but not lunch. Before you head out, make sure your preferred restaurant will be open.

The following descriptions attempt to paint a picture of the restaurant's atmosphere, describe the food offered, and arm you with enough information to make an intelligent choice. Under "STYLE," the restaurant is described in a few words to make comparisons easier. Under "NOTES," specific strong points — and weak ones — are outlined. "Inexpensive," "Moderate," or "Expensive" rates the cost of entrees, though few sit-down restaurants are inexpensive. Moderate entrees range between $10 to $20.00. Expensive ratings include those with entrees starting around $20.00. In a few instances, restaurants are rated as very expensive. End codes describe the meals served: B=Breakfast, L=Lunch, D=Dinner. Once again, to make a reservation, call (407) WDW-DINE up to 60 days ahead of time.

Ariel's — Yacht & Beach Club
STYLE: Upscale steak and seafood dining.
NOTES: Ariel is the name of the lead character in Disney's film *The Little Mermaid*. The restaurant is not, however, cartoonish. The name suggests a family restaurant, but it appeals to adults more than children. Decked out in a nautical theme with a 2,500-gallon aquarium centerpiece, it is elegant but without a dress code, meaning some people show up in shorts — shocking elsewhere but understandable at Disney World. Expensive. D.

Artist Point — Wilderness Lodge
STYLE: Western steaks and seafood.
NOTES: Artist Point has a panoramic view of Bay Lake and the themed areas of Wilderness Lodge. With Pacific Northwest decor and murals, it has a rustic elegance, if "rustic" and "elegant" are not mutually exclusive. Specialties include salmon and steak. A character breakfast features Pocahontas. Expensive. B, D.

Boatwright's Dining Hall — Dixie Landings

STYLE: Southern/Cajun casual.

NOTES: While not romantic nor formal, Boatwright's can be fun. Theoretically, it's a boat building warehouse and, indeed, a half-finished boat is part of the decor. It's called a dining hall and the open room feels that way. If looking for a good meal with a unique theme, stop by. If searching for a touch of formality, look elsewhere. Moderate. B, D.

Bonfamille's Cafe — Port Orleans

STYLE: Moderately elegant American/Creole cuisine.

NOTES: Bonfamille's (meaning "good family") is a good choice for those who do not wish to spend much money but still want a pleasant meal in enjoyable surroundings. Reminiscent of New Orleans' French Quarter, the menu includes both Creole recipes and traditional American favorites. Moderate. B, D.

The California Grill — Contemporary Resort

STYLE: Upscale casual with great view.

NOTES: At the California Grill, food preparation and service are part of the show. Featuring an open kitchen, the modern styling encourages diners to see beyond their own table. Food is extremely fresh and prepared to order. Fun and well worth enjoying, it's also not the top choice for one of those intimate, romantic dinners. Located on the best floor of the Contemporary — the former home of Broadway at the Top — the restaurant has a magnificent view of the Seven Seas Lagoon, the Magic Kingdom, and the evening fireworks. Expensive. D.

Cape May Cafe — Yacht & Beach Club

STYLE: New England clambake buffet.

NOTES: Cape May Cafe offers relaxed dining. Like a beach party — but indoors and air-conditioned — chefs steam seafood in full view of diners, all served for one price but with a surcharge for lobster. Character breakfast. Moderate. B, D.

Captain's Tavern — Caribbean Beach

STYLE: Family-style casual

NOTES: Fairly traditional American food served in a Caribbean atmosphere. Not expensive and located in a kid-friendly resort, it might feel a bit more congested than other restaurants. Moderate. D.

Chef Mickey's — Contemporary Resort

STYLE: Fun, moderate restaurant.
NOTES: Located on the grand concourse of the Contemporary, Chef Mickey's looks open and unprotected. But from within, it's somewhat small, albeit with a 90-foot ceiling and monorail overhead. It's a fun choice for a decent meal if you're spending the day in the Magic Kingdom. Moderate. B, D.

Concourse Steakhouse — Contemporary Resort

STYLE: Pleasant dining at reasonable prices.
NOTES: Best described as a traditional restaurant, it has decent food, reasonable prices, and efficient table service. Moderate. B, L, D.

Coral Café — The Dolphin

STYLE: Casual buffet.
NOTES: Guests can choose a buffet option for breakfast and dinner or eat à la carte. Decorated in a traditional Florida style, it's serves good food to people on the go. Moderate. B, L, D.

Coral Isle Café —Polynesian Resort

STYLE: Coffee shop.
NOTES: Features American cuisine along with Polynesian specialties. The Coral Isle Café is better-than-average, almost-fast food served by a waiter or waitress. Moderate. B, L, D.

Flying Fish Café — Boardwalk Resort

STYLE: Upscale seafood.
NOTES: All seafood is fresh, much of it unique. For non-seafood-lovers, steaks are also served. Expensive. D.

The Garden Gallery — Shades of Green

STYLE: Military-only, casual dining.
NOTES: Shades of Green was formerly The Disney Inn, located close to The Grand Floridian but not on the monorail system. The Garden Gallery has a good breakfast buffet and caters mainly to people staying in the hotel. Inexpensive to moderate. B, L, D.

Garden Grove Cafe and Gulliver's Grill — The Swan
STYLE: Upscale American food.
NOTES: There's no strong theme to the Garden Grove, just the beauty of nature in pleasant surroundings. It has a tropical atmosphere for those Northerners vacationing in the winter. Expensive. B, L, D.

Grand Floridian Café — The Grand Floridian
STYLE: Light dining.
NOTES: Relaxed dining that doesn't take too long. Serves light meals, sandwiches, and salads. Moderate. B, L, D.

Flagler's — The Grand Floridian
STYLE: Upscale Italian.
NOTES: Large windows overlook the Grand Floridian marina in this turn-of-the-century Italian restaurant. Somewhat large, it's the first choice for folks who wish to enjoy an upscale meal in Disney's finest hotel. It doesn't match Victoria & Albert's in style or price, but it's as formal as many people wish to go. Expensive. D.

Harry's Safari Bar & Grille — The Dolphin
STYLE: American food in a jungle atmosphere.
NOTES: Expensive food is generally associated with formal dining that includes low lights, fine service, linens, crystal, silver, etc. But at Harry's, it comes with a jungle. If you want good food and a fun atmosphere, dine at Harry's. Expensive. D.

Juan & Only's — The Dolphin
STYLE: Upscale Mexican.
NOTES: A downscale Mexican jail theme supports an upscale Mexican restaurant. While the jail atmosphere is decidedly casual, the food rises above Taco Bell and the entire dinner, while not exactly formal, can be a great mealtime adventure. With few Mexican restaurants located nearby, those who love a South-of-the-Border flavor find solace here. Moderate. D.

Kimono's — The Swan
STYLE: Upscale Oriental
NOTES: A Japanese style restaurant and lounge that serves sushi. Expensive. D.

Narcoossee's — The Grand Floridian
STYLE: Victorian seafood and steak.
NOTES: Narcoossee's is located in a free-standing octagonal building on the banks of the Seven Seas Lagoon. It fits well with the Grand Floridian styling, but also has a great view of the Magic Kingdom and the evening's Electrical Water Pageant. It has an open kitchen and is a formal, yet relaxed, restaurant with up-scale prices. Expensive. L, D.

1900 Park Fare — The Grand Floridian
STYLE: Nice buffet dining.
NOTES: 1900 Park Fare serves good food fast. It's a great place to eat if you want an above-average meal without wasting time. The style follows the Victorian themes of the Grand Floridian, but on a casual level. Big Bertha, an antique band organ imported from Paris, sits high above diners. Buffet selections include prime rib, seafood, vegetables, and salads. It currently features Disney characters for both breakfast and dinner. Moderate. B, D.

'Ohana — Polynesian Resort
STYLE: Casual open-pit dining.
NOTES: Polynesian style restaurant has an open fire pit, meaning the food preparation is also the entertainment. The set price includes skewers of food prepared over an open fire. If you're looking for unique dining, this is a distinctly change-of-pace meal. Overlooking the Seven Seas Lagoon, the open feel of the room adds to the outdoor, tropical atmosphere, as do tropical evening dancers. Character breakfast. Moderate to expensive. B, D.

Olivia's Café — Old Key West
STYLE: Casual
NOTES: The only full-service restaurant at Old Key West, Olivia's serves a heavy dose of Key West favorites as well as traditional food like burgers and crab cakes. Moderate. B, L, D.

Palio — The Swan
STYLE: Italian.
NOTES: A pleasant restaurant serving good Italian food for those who need their pasta fix for the week. The pleasant atmosphere includes a strolling musician. Moderate to expensive. L, D.

Season's Dining Room — The Villas at the Disney Institute
STYLE: Upscale.
NOTES: As the sole restaurant at the Disney Institute, meals tend to be a learning experience and diners have choices to make, including which of the four dining sections they wish to eat in (themed after the four seasons) and whether they want to eat family style or à la carte. They should even choose which night of the week they prefer, since each features a different culinary theme. Out-of-the-way, it's a great place for a casually elegant meal in a relaxed atmosphere. Expensive. B, L, D.

Spoodle's — Boardwalk Resort
STYLE: Relaxed Mediterranean cuisine.
NOTES: Casual but not tacky, Spoodle's serves food from the countries bordering the Mediterranean, encouraging diners to share dishes and try new foods. For those who like dishes from Greece, Italy, Spain, and North Africa, it's a fun discovery. For those who want to discover new things, it's one of Disney's best. Moderate to Expensive. B, L, D.

Sum Chows — The Dolphin
STYLE: Upscale Chinese.
NOTES: The cuisine is not strictly Chinese, but favors Asian spices and cooking styles. While no formal dress code exists, the average outfit is a bit dressier than that of other restaurants. Guests who like Asian food and formal dining will enjoy Sum Chows. Expensive. D.

Trail's End Buffet — Fort Wilderness
STYLE: American buffet.
NOTES: Themed with a back-to-the-West atmosphere, dining is family-oriented. Guests at other resorts rarely travel to Fort Wilderness for a buffet dinner, but a large selection of reasonably priced food keeps most campers content. Inexpensive to moderate. B, L, D.

Tubbi's — The Dolphin
STYLE: Good food fast.
NOTES: A good buffet with decidedly unusual — bright, loud, and fun — decor. Moderate. B, L, D.

Victoria & Albert's — The Grand Floridian
STYLE: Top notch formal dining.
NOTES: This is the finest restaurant in Walt Disney World, one of the smallest, and the only one requiring jackets for men. Table settings include fine china, crystal, and silver. Each person pays $80.00 to dine, which includes all food; for $105.00, each course includes an appropriate glass of wine. Dining at the Chef's table costs $20 more but worth the extra money. Specific entrees change daily, but always include a choice of fish, fowl, red meat, veal, and lamb. One Disney touch separates Victoria & Albert's from other fine restaurants: each table has two servers, a maid and a butler and, according to their name tags, each maid is named Victoria and each butler is named Albert. Very expensive. D.

Whispering Canyon Cafe — Wilderness Lodge
STYLE: Western, family-style dining.
NOTES: Overlooking the main lobby in Wilderness Lodge, Whispering Canyon Cafe serves up all-you-can-eat comfort food — fried chicken, ribs, corn and such — family style. While not extremely convenient to any of the parks and serving the kind of food that most people enjoy but don't go out of their way to find, it's still a good choice if you're exploring WDW and want a fun place to eat. Moderate. B, L, D.

Yacht Club Galley — Yacht & Beach Club
STYLE: New England casual.
NOTES: Decorated in light colors with a New England theme, menu selections include seafood and American cuisine. It's not the first choice for a formal or romantic dinner, but ideal for a pleasant lunch or non-fast-food evening meal. It's also convenient to Epcot if you want to avoid the lunch-time crowds. Breakfast buffet. Moderate. B, L, D.

Yachtsman Steakhouse — Yacht & Beach Club
STYLE: Upscale country dining.
NOTES: As the name says, they specialize in steaks, but chicken and seafood are also served. Service is upscale, but knotty pine decor lends a relaxed feel to a good meal. It's made for those who love a good steak and don't mind paying a little more to get one. Expensive. D.

THE SPORTING LIFE: DISNEY STYLE

14

237 Golf

241 Tennis

242 Boating

242 Fishing

243 Skis, Horses, and Bikes

Chapter Fourteen

THE SPORTING LIFE: DISNEY STYLE

Walt Disney World has always had golf and tennis, but they've been overshadowed by the grandeur of the theme parks. After all, a number of world-wide destinations offer great golf, but few also have Mickey Mouse and Space Mountain.

Things have changed, however. With the completion of their new racetrack in 1996 and the Walt Disney World Sports Complex in 1997, Disney jumps into the athletic arena with both feet, attempting to conquer the sports world the same way it conquered the entertainment world. Sports fans who shunned the idea of a Disney World vacation as "kid's stuff" may soon eat their own words as they spend hard-earned vacation dollars in Central Florida. Even armchair athletes can now compete in Fantasia Gardens, their new 36-hole miniature golf course.

GOLF

Walt Disney World is one of the biggest golf resorts in the country with 99 holes of play on 775 acres of prime Central Florida real estate. The Oak Trail course offers up only nine holes, great for practice or the golfer just starting out; at the other end, the Palm Course was rated by *Golf Digest* as one of the nation's "Top 25 Resort Courses." Each course has an assortment of tees and yardage, serving everyone from the beginner to the seasoned pro. Disney courses host the annual LPGA HealthSouth Inaugural as well as their most famous sports competition, the Walt Disney World/Oldsmobile Golf Classic.

On opening day in 1971, WDW had two golf courses, The Magnolia and Palm. The following year, the Lake Buena Vista course opened followed by the Oak Trail course. Twenty years later, as the rest of Walt Disney World grew at break-neck speed, Disney built the Bonnet Creek Golf Club, home base for their two newest courses, Osprey Ridge and Eagle Pines.

For play on any course, tee times may be reserved ahead of time by calling (407) WDW-GOLF, which translates to (407) 939-4653. Guests who booked a golf package may reserve tee times 90 days in advance; guests staying at a Disney resort may book 60 days in advance; all others book 30 days in advance. For a reservation on the day of play, call the course directly at the numbers listed under individual descriptions. To get a discounted rate, try to play during traditionally slow times, specifically in the summer and/or after 3 p.m. From late spring through December, they also offer a seasonal badge that qualifies golfers for substantial discounts.

On-site guests' greens fees for full 18-hole courses start at $85 and go as high as $105 depending on both course and season of the year. Price includes cart rental. Fees run $95 to $120 for golfers staying off-site. After 3 p.m., greens fees cost roughly half that amount. The nine-hole Oak Trail course costs $24 for nine holes and $32 for 18 holes. Pro shops rent equipment for those who find it inconvenient to travel with golf paraphernalia. Clubs run $22 to $30. Shoes and balls also available.

Palm Course

Designed by Joe Lee, the Palm course allows water hazards to punish golfers for their mistakes. Hole 18 has been ranked as high as fourth toughest on the PGA tour. Located near the Magic Kingdom, the Palm course is shorter than its neighbor, the Magnolia, but makes up for it with additional hazards. Expect water on ten holes. With thick woods surrounding the fairways, it's a do-or-die game of golf.

Tees	Yardage	Course Rating	Slope Rating
Blue	6957	73.0	133
White	6461	70.7	129
Gold	6029	68.7	124
Red	5311	70.4	124

Same day tee times, call (407) 824-2288.

Magnolia Course

This sister to the Palm Course is longer and also designed by Joe Lee. Golfers used to Florida course designs will recognize the classic styling. The Magnolia has 97 bunkers with one sand trap shaped like Mickey Mouse, photographed extensively by those who play around the world. Six holes have water hazards and six bridges span creeks that cut through the course. Framed by 1,500 magnolia trees, it's featured in the final round of the Walt Disney World/Oldsmobile Golf Classic.

Tees	Yardage	Course Rating	Slope Rating
Blue	7190	73.9	133
White	6642	71.6	128
Gold	6091	69.1	123
Red	5232	70.5	123

Same day tee times, call (407) 824-2288.

Oak Trail Course

Designed by Ron Garl, Oak Trail sits near the Magnolia course. A par 36 walking course, it's made for beginners, warm-ups, and practice rounds. White tees play 2913 yards; red tees play 2532 yards. *Same day tee times, call (407) 828-3741.*

Lake Buena Vista Course

Another course in a somewhat classic Florida style, Lake Buena Vista is located near Downtown Disney. The course cuts through thick Florida wilderness, with natural foliage and grassy fairways. Unusual challenges make the Lake Buena Vista course different. No. 16 is a 157-yard island green while the final hole is a challenging 448-yard dogleg.

Tees	Yardage	Course Rating	Slope Rating
Blue	6819	72.7	128
White	6268	70.1	123
Gold	5919	68.2	120
Red	5194	69.4	120

Same day tee times, call (407) 828-3741.

Osprey Ridge

One of the two newest Disney courses, Osprey Ridge and Eagle Pines opened in 1992. Designed by Tom Fazio and one of his personal favorites, the Florida wetlands and moss hammocks serve as a backdrop for play. Diehard golf fans probably don't care, but the scenic beauty is breathtaking. Using a little Disney engineering technology to construct areas for nesting, actual osprey habitats have been included so golfers can see a real "birdie." (Bad joke. Sorry.)

Tees	Yardage	Course Rating	Slope Rating
Blue	7101	73.9	135
White	6680	71.8	128
Gold	6103	68.9	121
Red	5402	70.5	122

Same day tee times, call (407) 824-2270.

Eagle Pines

Unlike the other Disney courses, Eagle Pines breaks from tradition. Also designed by Tom Fazio, it's a "low profile course." That means the course sits even with — or lower — than the surrounding land. Fairways are dished, unlike traditional crowned fairways. And rather than grass, pine straw and sand make up most of the rough. Those unused to such play find it scary but, by the third or fourth hole, not as intimidating as it first appears.

Tees	Yardage	Course Rating	Slope Rating
Talon	6772	72.3	131
Crest	6309	69.9	125
Wings	5520	66.3	115
Feathers	4838	68.0	111

Same day tee times, call (407) 824-2675.

Golf Instruction

Those wishing to improve their game — or even those who never hoisted a club before — can take a class suited to their level of expertise. Costs vary. One-on-one instruction at any Disney course costs $50 per half hour. Group lessons including nine holes of play cost

$150. Ninety-minute sessions with PGA pros cost $75. For reservations, call (407) 939-4653. A complete golfing program, developed by Gary Player, is also offered at the Disney Institute.

Miniature Golf

New for Disney's 25th anniversary, miniature golf can now be found within the borders of WDW. Two side-by-side, 18-hole courses emulate both the old and new in miniature golf play. Fantasia Gardens reflects the old — traditional putting that requires players to avoid moving wood, flowing water, and sandy diversions. Adapted from Disney's film Fantasia, classical music and dancing vegetables make the play decidedly unique, even when compared to the mega-courses found just outside Walt Disney World.

The second 18-holes, Fantasia Fairways, reflects the newest trend and looks like an extremely small traditional course. In other words, the challenge includes sand traps, lakes, and bunkers made of real grass. Holes range from 40-feet to 75-feet. Both courses operate from 10 a.m. to midnight and cost $9 per adult, $8 for kids (3-11).

TENNIS

A number of WDW resorts have tennis courts, including the Grand Floridian which, in keeping with its Victorian theme, has two clay courts. Both the Contemporary and the Grand Floridian have on-site tennis pros that offer clinics and private instruction. The Contemporary even has a "Beat the Pro" challenge where you pay for a game only if you lose.

With six Hydrogrid clay courts, the Contemporary is WDW's major resort for tennis buffs. For program specifics, call them at (407) 824-3578. Court reservations for the Grand Floridian can be made by calling (407) 824-2694. Both resorts charge $12 per court, per hour, or $40 for length-of-stay; racquet rental and balls cost extra and reservations may be made up to 30 days in advance of play. The Sports Complex's 11 clay courts and tennis stadium expand Disney's tennis offerings into the professional arena.

The Disney Institute has four clay courts primarily used by Institute guests and the Boardwalk Resort has two. Hard-court options include three at Old Key West, two at the Yacht and Beach

Club, and two at Fort Wilderness. There is no charge to play these hard courts nor do they accept reservations. For the Swan or the Dolphin, which have a total of eight courts, call (407) 934-4000, extension 6000 to make a court reservation.

BOATING

With the Seven Seas Lagoon and Bay Lake connected by an unusual bridge (the water goes over the traffic rather than the traffic over the water), there are acres of Disney water to be explored and many on-site resorts rent boats. In addition to the lake boating available from the Magic Kingdom area resorts, Dixie Landings and Port Orleans sit on a canal system that connects to Downtown Disney. All three rent boats. At the Caribbean Beach, guests use their private lake.

Rental rates vary from about $6.00 to $20.00 per half hour, depending on type of boat. Guests can choose from an interesting array of craft, including little speedboats that zip around Bay Lake, canopy boats, pontoon boats, sailboats, pedal boats, and canoes (available only at Fort Wilderness for use on the canals).

For the strong of heart, parasailing is offered at the Contemporary marina for $60 per person. Price includes seven- to ten-minutes of floating in the air, pulled by a boat and held aloft by a kite. Much easier than it looks, it never-the-less does not appeal to everyone. For more information on parasailing, call (407) 824-1000, ext. 3586.

FISHING

A license is not required within the Walt Disney World resort, so avid fishermen can bring their tackle. You cannot, however, fish everywhere nor keep anything you pull out. Those who plan to actively fish away part of their vacation should consider staying at Fort Wilderness or the Villas at the Disney Institute where guests may cast a line in any of the nearby canals. Fishing is restricted in Bay Lake and the Seven Seas Lagoon, the two large lakes near the Magic Kingdom. For most expeditions noted below, reservations may be made up to two weeks ahead must be made at least 24 hours in advance.

Consider the following:

• **Captain Jacks Marina at Disney Village Marketplace.** With access to Disney canals, the Marketplace is one of two main ports-of-call for a fishing junket. Each morning expedition accommodates up to five people for one price. Costs, per boatload, run $137.00 for two hours, $187.00 for three hours, and $237.00 for four hours. Price includes boat, guide, gear, and snacks. Reservations: (407) 828-2204.

• **Fort Wilderness Marina.** The only way to fish in Bay Lake or the Seven Seas Lagoon — within sight of the Magic Kingdom or Discovery Island — is to schedule a trip out of Fort Wilderness, though guides will pick up guests from any resort fronting the lakes. The two-hour expeditions leave at 8:00 a.m., 11:30, and 3:00 p.m. Costs, per boatload, run $137.00 for two hours, $187.00 for three hours, and $237.00 for four hours. Price includes boat, guide, gear, and snacks. Reservations: (407) 824-2621.

• **Yacht & Beach Club or Boardwalk.** Two-hour excursions cost $130.00 and include boat, guide, fishing equipment, and snacks. Reservations: (407) 939-5100.

• **Dixie Landings.** Fishing is allowed near Ol' Man Island and poles rent for $3.00 per hour. Excursions depart at 6:30 a.m., travel the canal and Buena Vista Lagoon, and cost $35.00 per person. Price includes guide, gear, and snacks. Reservations: (407) 934-5409.

SKIS, HORSES, AND BIKES

Water-skiing

Two to five guests, per boat, may water-ski on Bay Lake, with departures available from all on-the-water resorts. Experienced instructors accept both professionals and novices. Cost is $82.00 per hour, plus tax. Reservations are required and can be made up two weeks before arrival by calling (407) 824-2621.

Horseback Riding

Based in Fort Wilderness at the Tri-Circle D Livery (near the main parking lot), this guided trail ride lasts about 45 minutes. Disney cast members lead the processional and keep the pace fairly subdued.

Guests must be at least nine-years old and weigh less than 250 pounds. Groups depart at 9:00 a.m., 10:30, noon, and 2:00 p.m. Cost is $17.00 per person. They have a minimal dress code: shoes must be worn, long pants are recommended, and hats are discouraged. Reservations: (407) 824-2832.

Bike Riding

Bikes are available almost everywhere where there's 1) enough room and 2) it's safe. Specifically, Old Key West, Fort Wilderness, Wilderness Lodge, Port Orleans, Caribbean Beach, Dixie Landings, Boardwalk, Villas at the Disney Institute, and Coronado Springs have areas for rental. Costs run $3 to $10 per day, depending on type of bicycle.

AND ALSO AT DISNEY...

246 Disney Weddings

247 Walt Disney World Sports Complex

248 Indy 200

248 Character Warehouse

249 Celebration

250 Disney Cruise Line

251 Disney's Animal Kingdom

Chapter Fifteen

AND ALSO AT DISNEY...

In the beginning, Walt Disney World was, first and foremost, a theme park with nearby hotel rooms. Additional attractions, the golf courses for example, were meant to complement the park and entertain non-theme-park lovers while the rest of the family explored the Magic Kingdom.

Today, however, many people visit WDW and never visit the theme parks. And if they do visit, it's because they feel obligated, being so close and all, but they *actually* came for a convention or a special event like the Indy 200. In the future, Disney will continue to diversify, entering areas not yet explored. Since many of these new Disney activities don't fit in other chapters, they're listed here.

WALT DISNEY WORLD WEDDINGS

It is not only possible to get married at Walt Disney World, but it can be done in a private Wedding Pavilion on the shores of the Seven Seas Lagoon with Cinderella's Castle in the background. Or, if you prefer, you can exchange vows inside the theme parks (after hours only).

The Disney wedding program is ideal for mature couples marrying for the second time. While a lot of people may not opt for the Disney-specific touches — a ride in Cinderella's glass coach, for example — the ornate splendor of the Grand Floridian or the Yacht & Beach Club creates a perfect backdrop for an unforgettable wedding.

For true Disney fans, not only can Mickey be the best man, but — for a fee — any Disney character will attend. Vows may even be exchanged in front of Cinderella's Castle with a private outdoor reception held in Fantasyland. If you want the carousel to remain open for your guests or a private fireworks display, all you have to do is pay for it.

The Wedding Pavilion, first opened in 1995 and located between the Polynesian and the Grand Floridian resorts, provides a white, off-white, and off-off-white backdrop for those who want a traditional ceremony. Weddings are big business for Disney and cast members work one-on-one with brides to coordinate all the details. Flowers, photography, gifts for members of the wedding party, and other wedding chores can be prearranged.

For couples who want Disney service and style but without cartoon characters, the gardens of Epcot create a refined wedding location. Those who can trace their lineage to Europe may marry in the (World Showcase) land of their ancestors.

Costs vary wildly depending on what you want but can run to $20,000 and more for a top-of-the-line ceremony. For information or brochures, call a Disney wedding specialist at (407) 363-6333. If you're marrying elsewhere and honeymooning at Walt Disney World, call (407) 828-0228 for honeymoon information.

WALT DISNEY WORLD SPORTS COMPLEX

The sports complex, opened in spring of '97, sits on 200 acres, carries a construction price tag of $87 million, and hopes to attract amateur sports events. Cynics see it as a marketing ploy. If Disney hosts events such as the Little League play-offs, they say, Disney not only gets added theme park visitors, but national exposure and free advertising.

But sports are, after all, entertainment. And Disney is entertainment. The two go together like peanut butter and jelly. For amateur sports associations, there is an advantage in returning to the same site year after year. They get to know the coordinators and the fields, don't worry about hotel space or transportation, and can reasonably expect that everything will be in working order.

With Disney's acquisition of ABC and ESPN, the Disney-Sports link should grow stronger. There's talk of professional football coming to Orlando and even rumors of a future Olympiad. In the meantime, the sports complex will keep amateur contenders happy. The array of sports available includes a 7,500 seat baseball stadium with an additional 2,500 seats possible, four major league baseball fields, four softball fields, two youth baseball fields, a track and field complex, four football/soccer grass playing fields, four outdoor volleyball courts, eleven tennis courts (including a 2,000 seat center stadium), a 5,000 seat field house with six basketball courts, and a fitness center with training rooms.

INDY 200

In January 1996, Indy racing arrived at Walt Disney World. In a track located behind the main entrance to the Magic Kingdom, world-class racing became another "major" attraction, an event to be replicated yearly. ("Major" sounds overused — applied to everything Disney creates. However, everything *is* major.)

CHARACTER WAREHOUSE

Within Disney World, it's not unusual to find a few sale items, generally marked with small, tasteful signs. As fall approaches, T-shirts are marked down. Alternately, in mid-spring, sweatshirts are discounted.

Do not, however, expect to find many bargains. For great deals, drive to Belz Factory Outlet World on International Drive. An enormous playground of shops, bargains, and not-really-bargains, Belz Factory Outlet World is a series of enclosed malls and strip malls surrounded by other malls and strip malls. The Character Warehouse, the only off-site, Disney-owned discount store, is located in Building Two. Drive North on International Drive until the it ends in a circular turn-around. The building on your immediate left holds the Character Warehouse which is in the center of the building.

The Character Warehouse should be the first place you shop. Selling factory seconds and discontinued items, sizes and selections don't approach what you find inside the parks or at the Downtown

Disney shops. But you find bargains, with prices generally 50% to 75% less than identical items sold on-site. The store usually has a special, such as a one-size-fits-all Mickey sweatshirt, originally $35, marked down to $9. There's a fair chance you'll find something for yourself and an excellent chance you'll find something for the folks back home. The more relatives you have, the more money you save. In addition to Mickey stuff, there's also an occasional deal on other merchandise. Pringle sweaters, 100% wool and a product of Scotland, recently sold for 75% off their original price in World Showcase. They also stock stuffed animals and knick-knacks.

For more information on the Character Warehouse, call (407) 345-5285.

CELEBRATION

When Walt Disney first envisioned Epcot (an acronym for Experimental Prototype Community Of Tomorrow), he didn't view it as a theme park. He hoped to create a town, possibly populated by employees, where the layout and style of neighborhoods encouraged interaction between people, where traffic flowed smoothly, and where residents could walk to work. Walt Disney's dream town was to retain the best aspects of old neighborhoods while embracing modern technology.

For pragmatic reasons and because Walt Disney died too young, the Epcot name stuck but the concept changed.

Today, the Disney-built town of Celebration renews many of Walt's original ideas for Epcot, though town developers make no comparison to Walt's vision. This new community, located on the southeast corner of Walt Disney World and not easily accessible to the parks, uses design concepts that make neighborhood life less stressful, including front porches (they encourage people to sit and talk), hidden garages (that take the emphasis off cars and put it back on people), and narrow lots (creating less yard work and closer neighbors). The architectural styles recreate pre-WW II housing, a sort-of Mayberry, R.F.D. near Orlando.

While a bit experimental, Celebration is not an attraction but a real estate project spearheaded by Disney. In other words, it's a really big housing development. Thus far, it's not even an actual town, though it may incorporate in the future. Never-the-less, Celebration businesses — like businesses in every American town — encourage outside participation and tourists may drive in, eat at local restaurants, watch local movies, or browse through local shops. For more information, visit their sales center on US 192 just east of I-4 or call (407) 939-TOWN, which translates to (407) 939-8696.

DISNEY CRUISE LINE

The premier of the Disney Cruise Line in 1998 should attract a lot of attention and, though no ship has yet sailed, excited Disney patrons can now make reservations. A cruise vacation has traditionally offered top quality service and a complete vacation package that includes entertainment and food for one all-inclusive price. With the entrance of Disney, expect the same, but with added Disney touches.

While many details mirror that of other cruise lines, some aspects are unique. For one thing, guests eat in different themed dining rooms each night, unlike most cruise lines that use the same dining room. Also, on-board entertainment is Disney, meaning better than that found on some lines. It will also be one of the few lines with top-notch entertainment for kids, though it will be competing with Premier Cruise Lines (The Big Red Boat) that also sails out of Port Canaveral, also markets to families, and also sails with cartoon characters (Bugs Bunny and pals).

As a plus for mature travelers, the Disney Cruise Line is not aiming its sights strictly at the under-40-with-kids market. Palos, an Italian restaurant with romantic decor, serves only adults. With segregated activities on board — children go one place, teens another, adults another — it's almost possible to completely ignore people under 30, privately enjoying activities that kids hate. In addition to a wine tasting class, for example, the line has complete spa facilities.

The Disney Cruise Line sells inclusive packages. You can book either the cruise alone or a one-week package that includes both cruise and a hotel stay at Walt Disney World. All packages include on-board meals, airfare from the city nearest your home (some have an add-on charge), and transfers to Port Canaveral. Seven-day packages also include transfers to Walt Disney World, hotel, use of the transportation system, and unlimited admission during your stay to all

Disney theme parks, water parks, and Pleasure Island. Hotel choice depends on cabin booked. Expensive suites on the ship grant passengers a stay at the Grand Floridian. Least expensive cabins qualify for Caribbean Beach, Dixie Landings, Port Orleans, or Coronado Springs. Other resorts fall somewhere in the middle.

Not included in the package price are meals during your stay at WDW, port charges of approximately $89 per person, and personal items. Like other cruise lines, Disney offers discounts for early booking. For more information, check with your travel agent. If booking a cruise, decide exactly what you want and call three or four agencies for quotes, making sure one or two specialize in cruises. When ready to confirm a reservation, however, go with someone you trust, even if the cost is marginally more than a quote you received elsewhere.

For grandparents, a Disney cruise offers the ideal opportunity to vacation with grandchildren. While Disney entertains the kids, you can also spend a quiet evening with your spouse. And, because meals and most activities are prepaid, the stress of what-do-we-do-next and how-much-does-that-cost makes a cruise less taxing than a comparable theme park vacation.

DISNEY'S ANIMAL KINGDOM

The biggest attraction coming to WDW, their fourth theme park, opens in spring of 1998. Some details still need to be worked out, but the 500-acre park promises to be a zoo with rides, similar to Busch Gardens in Tampa Bay. Like Epcot, it will educate visitors as it entertains them. And, like Sea World of Orlando, it will push an ecological theme, singing a we-are-one-with-the-environment song. Disney's largest theme park ever (five times the size of the Magic Kingdom), Animal Kingdom should be interesting to mature travelers equipped with a good pair of walking shoes.

The Tree of Life, a monstrous fiberglass tree with branches shaped like animals, will symbolize the park, just as Cinderella's Castle symbolizes the Magic Kingdom. Used in both the park's logo and advertising, the Tree of Life will be visible from all lands. Inside the tree, central figures from the Disney movie, *The Lion King*, will star in a 3-D movie about bugs.

Three themed lands — Safari Village, Africa, and Dinoland — are planned, with a fourth, Asia, opening later. Safari Village is the Animal Kingdom equivalent of the Magic Kingdom's Main Street. Africa focuses on real African animals — essentially a zoo — but with themed adventures. Dinoland focuses on extinct animals and gives Disney another chance to create dinosaurs that chew grass, flap wings, and attack tourists. While dinosaurs lurk at Epcot's Universe of Energy, expect bigger, better, and more cold-blooded behemoths here. Yet another land, Beastly Kingdom, was designed to highlight mythical creatures such as unicorns, but plans for that section have been put on hold.

While the trend in zoos today is to put animals in a natural setting, expect the Disney people to do it best, with settings so natural that even some animals can't tell the difference. Initial plans called for several roller coasters and thrill rides, but as things change, fall through, and develop, it looks as if guests will enjoy a series of high-tech adventures with mental thrills more than physical ones — good news for roller-coaster-haters. At one point on the safari, for example, a bridge collapses and guests find themselves face-to-face with alligators. It's scary, but not stomach-wrenching.

For mature travelers, Animal Kingdom promises to have plenty of shows, both in theaters and from vehicles that wind through the zoo. A walk-through exhibition is also planned.

OTHER BIG TOURIST DRAWS

254 Cypress Gardens

257 Sea World of Orlando

261 Splendid China

262 Universal Studios Florida

270 Busch Gardens, Tampa Bay

273 Church Street Station

275 Kennedy Space Center's Visitor's Center

276 Dinner Shows, Gators, and Other
Orlando Stuff

Chapter Sixteen

OTHER BIG TOURIST DRAWS

Every theme park in the Orlando area has something that appeals to the mature traveler — but some have more than others. Cypress Gardens, for example, attracts mainly mature travelers, as do smaller parks such as Splendid China and World of Orchids. Sea World, while not an adults-only destination, also intrigues the over-30 crowd.

Of course, some 88-year-olds ride roller coasters and some 42-year-olds avoid the carousel. Mature travelers are a diverse group and it's unfair to generalize. Still, a majority of adults prefer shows over fast rides, beautiful gardens over late nights at the bars, and relaxed touring over a hectic schedule. In the following park descriptions, the analysis is directed at the typical mature traveler, though the roller-coaster-loving adult is not forgotten.

In the descriptions, each park is summarized, followed by a list of specific highlights, handicapped information, directions, and costs. Prices are current at press time and do not include tax. Since rates are volatile, consider them guidelines rather than fact and assume a 5% increase when budgeting. If you need additional information, phone numbers are provided.

CYPRESS GARDENS

While it has grown, expanded, and diversified over the years, Cypress Gardens stays true to its roots, no pun intended. It debuted in 1936 — one of the few large parks that pre-dates Walt Disney World — and bills itself as "Florida's first theme park." It's also the "water-ski capital of the world."

Both the gardens and the water-ski show have competition nowadays — Disney has beautiful gardens everywhere and Sea World's ski show reaches more people. But for grandeur, substance, and style, Cypress Gardens still leads the pack.

First, Cypress Gardens' greenery does not complete a theme or exist as part of a larger fantasy. It stands on its own. Over 8,000 varieties of plants and flowers from over 90 countries exist together and, like a great painting, complement each other in form and fashion. The natural flow of the paths makes it appear as if it all happened naturally; that man did little more than help nature along by giving the plants room to grow. That's not true, of course. A lot of work went into Cypress Gardens. But rather than feel awed by the grandeur, the overall effect is far more relaxing.

For water-ski professionals, Cypress Gardens is *the* place to perform, the alma mater of champions. The show has fun moments, but choreographers go for a beautiful presentation, more like a ballet on the water. That's not to say that Sea World's ski show, the main competitor, is not good. It is. But at Sea World, the show strives for laughs and appeals to a younger crowd.

Cypress Gardens does not have the high-tech feel of Universal Studios or Disney. You can see how the park grew over the years. Unlike Disney which went up en masse, Cypress Gardens added a building here and a building there, growing over the years at a slow-but-steady snail's pace. From the style of the exhibits, it's easy to see where the park began and where, year-by-year, they expanded. But clean and meticulously groomed, the gardens have no equal in Florida or perhaps the world.

For those who live close enough to visit several times per year, Cypress Gardens schedules a number of seasonal festivals. While subject to change, they include:
• **Spring Flower Festival**, featuring large topiaries made of flowers. The only festival of its kind, these living statues are nurtured behind the scenes, then brought out when in bloom.
• **Victorian Garden Party**, running through the summer, features a number of topiaries themed to the 1860's, including women with parasols and gentlemen with top hats.
• **Mum Festival** displays over two million blooms in a variety of settings. Runs in October and/or November.
• **Poinsettia Festival** runs concurrently with the Garden of Lights,

from Thanksgiving into the New Year. In addition to 50,000 poinsettia blooms, the park changes into a winter wonderland of sparkling lights and Christmas displays, minus the snow and cold.

Most Cypress Gardens visitors are adults. While they have a few small rides that please the pre-teen set, there is little to keep older kids occupied. Operated by Anheuser-Busch for a number of years, the park was sold in 1995 to the on-site executive officers and is no longer affiliated with beer, though it is still served on property.

Along the way, the following exhibits can be enjoyed:

• **Carousel Cove**. Home to the limited number of rides at Cypress Gardens, Carousel Cove caters to the preschool crowd. Rides included in the admission price.

• **Cypress Junction.** Twenty model trains travel along 1,100 feet of track, visiting famous American landmarks such as Miami, New Orleans, and Mt. Rushmore.

• **Cypress Roots Museum.** Tracing the history of Cypress Gardens, the Cypress Roots Museum displays memorabilia dating back to the park's inception in 1936.

• **Island in the Sky**. The countryside in this hilly part of Florida can be viewed from 153-feet in the air in this tower that rises, spins, then returns to the ground.

• **Original Gardens.** This is the most famous area in Cypress Gardens, the place where visitors snap picture after picture of young women dressed as hoop-skirted Southern Belles. Guests explore these sixteen acres of free-form and sculpted gardens on foot and/or by canal boats that wind through the greenery and out onto Lake Eloise. While there's an educational aspect to the gardens, the primary emphasis is on beauty and the tropical plants. Keep an eye out for alligators sunning themselves on the edge of a canal or along the water.

• **Plantation Gardens.** Fruits, vegetables, herbs, and spices grow next to a formal rose garden and other backyard-styled vegetation.

• **Pontoon Lake Cruise.** For an additional fee, guests can tour Lake Eloise by boat. Lake Eloise sits in a chain of lakes, meaning connected by natural and man-made canals. An interesting journey, the tour gives passengers a feel for the area, but other Winter Haven boat operators found off-site give longer tours for those who want to really explore the back-water sections of Florida.

- **"When Radios Were Radios."** An exhibit that doesn't seem to fit into Cypress Gardens, "When Radios Were Radios" is none-the-less interesting and worth a stop. Hundreds of antique radios bring back memories to adults who can remember what the world was like before television.
- **"Wings of Wonder" Butterfly Conservatory.** One of the most recent additions, Cypress Gardens advertises their butterfly conservatory on billboards all around Orlando. Housed in a Victorian style greenhouse filled with thousands of butterflies, a single path winds through an indoor garden. Cocoon incubators line one wall and visitors can watch the butterflies-to-be develop. Once fully emerged, they exit the incubator and fly among the plants, waterfalls, and visitors. The effect — swatches of color dancing around you — feels almost unreal, something seen only in movies.

WHEELCHAIR ACCESSIBILITY: Good. Since there are few rides, wheelchairs can access everything, though there are a few steep hills to climb. For the boat tour, guests must be able to transfer themselves from wheelchair to boat. Wheelchair rental is available and suggested for those with difficulty walking.

DIRECTIONS: Cypress Gardens is about a half hour from Walt Disney World. From the Disney area, take I-4 west to US 27 south. From US 27, turn right (west) on state road 540, towards Winter Haven. Follow signs.

COSTS: Adults $27.95, senior/AARP (55+) $22.95, children (6-12) $17.95, under 6 free. Year-round admission is $59.95 adult, $49.95 senior, $29.95 child. Open every day of the year, 9:30 a.m. to 5:30 p.m. Parking is free. Information: (800) 282-2123 or (941) 324-2111.

SEA WORLD OF ORLANDO

A park marketed to the entire family, Sea World is none-the-less a treat for the mature traveler. If you have no interest in sea life and find zoos boring, move on to other things. But if you enjoy animal shows, a smattering of educational information, and a relatively line-free day, visit Sea World.

Because most Sea World attractions are some type of theater production, guests arrive en masse at scheduled showtimes. Front and center seats fill up first, though even late arrivals find some kind of seating in the off season. The park emphasizes the protection of endangered animals, a concept slightly at odds with their animals-in-cages format, but a theme that is none-the-less noble. Unknown to many out-of-state visitors, an on-site animal rescue team responds to emergencies — essentially an aquatic ambulance service — saving injured manatees, stranded dolphins, and even an occasional whale.

A day at Sea World does not have the Disney magic, that feeling that as you turn a new corner, you've discovered a new land or adventure. The term "theme park" once described a unique *type* of park, one where different sections recreated different fantasies. Sea World is not themed; the entire park follows the single idea of "marine life." Shamu's Happy Harbor, for example, is a kid's playground but not like any real land or place. The killer whale show takes place in a stadium that looks like a stadium. Italian restaurants sit near penguins without either building exterior looking particularly "Arctic" nor particularly "Italian." There is one notable exception: Key West at Sea World, an area opened in 1996, follows a single theme. Exhibits, shops, and restaurants in that single section adhere to one idea — The Conch Republic. It is, perhaps, the wave of the future. (Pun intended.) Key West contains Dolphin Cove, Turtle Point, Stingray Lagoon, and the newly renamed Key West Dolphin Fest.

And Sea World has beer. Free beer. As one of several Anheuser-Busch parks, guests over 21 may enjoy a choice of beers during their stay. The limit is two per guest, but there's no easy way to police those who return later in the day. More than one family member has ordered a beer, staked out an air-conditioned table, and relaxed while the rest of the family rode Wild Arctic or shopped.

The following list briefly describes the major attractions:
• **Baywatch at Sea World.** Tapping into the most famous TV show in the world, Sea World's ski show has lots of action. The Baywatch television show never has much of a plot and that holds true for the ski show, but acrobatic ski stunts make up for any missing story-line. Guests sit in an enormous lake-side theater that's shaded but not air-conditioned.
• **Dolphin Cove.** A 700,000-gallon aquarium, Dolphin Cove has an artificial beach with waves, as well as an underwater viewing area where visitors can watch dolphins at play. Covering 2.1-acres, it's the centerpiece of the Key West themed area.

- **Hotel Clyde and Seamore.** For some reason, sea lions are the clowns of the water world. While this show's humor and story-line entertain the younger generation, the sea lion tricks amuse all ages. Theater is outdoors but shaded.
- **Key West Dolphin Fest.** Bottlenose dolphins and false killer whales perform stunts, acrobatics, and comedy routines. Outdoors but shaded.
- **Manatees: The Last Generation?** For those living outside Florida, the manatee looks like something from another world. In this exhibit, guests view the animals first from above the water and then from below. A short 3-D presentation describes the manatee, their environment, and their chances for survival. Movie and underwater shows are indoors and air-conditioned.
- **Laser Fireworks Spectacular.** (formerly Mermaids, Myths and Monsters) Sea World's answer to Epcot's IllumiNations, fireworks, laser lights, and walls of water create a patriotic grand finale. Great special effects. Outdoors.
- **Pacific Point Preserve.** Craggy rocks border an enclosed sea lion exhibit. With ocean waves pounding against boulders in this recreation of a rough California coastline, the exhibit looks extremely natural. Adventurous souls can buy baskets of raw fish and feed the barking mammals. Outdoors and in full sun, it's best to visit in early morning or late afternoon.
- **Penguin Encounter.** Hundreds of penguins dive, swim, and leap from the water in an Antarctic ice flow located smack in the middle of hot-and-sticky Central Florida. A slow moving sidewalk transports lower level viewers past the exhibit, giving everyone a momentary front row view. There is also a higher, non-moving level for guests who want to stay longer. Indoors and air-conditioned.
- **Sea Turtle Point.** Another beach-style attraction within Key West, many Sea Turtle Point turtles were rescued from the ocean and nursed back to health. Those with permanent disabilities found a home here.
- **Shamu's Happy Harbor.** Shamu's Happy Harbor is similar to McDonald's playlands but twenty times bigger. A separate water-based playground gives kids ample opportunity to get soaked. If you visit with children, bring a towel. Outdoors but shaded.
- **Shamu World Focus.** All killer whales are named Shamu at Sea World. Housed in a huge, semi-circular arena, guests enjoy tricks per-

formed by the huge mammal. While Shamu's maneuvers are performed by dolphins elsewhere, watching a five ton animal defy gravity can take your breath away. It shouldn't be missed. One word of warning: treat the designated "splash zones" (seats down front) with respect. "Splash" is too nice a word. Even if you think a little water might feel refreshing, remember that it's not a little. Also, it's salt water, so once evaporated, a thin film of salt will stay with you. It's also very cold. Theater is outdoors but shaded.

• **Stingray Lagoon.** In addition to a nursery for newborn stingrays, Stingray Lagoon houses over 200 adults. In one area, guests may touch (pet?) the elusive creatures.

• **Terrors of the Deep.** This attraction's bark is worse than its bite. The "terror" is visual — sharks, moray eels, and lionfish. Guests travel on a moving sidewalk through a clear, circular tunnel on the bottom of a shark infested aquarium. In a separate area at the end of the sidewalk, guests can view the animals at their leisure. Exhibit is indoors, air-conditioned, and suitable for anyone.

• **Wild Arctic.** For Sea World veterans, Mission: Bermuda Triangle is out and Wild Arctic is in. Using the same motion simulator vehicles as its predecessor, Wild Arctic takes guests on an action-packed helicopter trip to the frozen tundra. For the ride, guests sit in an enclosed room while a movie plays in front. Because the room moves, it *feels* as if you're in a real helicopter. Seats tilt left as the helicopter tilts left and seats tilt right as the helicopter tilts right, many times rapidly. While you actually don't go anywhere, movements are jerky and those subject to claustrophobia or motion sickness should avoid it. At the conclusion of the ride, guests tour Sea World's new polar bear exhibit on foot, which can be viewed without taking the ride first.

Sea World also has a number of smaller attractions. Tropical Reef, an aquarium, features thousands of colorful fish. Caribbean Tide Pool has fish, sea urchins, starfish, and more. Hawaiian Village has a live show featuring traditional Polynesian dances.

WHEELCHAIR ACCESSIBILITY: Good. Most Sea World attractions are accessible to the handicapped with the possible exception of Wild Arctic. (Guests must transfer themselves from wheelchair to seat.) Wheelchair rentals are available on site.

DIRECTIONS: Sea World is located at the south end of International Drive. Guests staying on-site at Disney World and on US 192 should take I-4 East (it feels like north) and exit at 27A. Watch for the signs. **COSTS:** Adults $39.95, children $32.80, 10% discount for seniors; two-day pass $44.95 adults, $37.80 child, and no discount for seniors; a 12-month pass $69.95 per adult, $59.95 for seniors over 55. Information: (407) 363-2249. A separate package, the Vacation Value Pass, offers unlimited admission for five consecutive days to Sea World, Universal Studios, and Wet 'n Wild. It costs $89.95 for adults and $72.95 for children. For more Vacation Value Pass information, call Universal City Travel Company at (800) 224-3838. For Sea World information call: (800) 432-1178 or (407) 351-3600

SPLENDID CHINA

It's a mistake to lump Splendid China in with the other theme parks. Unlike competitors, everything — food, shows, and exhibits — highlight a single theme, specifically the people, climate, and culture of China. Splendid China is like the *Reader's Digest* condensed version of an entire country. For mature travelers interested in seeing beautiful gardens and ornate exhibits in a relaxing atmosphere, it's a perfect stop. Those expecting rides and technological entertainment will be disappointed.

Owned indirectly by the People's Republic of China, Splendid China has had trouble competing in the Orlando market. While millions of tourists flock to the state, it's tough to wage head-to-head combat with Walt Disney World and the other parks, and few children want to visit anything with no rides or cartoon characters. Many mature travelers, of course, see smaller crowds and fewer children as Splendid China's strongest selling point.

If nothing else, Splendid China is authentic. It is a 76-acre travel brochure, recreating the best-loved Chinese art and architecture on a small scale. For those who will never visit China, it's the next-best-thing. More than 120 Chinese artisans created 60 scaled-down replicas of famous tourist sites. From the half-mile long Great Wall of China to the politically charged Potala Palace, home of the Dalai Lama, visitors can, in a small way, glimpse the grandeur of the originals while they marvel at Chinese craftsmanship.

Food remains a strong part of every culture and Splendid China has a number of excellent restaurants, albeit expensive. But eating Chinese food when in China — or in this case, when it *seems* as if you're

261

in China — adds to the total experience.

In addition to the exhibits and food, many Chinese performers — most Chinese citizens staying in the United States — recreate traditional folk dances. Immersed in the Chinese culture for a few hours, guests get a true taste of the country. When it first opened, visitors had to pay a single admission price to even access stores and restaurants. As a result of slow demand, however, guests may now visit Chinatown — the area by the front gate with shops and restaurants — free of charge. Should the park continue to lose money, more changes will inevitably follow.

WHEELCHAIR ACCESSIBILITY: Good. Since Splendid China has no rides, accessibility is not a problem. Wheelchair rental is available.

DIRECTIONS: Guests from both directions on I-4 should take exit #25B (US 192), the same exit used for the Magic Kingdom and Disney-MGM Studios. Those staying in Kissimmee/St. Cloud take US 192 west. Splendid China is three miles west of I-4 on the left. Look for the large dragon.

COSTS: Adults $23.55, children $13.90. information: (800) 244-6226.

UNIVERSAL STUDIOS FLORIDA

Universal Studios is second only to Disney World in tourist drawing power and prestige; its current expansion promises even more head-to-head competition. While most mature travelers know little about Nickelodeon Studios (though they might watch old television shows on Nick at Night), this large cable channel makes its home inside Universal Studios. In addition, other syndicated shows — again, not directed at the mature market — were filmed at Universal including *Superboy* and *Swamp Thing*.

With a sister park located in Hollywood, Universal Studios is first and foremost a theme park. In Hollywood, the memorabilia was actually used nearby in movies or TV, as were the backlot sets seen by tram. Florida also has memorabilia, but most was shipped from Hollywood. And, while some backlot sets were used in TV production, they were created for the park first.

The park is semi-themed, meaning it has distinctively different areas. It's confusing, however. It seems as if the designers could not decide if they were building a movie set that *looks* like New York City or if they were *actually* recreating New York City. Some buildings are one-dimensional facades, reminding guests that once they look past the exterior, movies use building fronts that must fool only the camera. But beside those movie buildings, a three-dimensional building might house a themed restaurant or ride. Those 3-D buildings break the movie-making fantasy and prove that Universal Studios is more theme park than movie set, while the facade-only structures break the it's-really-New-York fantasy. This mixed-bag detracts from a visit because guests are never sure which fantasy to go with.

But having said that, the confusing theme is only a minor distraction.

In general, Universal Studios has few action rides. Only Back To The Future, a motion simulator akin to Disney's Body Wars, really jerks riders around. Other attractions, such as Jaws or Earthquake, shake riders, but not enough to keep most mature travelers from enjoying them.

To avoid long lines at Universal, use the same tactics suggested for Disney parks: arrive early, wear good walking shoes, and start in the back of the park. Unfortunately, this also turns the day into a competition rather than an enjoyable outing. In addition, many people use this plan of attack, so you might discover that back-of-the-park lines are just as forbidding at mid-morning as others later in the day.

Consider the following suggestions:
• Ride Jaws, Back to the Future, and Terminator 2 3-D in the very early morning or in the evening.
• If you don't want to walk to the back of the park first thing, start with Terminator, then see E.T. or Kongfrontation.
• On arrival, make sure to pick up a daily schedule of events. Refer to it often for show times, adjusting your pace or taking a shopping break if a nearby show starts soon.
• Save Alfred Hitchcock and Murder She Wrote for the early afternoon. If you go too early, you meet the first-in-the-door crowd who have no plan and ride the first thing they see. If you wait too long, you meet the people who arrived early, rode everything, and now want something relaxing.
• See Nickelodeon Studios. It's not familiar to many mature travelers, but more TV production takes place on these sound stages than any-

where else in Orlando. In addition, seeing what kids now watch can be a real eye-opener to those who haven't followed the progression of children's programming.
• Eat lunch in the middle of the afternoon. It provides a break when the sun is hottest, you avoid the longest lines of the day and later, when everyone else eats dinner, you enjoy the shorter lines.

Think of the park as a giant egg-shape. The main entrance sits at the bottom of the egg with the widest part straight ahead and the tallest part off to your right. Most attractions sit along the egg-shaped walkway, though Nickelodeon Studios sits just outside. All of Universal can be seen with a minimum of back-tracking.

The following list outlines rides and details the amount of movement. Decide what you can take. The order assumes you make a right immediately after entering the park and continue to tour counter-clockwise.
• **Terminator 2 3-D.** Universal's newest attraction, it may also be the best. In truth, it's a theater presentation with no movement at all. The show artistically blends a 3-D movie with live action, seamlessly allowing actors to move from stage to screen. They also throw in live effects such as fog, drops of water, and other surprises. The bottom line: it's perfectly safe but expect to be startled more than once.
• **The Gory, Gruesome & Grotesque Horror Make-Up Show.** It's gory but not very scary. A talented crew combines education with humor to demonstrate how make-up artists create weird effects such as moving hands, oozing blood, and other visual heebie-jeebies. One or two things make you jump (because they startle you — not out of fear), but otherwise, most people over the age of five enjoy it. Indoors and air-conditioned.
• **E.T. Adventure.** Taken from the Steven Spielberg movie, the first half of the E.T. Adventure recreates movie scenes with riders playing the part of Elliot, E.T.'s earth-bound friend. At one point in the movie, police attempt to capture E.T., whom Elliot is transporting in the basket of his bicycle. In the E.T. Adventure, the vehicles imitate that scene and riders sit on a bicycle-styled seat vehicle. Attached at the top, the action takes place beside and below riders, creating the illusion of flight. For those who prefer a non-bike experience or who wish to remain in a wheelchair, selected cars look like spaceships and are more accessible. Indoors and air-conditioned for all but the first

parts of the waiting line.

• **Fievel's Playland.** Fievel is the hero of *An American Tale*, a cartoon roughly following an immigrant family's trip to America, circa 1900. In the movie, mice leave their homeland for the land of milk and honey, make the perilous boat trip across the Atlantic, and struggle to make a life in America. Fievel's Playland — a self-toured playground strictly for the under-ten set — is worth a look but offers little to anyone past puberty. Outdoors and partially shaded.

• **A Day In the Park With Barney.** Barney, the big purple dinosaur from television, holds a strange fascination for the preschool set. Debuting in 1995, the Barney attraction is the highlight of a park trip for many children. Adults, generally confused about the violet reptile's appeal, do not enjoy this live show as much. Indoors and air-conditioned.

• **Animal Actor's Stage.** Famous on-screen animals strut their stuff in this live-action stage show. The changing cast could include Mr. Ed, Lassie, and Beethoven. It's fun and many times unpredictable. Outdoors but shaded.

• **Back to the Future Ride.** Some say this is the best ride at Universal Studios; others won't touch it. The motion simulator rides at Universal Studios (Back to the Future and the Funtastic World of Hanna Barbera) operate differently than those at Disney World (Body Wars and Star Tours). Like Disney, Universal's ride vehicles also react to a movie, turning left when the movie pitches left and right when the movie jerks right. But rather than a small movie seen only by the riders in a single vehicle, Universal's movie screens are huge, serving a number of different vehicles at one time. That gives Universal's rides a depth and clarity not found at Disney. In addition, the Universal people don't mess around. The vehicle (a DeLoreon car) makes some monumental jerks. If you ride, hold on tight.

The story line roughly follows the movie of the same name. For some reason that's explained but that makes little sense, your car has to bump the car in front of you (a car that's in the movie). That fact is somewhat important and easy to miss. It's a wild ride and great for the roller coaster crowd. For the squeamish, save your scares for Jaws or Kongfrontation. Indoors and air-conditioned.

• **Wild, Wild, Wild West Stunt Show.** It may not be Broadway, but it's fun. They must have first decided what stunts to perform and then concocted a plot that fit the action. It's easy to follow and enjoyed by

265

any age group. Outdoors but shaded.

• **Jaws.** A long time in the making, Jaws is one of Universal Studios most popular rides. Taken from the movie of the same name, you don't have to know squat about the film to enjoy the adventure. Guests ride in a boat (of course), that rocks back and forth at different times, though the movement is not wild enough to deter anyone from riding. You might get wet depending on where you sit; a few will get very wet. Expect long lines from early in the morning through the afternoon, but they sometimes thin later in the day. Ride and line are outdoors but shaded.

• **Earthquake: The Big One.** Earthquake is the only action ride that includes movie-making information, showing how Hollywood builds models and uses matte paintings to create scenes. After seeing two educational pre-shows, the audience spills into a subway station and boards an awaiting subway train.

There is little motion to the train car. At one point, it falls a few inches and then rocks back and forth, simulating the 8.3 earthquake. The sudden drop startles guests because it's unexpected, but most scares are visual rather than physical. While the ride has good special effects, it's scarier than others, perhaps because it simulates a real disaster. Deep down, most people don't believe in giant apes, time travel, or even giant sharks. But earthquakes happen. The line is outdoors and shaded, but both preshows and the main ride take place indoors and are air-conditioned.

• **Beetlejuice's Graveyard Review.** Beetlejuice is a wacky dead guy, white-skinned, with disgusting stuff on his face. He's starred in a movie and had his own cartoon show, though you don't have to know anything about him to enjoy this theater performance. Hopefully, you like rock and roll. The stuff they play in this live show is generic and invigorating, incorporating lots of on-stage pizzazz. Everyone should enjoy it. The best seats go first, but back seats offer an acceptable view. It can also be fairly loud at times. Outdoors but shaded.

• **Kongfrontation.** Everyone knows King Kong, but if they don't, it doesn't matter. This technologically magnificent ride takes scared New Yorkers (that's you) on a cable car ride as they escape the giant ape. It should come as no surprise that riders do not avoid him altogether. The cable car rocks some and, at one point, seems to fall in slow-motion, but all-in-all, it's a tame ride that anyone can enjoy.

Indoors and air-conditioned.

• **Murder She Wrote.** Unlike pure entertainment rides, Murder She Wrote educates viewers on movie post production techniques. Post production covers all those things done after filming, such as dubbing, editing, adding background music, etc. In this case, they use the TV show *Murder She Wrote* as an example, moving the audience through a series of four theaters to show how a single scene can be manipulated. They assume you've seen *Murder She Wrote* at least once. If you have not, it still makes sense, but you miss a few inside jokes. Because it's indoors, air-conditioned, and takes over half an hour to view, it's a good choice for the hottest part of the day.

• **Alfred Hitchcock: The Art of Making Movies.** Half a tribute to Alfred Hitchcock and half an explanation of a movie director's job, this attraction throws in a little horror to shake things up. The presentation takes place in a couple of theaters, including one that reenacts the famous shower scene in *Psycho*. No one should be bothered, but those who hate horror and/or Alfred Hitchcock movies might want to pass. It's also not recommended for children under 13. Due to the length of the air-conditioned show, it's another good choice for the hottest hours of the day.

• **The Funtastic World of Hanna Barbera**. Like Back to the Future, this ride is a motion simulator. Groups of riders sit in individual cars, each watching a large movie that plays in front. After seat belts are fastened, the cars rise upward about a foot and then bend left and right in response to the action on the screen. There's a separate area for wheelchair guests and those who want to view the movie without being tossed all around. By opting for the non-moving seats, fearful guests can see what a motion simulator does and decide if they're willing to chance it. Line is outside but shaded; attraction is indoors and air-conditioned.

• **Nickelodeon Studios Walking Tour.** If you don't know any kids in the three- to fifteen-year old age group, the Nickelodeon shows and sets won't look remotely familiar. The game shows on Nickelodeon have little resemblance to *Wheel of Fortune* or *Jeopardy*. The Nickelodeon Studios tour does, however, show a working studio. As an educational tour, it doesn't compare to Disney-MGM Studio's tour, but it usually has a lot more filming going on. For kids too old for Barney, it's the highlight of their trip to Orlando. If you do want to tour Nickelodeon, try to visit during normal business hours since that's when most filming takes place. Tour is indoors and air-conditioned; line is outdoors but shaded.

• **Dynamite Nights Stunt Spectacular.** An exciting presentation on the lagoon, the accent is on thrills as the Universal folks bring an action-adventure movie to life. Bad guys in boats chase good guys in boats. Things crash, explode, burn, and ultimately resolve themselves. The plot is simple and immaterial. Central spots with a view of the entire lake are best, but expect crowds to start forming at least a half hour before show time. Try not to stand on either end of the lake (by the Wild, Wild, Wild West Stunt Show or near Mel's Diner) where your view of the entire lake is obstructed. Additionally, when the show ends, crowds stream like ants for their parked cars. If you have the stamina, find a nice place to relax or, if you're a die-hard shopper, fight the crowds for souvenirs at still-open stores near the entrance.

• **Smaller Shows.** Smaller shows take place throughout Universal Studios, outdoors and with no seating. Rocky and Bullwinkle, the famous cartoon duo, and The Blues Brothers perform on New York Streets. A walk-through exhibit near the park entrance, titled *Lucy, A Tribute*, features costumes and memorabilia from the life of Lucille (Ricardo) Ball. In addition, recent Universal films ship props and sets to the park as soon as shooting is completed. The movie gets extra publicity from the park's advertising and the park has something new each summer to attract visitors.

There are a number of restaurants at Universal Studios serving everything from the standard theme park fare — burgers, shakes and fries — to more exotic entrees. While Universal has upscale waitress-service restaurants, nothing is top-of-the-line gourmet. Consider Lombard's Landing for a better meal. For non-American food, visit the New York backlot or, for fast food, the food court located next to the Animal Actors Stage Show. Food prices are all higher than that found off-site — expensive, but not quite high enough to call it price-gouging.

The Hard Rock Cafe is Universal's most famous eatery and the first themed restaurant in Orlando. With sister restaurants in large cities around the globe, The Hard Rock celebrates rock and roll. Inside, music memorabilia lines the walls including gold records, clothing, and band instruments. The Hard Rock sits to the right of Universal Studios' main entrance and can be visited without park admission. Parking is also free. Expect fairly expensive prices for salads, specialty items, and basic burger-and-fries entrees.

Shopping inside Universal Studios follows the theme of nearby rides. A gift shop at the exit from Kongfrontation, for example, sells wildlife T-shirts, stuffed animals, and jewelry — heavy on the gorilla decor. Near Back to the Future, they sell high-tech toys. Some merchandise reflects classic Universal films.

Universal's expansion plans rival only Disney. The final product, to be called Universal City, will include a number of resorts, recreation areas, theme parks, and restaurants. Currently, a huge tract of land next to I-4 has been cleared for their latest project, a second theme park called Islands of Adventure. Set to premier in 1999, the new park will have an area called Seuss Landing dedicated to the books of Dr. Seuss, a Jurassic Park ride, Popeye's hometown of Sweethaven Park, an area featuring Marvel Comic heroes, and other yet-to-be-announced sections.

In 1998, Universal's E-Zone, located near the current park, will give Downtown Disney some competition. In addition to revamping the Hard Rock Café, other restaurants, bars, movie theaters, and shops will entice visitors to spend their nights partying. Subject to change, the zone will include B.B. King's Blues Club (restaurant and lounge), a 16-screen movie complex, E! Entertainment Television Production Center (television studio for E! television), Emeril's of New Orleans (Creole "kicky cuisine" restaurant), Marvel Mania (comic book-themed restaurant), NASCAR Café (officially sanctioned NASCAR restaurant), Pat O'Brien's (New Orleans-style lounge), and Bob Marley — A Tribute to Freedom (Jamaican music and history).

Hotels will be added in stages until the year 2005, and long-term plans call for four upscale resorts, an 18-hole championship golf course, a tennis complex, and the world's largest parking garage. As at Disney, all guest areas will be connected by a mass transit system that includes boats, trams, ferries, buses, and people-moving systems. If all goes as planned, Orlando will build a small rail line from Universal to Disney by way of International Drive and the Orange County Convention Center. That means that convention visitors can stay at Universal's top-of-the-line hotels or, if they prefer to stay on International Drive, easily commute to Universal's series of bars for nighttime entertainment.

WHEELCHAIR ACCESSIBILITY: Wheelchairs are welcome at Universal Studios. Selected attractions, such as Back to the Future, demand some upper body strength and the ability to transfer into the ride vehicle.

DIRECTIONS: Universal Studios is easy to find if you can follow signs. Two exits from I-4 will work indirectly. Expect confusion. After exiting, you may find yourself traveling *away* from the park, circling, and then returning. Use exits 29 or 30B off I-4 and, again, keep an eye out for signs. Parking costs about $6 per day.

COSTS: A one-day admission costs $38.50 for adults, $31 for children (3-9), and under 3 free. Membership in AARP will get a 15% discount, per person, for a party up to six. An AAA membership will do the same. For more information, call Universal Studios at (407) 363-8000. A separate package, the Vacation Value Pass, offers unlimited admission for five consecutive days to Sea World, Universal Studios, and Wet 'n Wild. It costs $89.95 for adults and $72.95 for children. For more Vacation Value Pass information, call Universal City Travel Company at (800) 224-3838.

BUSCH GARDENS, TAMPA BAY

Busch Gardens is almost too far from Central Florida to include it under "other attractions," but with its major advertising presence along Florida highways and its unique (until Disney opens Animal Kingdom) product, it deserves mention. Unlike Disney, many Busch Garden rides are standard amusement park thrills, like roller coasters and stationary beasts that spin in tiny circles while jerking you up and down. Kid stuff. But because they heavily feature these rides in advertising, it's easy to dismiss the park out of hand, not realizing that they also have shows, themed lands, tame rides, and wild animal exhibits. Furthermore, their action rides siphon off kids and young adults, leaving shows and animal exhibits accessible to mature travelers. Popular with the high number of seniors living on Florida's Gulf Coast, the Anheuser-Busch Company reported that of their total visitors in 1994, an incredible 26% were over the age of 65.

Built in 1959, the park is not only the first Anheuser-Busch theme park, but it also predates Walt Disney World. It's also big. Even if you make a single complete circle around the park with little back-tracking, plan to spend considerable time on your feet. Much of the park has a garden feel, shaded by mature trees. Older areas are located near the entrance and have more animal exhibits. Areas in the back of the park feature newer rides, such as Kumba, their killer roller coaster. The newest land, Egypt, exists to the far right of the entrance.

Animals are housed in two separate areas. The first is a large grassy field, called the Serengeti Plain, where most grazing animals live in a natural setting. Explored by train, monorail, or skyride, it's the most zoo-like section of the park. Future plans call for the exhibit to be expanded further with more realistic habitats and a walk-through tour that recreates villages of Africa. All other animals live in smaller cages throughout the ride area. Guests explore some exhibits, like the "Myombe Reserve: The Great Ape Domain," by path. Other animals live in a cage beside the walkway while still others are seen only by guests waiting in line for a ride, the queue winding around a cage.

That can be confusing, but discovering animals at every turn also adds to the adventure. Planning your day becomes easier too. If you want to see a show at 1:00 and it's 12:15, you simply spend a little more time viewing animals. With various exhibits and no time-limit on watching zoo creatures, the clock does not rule your visit.

On its map, Busch Gardens is broken down into separate lands, notably the Congo, the Crown Colony, Egypt, Morocco, Nairobi, Serengeti Plain, Stanleyville, Timbuktu, the Bird Garden, and a new children's area, Land of the Dragons. Unlike Disney's Magic Kingdom where there is a clear distinction between Tomorrowland and Fantasyland, most Busch Gardens visitors don't appreciate the difference between, for example, Nairobi and Stanleyville. No clear boundary separates one from the other. For most visitors, it's best to think of the entire park as Africa and leave other distinctions for the tour map. Since most of Busch Gardens' rides are amusement park attractions, they're not listed here. Only one ride — Questor — is a motion simulator, meaning you can't see the ride from the outside and, while it goes nowhere, the ride vehicle jerks around a lot. All other high motion rides are visible from the queue, some painfully so. One note: for those who love roller coasters, the front seat of their newest roller coaster, Montu, is worth the extra wait-time in line.

The following shows currently play at Busch Gardens:

• **Hollywood on Ice.** Six skating segments create a retrospective on the history of Hollywood, from the silent films to today's movies. It's a well-done song-and-dance program. Playing in Morocco's Tangier Theater, the show is indoors and air-conditioned.

• **Bavarian Colony Dancers and Band.** Timbuktu's Festhaus provides German dining in an African setting. In other words, it's out-of-place. But if you're willing to overlook a bit of Bavaria in the heart of the dark continent, it's a fun show and a good place to enjoy German food. Also playing in Timbuktu's Festhaus and alternating with the German show, the "International Show" features other countries' traditional dances. Indoors and air-conditioned.

• **World of Birds.** Different breeds of birds strut their stuff, from macaws and cockatoos to birds of prey. Outdoors but shaded.

• **Morocco's Marrakesh Theater.** Different shows play here but are usually music revues. Outdoors but shaded.

• **Dolphins of the Deep.** It's not Sea World, but the bottlenose dolphins jump, dance, and wave. Outdoors, mostly shaded.

• **Stanleyville Theater.** Variety show. Outdoors but shaded.

• **Children's Theater.** Located in Land of the Dragons, this is kids-only. Outdoors but shaded.

• **Tut's Tomb.** Not a show exactly, Tut's Tomb is a replica of the tomb of Tutankhamen, Egypt's boy king. With artifacts stored just as they were when the original tomb was discovered by Howard Carter in the early 1920's, the boy king himself narrates the walking tour and describes each artifact's place in Egyptian history. Educational and, unlike the original tomb, air conditioned, this high quality, history-based exhibit generally has a short line and is ignored by the roller coaster crowd.

Food at Busch Gardens is plentiful, most of it fast food burgers and fries, but with other interesting spots such as the German Festhaus. For an upscale meal, they have one full-service restaurant, the Crown Colony House. While not five-star material, it's a pleasant place to eat and watch animals roam on the Serengeti Plain. Prices are on the high side of reasonable.

WHEELCHAIR ACCESSIBILITY: Generally good to shows and animal viewing. Most rides, including the train and skyride, demand an ability to transfer from wheelchair to vehicle. Many action rides are not accessible to wheelchairs. Wheelchair and stroller rental is available.

DIRECTIONS: Take I-4 west from the Orlando area for about an hour. Exit north onto I-75. Take the Fowler Ave. exit, (#54) and follow directional signs.

COSTS: $38.45 adults, $34.60 senior citizen (a 10% discount for those over 55), $32.05 child. Parking $4.00 per day. Information: (813) 987-5082.

CHURCH STREET STATION

Not a theme park like the others, Church Street has restaurants, lounges, and stores located in a refurbished section of downtown Orlando. "Church Street *Station*" represents the core business that most people know, a complex of 50 specialty shops, three restaurants, and five bars that simultaneously serve alcohol and entertainment to the country crowd, the disco crowd, and the Ragtime crowd. But a number of other businesses, also located on Church Street (the street existed *before* the attraction), siphon off some of the ever-increasing masses, primarily the younger flock. Terror On Church Street, for example, is a haunted house that few older travelers pay to visit. Specialty bars, such as Hooter's and Fat Tuesdays, find their own crowd.

After 5 p.m., Church Street Station charges a single price for admission to all show-bars. The area itself is not enclosed, meaning anyone may visit the stores and restaurants. At each lounge entrance, paying guests show their pass for admittance. If you prefer to shop in a unique atmosphere and, while you're in Orlando, see what Church Street Station looks like, visit in the early afternoon when crowds are thin. Enjoy the decor, inhale the atmosphere, and preview the style. But for good entertainment, visit at night. If you drink, expect to pay resort prices.

Three restaurants serve guests. Lili Marlene's is the most elite, followed by Cracker's Oyster Bar, and the Cheyenne Barbeque. But the reason most people visit Church Street is for the bars and entertainment. Those include:

• **Rosie O'Grady's Good Time Emporium.** Probably the most

famous bar at Church Street, Rosie O'Grady's offers a little bit of the Old West coupled with Jazz, Ragtime, and theatrics.

Rosie's is fun. Certain things, like the can-can girls, are not unique to Orlando. But unlike other tourist bars, Rosie O'Grady's band plays good music. Tried-and-true Dixieland jazz has a fresh feel against a backdrop of ornate wood moldings and grand chandeliers. While people of all ages visit, it's a favorite hang-out for many mature travelers.

• **Cheyenne Saloon and Opera House.** Country music cuts across generational lines better than other forms of music. In the Cheyenne Saloon and Opera House, a detailed western motif with cut glass doors comes dangerously close to elegant. Those who don't care for country music should still take a quick walk-through. Those who like country music don't leave. As one of the best — albeit expensive — country and western bars in Central Florida, it attracts a local crowd too. Featuring quality acts nightly, expect elbow-to-elbow crowds, notably on the weekends.

• **Phineas Phogg's Balloon Works.** Disco at its finest, featuring darkened lighting, heavy downbeats, and dancers younger than 35.

• **Apple Annie's.** With no entertainment and light background music, Apple Annie's is perfect for those who want to talk and/or take a break from the more active lounges.

• **Orchid Garden Ballroom.** This rock 'n' roll lounge appeals to some mature travelers, though everyone should stop by to see the decor. A statue of Marilyn Monroe near the entrance features her famous pose — fighting to push her dress down while a wayward gust of air fans it in all directions.

WHEELCHAIR ACCESSIBILITY: In general, sections of each lounge are accessible by wheelchair though certain balconies may be off limits. They do not rent wheelchairs.

DIRECTIONS: Because it is located on a refurbished section of downtown Orlando, Church Street Station is not as easy to get to as other Central Florida attractions. From I-4, guests from both directions should take exit 38 (Anderson St.). Turn left onto Boone Ave. Left onto South Street. Then right on Garland Ave. Watch for signs at every turn.

Church Street Station does not have a private parking lot, but ample spaces are available nearby in Orlando city parking garages.

The easiest to find sits beneath I-4 itself. (Church Street Station starts only a few hundred feet from the interstate.) Valet parking attendants will wave you in as you get close to Church Street. If you want valet parking, pull in. If you prefer to save the extra change and park the car yourself, ignore them and continue on.

COSTS: $16.95 for adults, $13.95 for seniors (AARP membership), $10.95 for children (4-12). Information: (407) 422-2434.

KENNEDY SPACE CENTER VISITOR'S CENTER

Exploring Kennedy Space Center is exciting for anyone who remembers the United States' first manned flight into outer space or Neil Armstrong's walk on the moon. It's also exciting to anyone who hasn't. The thrill of space exploration — of taking off into the unknown and facing certain death should anything go wrong — still lives in the collective memory of most mature travelers.

Studying old rockets and space memorabilia and moon rocks is more than intellectually stimulating. It commemorates an era, dredging up feelings of pride and sometimes fear. And visiting the Space Center is a rare commodity in tourist-heavy Central Florida — it's free. Three IMAX movies — a film technique that produces sharper images — and a bus tour (highly recommended) cost a few dollars each, but it's still possible to visit for a day, pay nothing, learn a lot, and have a good time. In addition to the IMAX films, the space center shows regular movies that detail the history of space exploration. They have spacecraft replicas for hands-on exploration and even maintain an art gallery with mixed-media work, all of which relates to space exploration.

In 1996, their name changed from "Spaceport U.S.A." to "NASA Kennedy Space Center's Visitor's Center." The name "Spaceport" confused too many visitors who didn't realize it was the *official* visitor's center, thanks in part to local businesses that used the word "Spaceport" to sell cars, fast food, and everything else. The new name, while less original and fun, clearly describes its mission to visitors.

WHEELCHAIR ACCESSIBILITY: Good. Guests may remain in wheelchairs throughout. Wheelchair rental not available.

DIRECTIONS: It takes about one hour to reach Kennedy Space Center from the Disney World area. It's located on U.S. Highway 1 on NASA Parkway, 10 miles south of Titusville. Directions are well marked from Disney. Take the Beeline Expressway east, exit #28 off I-4. Expect to pay a couple dollars in tolls. From there, follow the signs.
COSTS: Free parking and museum exploration. IMAX movies cost $4.00 for adults, $2.00 for children (3-11). Kennedy Space Center bus tours cost $7.00 for adults and $4 for children. For information on tour departure times, call (407) 452-2121.

DINNER SHOWS, GATORS, AND OTHER ORLANDO STUFF

Central Florida competition is fierce for tourist business and one successful venture inspires duplicates. Dinner shows come and go, each new theme hoping to tap into tourist's latent desires. For specific information on an existing attraction, call the numbers listed after each one. Most prices are quoted before tax. While senior rates are quoted where appropriate, many of these offer a smorgasbord of discounts for everything from AARP membership to AAA membership. When buying tickets, mention any group affiliation that may net you a few dollars off and don't be afraid to ask a general question like, "What groups receive discounts on admission?"

• **Arabian Nights.** The name is a bit of a misnomer. While it has an Arabian theme, the actual dinner show highlights horses of the world, both Arabian and others. Guests sit in tiers facing a dirt courtyard. During the meal, horses strut, race, do dressage, and entertain the crowds. The show's loosely defined plot allows a genie to circle the world, watching horses of every kind. It's great for horse lovers; less wonderful for those who are not. Located at the intersection of I-4 and US 192. Adults $36.95, children 3-11, $23.95. They also offer various discounts throughout the year. Information: (407) 239-9223 or (800) 553-6116.
• **Central Florida Zoo.** While this zoo cannot compete with Busch Gardens or the big city zoos found across America, the price is reasonable. Explored on boardwalks, an area in the back winds through natural Florida wetlands. For those wishing to relax for a day, it's a

pleasant escape. Take I-4 east to exit # 52, highway 17-92. Turn right. Adults $7.00, seniors $4.00, children (3-12) $3.00. Information: (407) 323-4450.

• **Citrus Tower.** A pre-Disney tourist landmark, Citrus Tower rises high over orange groves, allowing visitors to see for miles across Florida's flat landscape. Candy, food, and ice cream are served alongside a citrus packing house. Take I-4 west to US 27. Follow signs. Adults $3.00, children under sixteen free when accompanied by paying adult. Information: (904) 394-4061.

• **Daytona USA.** About an hour from Walt Disney World, the Daytona International Speedway is a strong draw for race fans but, before Daytona USA opened in 1996, there was little to see. Featuring displays, games, and movies, Daytona USA focuses on the sport. Located one mile east of I-95 at 1801 International Speedway Boulevard in Daytona Beach. Adults $10.00, seniors $8.00, children (6-12) $5.00. Information: (904) 254-2700.

• **Fantasy of Flight.** This museum-styled park appeals mainly to those interested in aerial history, though most visitors enjoy flight simulators that allow guests to feel what it's like to fly an airplane. Adults $10.95, seniors $9.95, children (5-12) $7.95. Information: (941) 984-3500.

• **Gatorland.** Open before Walt Disney World, Gatorland grew thanks to its proximity to the famous mouse. In a back section of Gatorland, guests view alligators in a near-natural setting. In the front of the park, in large pens, the sheer number of alligators astounds most people. They also host a "Gator Jumparoo," where they string dead chickens to a chain, suspend them over a pit of alligators, and coax the giant reptiles to jump for their dinner. If it wasn't so fascinating, it would be disgusting. Located on S. Orange Blossom Trail (Highway 441) Adults $10.95, seniors $8.76, children (3-11) $7.95. Information: (407) 855-5496 or (800) 393-5297.

• **Jungle Adventures.** Located between Orlando and the Atlantic Coast, Jungle Adventures feels more authentic than parks closer to Disney that see a high number of tourists who want to see a gator. Convenient only if included in a trek to the beach or Kennedy Space Center, it's a pleasant diversion. Adults $9.97, seniors and children (3-11) $7.50. Information: (407) 568-2885.

• **Jungleland.** Located on US 192 between Walt Disney World and Kissimmee, Jungleland is fronted by a huge concrete alligator and contains over 400 animals and birds. Adults $9.95, children (3-11)

$6.95. Information: (407) 396-1012.

• **King Henry's Feast.** A kid-heavy dinner show that features fire-eaters, jugglers, and comedians in a Tudor setting. Adults $34.95, children (3-11) $21.95. Information: (407) 351-5151.

• **Medieval Times.** The legend and times of King Arthur are recreated in a dinner show featuring knights jousting and fair maidens performing. Located on US 192 in Kissimmee. Adults $34.95, seniors $31.55, children (3-12) $22.95. Information: (800) 229-8300.

• **Ripley's Believe It or Not Museum.** If you like weird stuff, stop in. Some exhibits amaze, like the writings on the head of a pin. Some rank up there with freak shows at the carnival. Either way, it's a feast for the mind. Located on International Drive, most traffic can be avoided from the Disney or Kissimmee area by taking I-4 to the Beeline Expressway, then exiting at International Drive and traveling north. Adults $9.95, children(4-12) $6.95. Information: (800) 998-4418.

• **Silver Springs.** Most water in Central Florida has a brownish color, but a number of crystal clear waterways form when natural springs bubble up from deep within the earth. Silver Springs is one of these natural springs and alligators, fish, and an occasional manatee swim in their waters. Florida's "oldest theme park," Silver Springs is famous for glass-bottom boat tours, but it also has a reptile institute, jeep tours, and a small zoo. It takes about an hour and a half to reach Silver Springs from Walt Disney World by way of the Florida turnpike. Adults $27.95, children (3-10) $18.95. For Florida residents, the rates are: adults $15.00, seniors $13.50, children $10.00. Information in Florida: (800) 234-7458. Outside Florida: (352) 236-2121.

UN-TOURIST THINGS WORTH YOUR TIME

17

281 Wekiwa Springs State Park

282 The Rivership Romance on the
St. Johns River

283 Harry P. Leu Gardens

284 Lake Kissimmee State Park

284 Bok Tower Gardens

285 Blue Spring State Park

Chapter Seventeen

UN-TOURIST THINGS WORTH YOUR TIME

A number of small attractions call themselves the "real Florida," the "natural Florida," or "the original Florida," and they sell everything from fishing trips to swamp buggy excursions and airboat rides. But the "real Florida" can be found not far from Disney World and it can be explored for very little money.

Florida's nickname, The Sunshine State, is a bit of a misnomer. The fact is, on most summer afternoons, the blue skies of morning give way to black clouds, lightning, thunder, and rain. Storms don't last long, but the daily watering produces lush vegetation that, in turn, produces an abundance of animal life. In Florida, birds are bigger, fish are bigger, and the lizards... well, you know.

Because of the rain, proximity to sea level, and rolling hills, Central Florida has more lakes than any other area of the United States. In relatively flat areas, water covers the ground for months at a time, forming wetlands. This unique land — wet much of the time, damp almost all the time — supports a vast array of life and is protected from development by state law. To see these wetlands and other natural environments, visitors can either book a boat ride or explore on foot in national, state, and local parks. They're not hard to find. But since no one makes big money off them (There's no theme park called "Real Florida Land"), they must be sought out.

The following attractions make excellent day trips, best explored between visits to the major attractions. All require a certain amount of walking, but without the hot asphalt, thick crowds, and long lines. Not all attractions are natural — notably Harry P. Leu Gardens and Bok Tower Gardens — but all rely more on nature than man.

280

For those who want to see alligators, they live in virtually every river and lake in Florida, but you have to look closely. Unless they're sunning themselves — mainly during the colder months — or actively pursuing dinner, alligators rarely move, sticking only their nose and eyes out of the water close to the shoreline. If you look for movement, you'll probably be disappointed. If you look for a bumpy log sticking out of the water, you stand a better chance for success.

One more word on alligators: they're not dangerous. Not much, anyway. In Florida, lightning kills more people than alligator attacks, and most attacks occur to people who foolishly (and illegally) feed them. Alligators — none too bright — cannot tell where food ends and human hands begin.

Insects are also not as bad as people fear most of the time. Depending on weather and season of the year, however, they can get thick in spots. Mosquitoes come out around dusk and again in the early morning hours, so daytime is best for touring. While Walt Disney World and other Orlando attractions spray and use natural methods to control insects, the "real Florida" does not. So pack a good insect spray, especially if you plan to tour the Florida Everglades where they call the little bloodsuckers their "swamp angels."

The following list is not all-inclusive, but concentrates on parks within an hour of Walt Disney World.

WEKIWA SPRINGS STATE PARK

Wekiwa is a Native American word meaning "spring of water." Wekiva (with a "V") means "flowing water." Both words are used in the area, somewhat interchangeably, so don't be confused.

Wekiwa Springs State Park offers a complete sampling of the "real Florida." The spring itself pumps 42 million gallons of crystal clear water per day from the depths of the earth. With year-round temperatures in the low 70's, it's ideal for swimming. The spring looks like a spa or health retreat, with the water forming an attractive contrast against a canopy of trees. A park walkway winds through different Florida landscapes, from wetlands to hills.

For the adventurous, canoe rentals are available. The Wekiva River is like rivers farther north with solid banks rather than meandering wetlands, but palm trees, Spanish moss, and indigenous wildlife make it a uniquely Florida waterway. For those wary of paddling, you don't have to travel far from the canoe rental area to get an "out in the wilderness" feeling.

There's a playground for children, campsites for those who RV, and eight miles of riding trails for horse connoisseurs. Campsites include water hookups, restrooms, and a dump station. The stout of heart can also enjoy thirteen miles of hiking trails. For a full day of relaxing exploration, pack a lunch (or buy sandwiches) and stay all day.

WHEELCHAIR ACCESSIBILITY: Wheelchair guests may enjoy the park, but will find it difficult to get around in spots since paths and walkways follow the shape of the land.
DIRECTIONS: From the Walt Disney World area, take I-4 east through downtown Orlando, and get off at exit # 49 (SR 434, Longwood). Drive west. Make a right onto Wekiva Springs Road. After a few miles, the park is on the right.
COSTS: Admission is $3.25 per carload, up to eight people. (407) 884-2009.

THE RIVERSHIP ROMANCE ON THE ST. JOHNS RIVER

The St. Johns River is, for most East Coast folks traveling I-4, just another of the many rivers that flows under one of the many bridges that they cross en route to Walt Disney World. But this unique Florida river (it's the world's only one other than the Nile that flows north) is an ideal way to see the real Florida for those who also wish to dress comfortably and enjoy a meal or cocktails from the comfort of a deck chair or air-conditioned table.

Most sailings on The Rivership Romance last three or four hours, with either lunch or dinner served en route. At times, they schedule special two-day cruises that include an overnight hotel room.

WHEELCHAIR ACCESSIBILITY: Poor. Wheelchair bound guests may enjoy the cruise, but the bathrooms are not accessible. Guests must be able to transfer from wheelchair to toilet.
DIRECTIONS: Take I-4 East from the Walt Disney World area. Pass through downtown Orlando and continue for about fifteen minutes. Take exit # 51 (SR 46) and go right (east) about four miles.

Boat docks are on the left near downtown Sanford.
COSTS: Lunch cruises, depending on length, run $35.00 to $45.00. Friday and Saturday evening cruises cost $50.00. They do not offer a senior discount, but AAA members receive a 10% discount off all fares. (800) 423-7401.

In addition to the Rivership Romance, other St. Johns boat tours set out daily and are located nearby at St. Johns River Cruises and Tours. Specializing in two-hour nature tours conducted by a trained guide, they also offer sunset cruises, airboat rides, and charters. Call for more information. (407) 330-1612

HARRY P. LEU GARDENS

Located in Orlando proper, Harry P. Leu Gardens has a deep South, antebellum feel. While most Florida attractions emulate the Caribbean, this reminds visitors of Florida's connection to the land of Robert E. Lee.

The gardens take up 47 acres on Lake Rowena. Rolling hills, sculpted lawns, rose gardens, walkways, Spanish moss, and 100-year-old buildings preserve the well-to-do lifestyle of early Florida inhabitants. Unlike Cypress Gardens and Epcot Center, the entire complex has the feel of a home, with camellias, palms, orchids, and other flowers arranged as if people still lived in the house and paid servants to tend the estate. Vast expanses of lawn join the various buildings.

Included in the house tour are antiques and memorabilia from the days before air conditioning, when the first "re-located Northerners" moved south. While the main buildings are now air-conditioned, they still depict a rich-folks version of early Florida history.

WHEELCHAIR ACCESSIBILITY: Fair. There are few steps but many hills. To tour the second floor of the home, guests must walk up stairs.
DIRECTIONS: From I-4 take Exit #41 onto State Road 50 (Colonial Drive). Go east. At Highway 17/92, turn left. Travel north for 3/4 mile, then turn right (east) onto Virginia Drive. Look for signs.
COST: Adults $3.00; Children (6-16) $1.00. (407) 246-2620.

LAKE KISSIMMEE STATE PARK

If the rich lived at Harry P. Leu Gardens, then the turn-of-the-century working stiffs lived in cow camps, found today at Lake Kissimmee State Park. The camp recreates an 1876 stop-over point used by cowboys who drove herds across Florida, including a stilt house and open pit fire. More important than buildings, however, is the cow camp atmosphere created by rangers dressed and acting the part of cattlemen. They don't acknowledge the existence of modern conveniences and, while telling tales of early Florida, serve up a bit of history along with a cup of boiled coffee "so hot you can't point at it and so thick it will float a lead bullet." The rest of Lake Kissimmee State Park is natural wilderness. Patient hikers can see a number of native birds including the bald eagle. Florida panthers also call the area home.

Lake Kissimmee, Lake Tiger, and Lake Rosalie form the headwaters to the Everglades. With 13 miles of hiking trails, fishing, canoeing, boating, and camping, Lake Kissimmee State Park is a great place to escape the Central Florida tourist rat-race.

WHEELCHAIR ACCESSIBILITY: Fair. While accessible, it has all the pitfalls associated with boardwalks and paths through the woods. **DIRECTIONS:** While relatively easy to find, it's about an hour's drive from the Walt Disney World area. Take I-4 west to Exit #23 and follow 27 south. At Lake Wales, turn east (left) on SR 60. Look for signs. **COST:** $3.25 per vehicle. (813) 696-1112.

BOK TOWER GARDENS

Florida has its own mountain range, a fact unknown to most of the world. Of course, the range is not too high nor does it have sharp cliffs. There is, none-the-less, an unmistakable rise in the land that runs north to south called the Lake Wales Ridge.

On top of a peak in this "mountain" range — the peninsula's highest point at 298-feet — is Bok Tower Gardens, centered by a giant carillon tower built of pink and gray Georgia marble and coquina stone (a seashell mixture) from St. Augustine. The carillon consists of 57 bronze bells that play each day at 3 p.m. Unfortunately, visitors may not tour the tower itself.

The surrounding 128 acres are a landscape garden, meaning that the gardeners mix plant colors and textures to create a botanical work of art, just as a painter mixes colors on canvas. Unlike most Central Florida gardens, the garden does not strive for plant diversity over cohesion and individual plants are not as important as the overall beauty of the park. It's a masterpiece created with living things.

As a landscape garden, Bok Tower does not have the feel of "real Florida," though one area with a path is left in its natural state. Rather, the park feels like an elegant estate, with rich shades of green and pockets of flowers. Squirrels expect handouts and can be very friendly, depending on your opinion of squirrels.

WHEELCHAIR ACCESSIBILITY: Fair. Many sidewalks are completely accessible but a couple mulched paths make getting-around more difficult.
DIRECTIONS: Take Exit #23 and follow US 27 south. You can see the tower on the left before you arrive, located near the crossroads for SR 60. Watch for signs.
COST: $5.00 for adults, $4.00 seniors, children (5-12) $1.00, under 5 free. (941) 676-1408.

BLUE SPRING STATE PARK

Another of Florida's natural springs, Blue Spring has one thing the others do not — manatees. It is one of the few places in Central Florida where visitors can expect to see these creatures in the wild. And, because the water is crystal clear, guests can see the entire animal. Unfortunately, this holds only in the winter months when the water of the St. Johns River turns colder. The manatees live in Blue Springs but must travel into the river for food. If you're visiting between December and March, call first to confirm that the manatees are there. Camping, picnicking, swimming, and canoeing are also available.

WHEELCHAIR ACCESSIBILITY: Fair. All spring areas are explored by boardwalk with slight inclines at times.
DIRECTIONS: Take I-4 West and travel about 20 minutes past Orlando. Take exit #53 and follow the signs to Orange City.
COSTS: $3.25 per vehicle, up to eight people. (904) 775-3663

TRAVEL TIPS FOR
FIRST-TIMERS

287 Flying

291 Trains

292 Car Rentals

295 Hotel Rooms

Chapter Eighteen

TRAVEL TIPS FOR FIRST-TIMERS

For some people, a trip to Orlando is their first major vacation. While they may have camped, driven to the beach, or spent a week with relatives during past vacations, the trek to Walt Disney World somehow ranks as a bigger adventure. It's certainly more expensive.

For some, an Orlando vacation is also their first time flying in an airplane or renting a car. The following descriptions hold no surprises for seasoned travelers, but for those who travel infrequently, they answer basic questions about the trip.

FLYING

If planning to fly for the first time, a good travel agent is invaluable. If you don't know a good agent, ask friends and neighbors for a recommendation. With thousands of airline fares that change daily — and 50 rules and regulations that accompany each one — even the best travel agent won't have all the answers memorized. But at least he/she will know where to look. With the cards stacked against them, the general public has little choice but to trust an agent's expertise.

If you live close to a small airport served by only one or two airlines, you can call the airlines directly for information and reservations. In general, an airline's reservationist won't volunteer as much price or flight information as a travel agent. For example, if the lowest published airfare is not available on the dates you request, the airline reservationist may quote you a higher price without explaining that you could save money by leaving a day earlier. A good travel agent should do that. In addition, a travel agent can issue boarding passes, saving time when you arrive at the airport on your day of departure.

Consider the following when making a reservation:

• When requesting information from a travel agent or airline, ask what the lowest fare is. Explain that you're very flexible and just want to find the best deal. While you may not wish to abide by all the rules that make that low fare possible, finding the dollar amount gives you a starting point. You might be willing to pay $40 more to leave on the date and time you want, for example, but if that convenience costs an additional $140, you may be willing to alter your plans.

• Airlines have frequent price wars but that may not do you any good. Price wars are best if a) you travel off-season, b) you're flexible with travel dates, and c) you're making reservations for travel within the next four months. Generally, fares drop just before an anticipated slow season. That means if you're planning an August trip in February, you won't find any bargains yet, though you may find some in April or May.

Also, not every seat on every flight is given up to a bargain fare. On low demand flights (evenings, for example), perhaps 40% of the seats are given over to bargain fares because the airline knows it will have trouble filling the plane. On flights departing at high demand times (morning non-stops, for example), only 5% of the seats may be assigned bargain-status because the airline knows it does not have to discount seats to fill the plane. (This is where you need that knowledgeable travel agent.) If the fare sale goes into effect on Monday at 1 a.m. and you don't call until Monday evening hoping to book a seat on one of the high demand flights, you'll be told "that airfare is no longer available on that flight."

The same is true for days of the week. Most people want to fly to Orlando on Saturday or Sunday morning. Therefore, midweek and evening departures have more space. For return flights, most people prefer afternoon departures on Saturday or Sunday. As a result, the least expensive fares usually have a mid-week travel requirement.

A good rule of thumb: If you must travel on specific dates, book early, before any possible price war. Most bargain tickets have an exchange clause, meaning you can get the lower fare — should one come out — for a penalty (most penalties are $50, but even this is tricky. Talk to your travel agent if considering this option). If you consider the $50 an insurance policy paid to guarantee your travel dates, it's a little easier to swallow, even if prices go down. If you're completely flexible in travel dates, wait for a fare war, but keep in mind that most bargain fares must be ticketed at least three weeks before departure.

There is no "best time" to buy an airline ticket. It's gambling — no different from that in Las Vegas or Atlantic City. Decide how much risk you're willing to take, talk to your travel agent, then decide.

• Check ticket penalties closely. A full fare ticket may come with minimal penalties — including money back if you fail to show — but can cost twice as much as one of the bargain tickets. Most of the time, airlines follow the ticket rules to the letter. Should you have a car accident on the way to the airport, yet still drag yourself wounded and bleeding to the airline ticket counter one day later in hopes of catching the next available flight, most airlines will still charge a penalty.

• Note the difference between non-stop and direct flights. If a flight is non-stop, you board the plane in your home city and fly straight to Orlando. If a flight is direct, you board the plane in your home city and don't deplane until you arrive in Orlando, but the plane itself lands in an intermediate city en route.

• If you prefer not to fly on smaller planes (turboprops), confirm with your booking agent that all connections use jets.

• Use a credit card to pay for flights. A number of new airlines only service a few markets, generally flying nonstop between cities. Financially, lines like AirTran and Vantage Airways make Orlando more affordable than ever. However, great news is always followed by a "but." Remember that 1) if an airline only has one Orlando flight scheduled per day, that leaves no back-up plan. If mechanical trouble grounds their only plane, you must either wait a day, wait hours until the plane is fixed, or wait for them to clear you onto one of their competitor's flights. Either way, you wait. 2) They may cancel their flight to Orlando if it proves unprofitable, a clearer danger if it's a new route and you're booking for anything six months or more in the future. And 3), there's always a possibility they will go bankrupt. If that happens, paid passengers find themselves with no transportation and worse — no money refunded. If you paid cash for your tickets you might get some money back, but it will not come for months (years?) and will not be the full amount paid. By using a credit card, you can at least deny the charge through the credit card company.

This can still cause problems if flights were booked months ahead of departure, but it at least gives you a measure of security.

• If you need a wheelchair at any point in your flight, request one when you buy your ticket. If a ticket requires a change of plane en route to Orlando, even some ambulatory people worry about making their connection. If in doubt, ask.

• Plan to arrive one hour before your scheduled departure, especially during peak travel periods (holidays). Arrive even earlier if booked on an airline that does not reserve seating. Flying is best described as "hurry up and wait; hurry up and wait." You may board a flight at any time, providing there is still room on the plane. But your seat is not guaranteed until you check in. A pre-issued boarding pass (from a travel agent) guarantees your seat longer than simply calling the airline for a seat assignment, but when it appears that no one else is boarding the plane, even those with a pre-issued boarding pass can lose their seat to others flying stand-by.

• Upon arrival at your local airport, proceed to your airline's ticket desk. If sky caps out front offer to take your luggage, they will need to see your ticket. They're not employed by the airline, but save you the trouble of carrying your bags into the airline ticket desk. It is customary to tip around $1 per bag. If you prefer to carry your own luggage, do so.

• After checking in and before reaching your plane, you'll pass through airport security. All bags are X-rayed and passengers walk through a metal detector. While harmless, the process can be time consuming during peak travel times or when airports beef up security. If you have film, either in a camera or on the side, ask the security guards to hand-check it to avoid damage. It's best to pack film in your checked luggage.

• Don't expect much leg room on the plane. A six-foot man's legs may even touch the seat in front of him. Also, don't expect much seat width. Overweight people who take up more than one seat create special problems for the airline and are many times charged a double fare. If in doubt, call the airline directly, explain your concerns, and ask their policy. As in any dealings with an airline, note the name of the person you talked to (get a last name or locator number) and the date of your call.

Once your plane arrives in Orlando, follow the crowd to baggage claim. Orlando has two terminals, "A" and "B". Both are served by different airlines and both are connected to the main terminal by a monorail. Since a monorail departs every few minutes, the wait time is minimal.

Once you arrive in the main terminal, baggage claim is one flight down and clearly marked by signs. Above each conveyer belt in the baggage claim area, a monitor lists airlines and flight numbers. (It's not uncommon to wait for half an hour, worried that your luggage is lost when it's actually spinning round and round a hundred yards farther down the terminal.)

After claiming your luggage, walk to the curb outside baggage claim if a transfer service (usually Mears Transportation) is included in your vacation package. For those renting a car, find the escalator that goes down one floor (to ground level — not the two-flight escalator that goes to the parking garage). On-site car rental companies are located at the bottom of the stairs. Off-site car rental companies have a van or bus parked just outside the door.

Welcome to Orlando.

TRAINS

Amtrak has a train station in downtown Orlando. In general, train fares cost slightly less than airline fares, though that varies, especially with today's budget air carriers. Most larger cities in the Northeast — New York City and Philadelphia, for example — have direct train service, but the ride still takes a full day. Seats are comfortable. Perhaps because of their semi-government owned status, service on trains does not match even that of the airlines. They also run round-the-clock, making travel times inconvenient. However, they're a fair alternative for people who like to keep two feet on the ground.

Amtrak offers more than one fare (discounted advanced booking, full-fare, etc.) but less than the thousands of fares found in "the friendly skies." Tell the reservationist or your travel agent that you're flexible and wish to know the lowest price first. Also mention your age if you're a senior citizen.

A second train alternative is AutoTrain, Amtrak's direct link between the Washington, D.C. area and Sanford, Florida, about thirty miles north of Walt Disney World. While AutoTrain falls under Amtrak's control, it operates as a separate entity.

The trip is simple. Trains leave Lorton, Virginia (20 miles south of Washington, D.C.) at 4:30 p.m. every day of the year, though cars must arrive by 3:30. The train travels all night and arrives in Sanford at 9:00 a.m. the following morning. For the return trip, the times are identical: 4:30 p.m. departure from Sanford with a 9:00 a.m. arrival in Lorton.

Included in the cost of transportation is the evening meal served with wine, a heavy Continental breakfast, evening movie, pillows, and blankets. Alcohol costs extra. Seats are spacious and recline, though most people have difficulty getting a good night's sleep. For an additional expense, sleeping cars are available. In addition to more comfortable and private accommodations, sleeping car passengers eat in a different dining car and enjoy upscale meals and service.

Round trip travel on AutoTrain can cost a little more than $500 for two people and their vehicle, depending on season and availability of bargain fares. Compared to the cost of driving, eating, and staying in a hotel both directions, AutoTrain compares favorably. Like airline prices, expect to pay top dollar if you wish to travel over holidays. In addition, retirees who winter in Florida use AutoTrain to move their car back and forth, so one-way prices to Florida are expensive around October and, for return travel, high around March.

Amtrak agents try to book "kiddy cars," meaning families with young children do not share space — or noise — with childless mature travelers. For reservations on Amtrak or Amtrak's AutoTrain, see your travel agent or call (800) USA-RAIL.

CAR RENTALS

An astounding array of car rental companies surround the Orlando airport. The most convenient companies are located at the airport, though they are also (usually) the most expensive. You pay a bit more for convenience.

Off-site car rental companies rent a parking space outside the terminal, one level below baggage claim. Big companies like Alamo run busses on a regular schedule; smaller companies wait for a phone call before they send a van to pick clients up.

Like airlines, car rental companies offer a number of discounts to groups such as AARP, AAA, and certain corporations. Once you reach a car rental agent, keep the following in mind:

• Have a major credit card with at least $1000 still available, even if your car rental is prepaid by a tour group. The car company will not immediately charge any expenses to your card, but it may block off credit to guarantee that you're a good risk. You do not get billed for the amount they block, but you can't use it for other purchases either. In other words, the car rental company effectively lowers your line of credit. If you plan to use that credit card to pay for part of your vacation, call the car rental company before you leave home and ask about their policy.

If you don't have credit cards, find out what the car company requires to rent a car. (Again, even if booked through a tour company.) Generally, they want a stiff deposit along with proof of residency such as a driver's license and perhaps electric bills with your name and home address. (A number of rental cars disappear every year to people with a fake ID. After all, even a $500 deposit is a small price to pay for a brand new car that can be stripped for parts.) At times, the car company will charge a "processing fee" or something similar. At any rate, call the car company ahead of time, ask what they require, and make sure you note the first and last name of the person quoting the information.

• Rental car agents are commissioned. Any additional upgrade or service that they talk you into nets them money. Be wary.

• Don't wait until the last minute to decide what size car you want. There are a number of different car codes, but most companies offer five sizes — one minivan and four types of cars. The largest car is a luxury model such as a Cadillac; the smallest car is an economy model such as a Geo Metro. One step up from an economy car is a standard size car such as a Ford Escort. One step above the standard car and directly below the luxury car is an intermediate model such as a Pontiac Grand Prix. If you wish to upgrade to a larger car at the car rental desk, it generally costs more than reserving it ahead of time. Also, some sizes may not be available if you wait.

At times, the car size you reserved will be sold out and they will give you a complimentary upgrade. Make sure it is "complimentary."

• "Unlimited mileage." Car companies continually change plans and sometimes offer both unlimited mileage and a pay-per-mile plan. If given the option, you must guess how many miles you plan to drive to determine which method is cheaper. A pay-per-mile plan usually has a base rate like "100 free miles per day and 10¢ per mile after that." For a one-week vacation, that gives you 700 "free" miles. Unless visiting relatives in Miami and driving to Florida's Panhandle, 700 miles should see you through the entire vacation.

• To save money, plan to return the car with a full tank of gas. The agent may offer you two other gas options, either a) prepaying for a full tank of gas, or b) allowing the car company to fill it up after your return.

When prepaying for a full tank of gas, the rate the agent quotes — per gallon — is cheaper than what is available in the Orlando area, but you prepay for every drop of gas in that tank. This option saves money if you return the car completely devoid of any gas, but few people can do that. If only a gallon or two remains in the tank, you've paid more for the "bargain" gas than you would have paid by filling the tank yourself. Allowing the car company to fill the tank after your return costs more per gallon than filling it yourself and paying local prices. But it is convenient. This is a fair option if you want to save a bit of stress on your departure day.

• Car insurance. Agents push this heavily. Like most insurance, it's overpriced and most people don't need it. But if you're involved in an accident, you'll wish you had it.

Before leaving home, check with your car insurance agent. Most — but not all — car policies include rentals. Should your policy include rentals, it generally covers them at the same rate it covers your own car. If you carry a $500 deductible on an accident, for example, expect your coverage to be the same for the rental car. Also, check your credit cards. Certain cards offer car insurance if used to pay for the rental. If offered, expect supplementary insurance, meaning coverage only for those portions of the damages not covered by another source. If you have that $500 deductible on your personal car insurance policy, the credit card people would reimburse you only the $500.

Many people — even those with coverage through credit cards and auto insurance — still buy the insurance offered by the car rental agent. One advantage is timing. With car company insurance, you usually get a replacement car within a few hours should you have an accident. Using your own coverage, a hefty chunk of your vacation could be spent talking to adjusters and local reps of your insurance company.

Think of insurance as a peace-of-mind option. If you're the type of person who will inspect the car every morning, worried that some hit-and-run driver dented it and cost you money, pay the extra $45 for a week's worth of peace-of-mind. If you're covered elsewhere and don't let life's little details get you down, forgo the insurance.

But either way, decide before you get to the car rental counter. Don't let an agent's scare tactics talk you into unwanted upgrades.

• Cars are rented to one driver only. If you wish to have someone else share the driving, plan to spend an extra $5 or more per day.

• Once you rent the car — and before you walk away from the counter — check the receipt. It will give an estimated cost for the rental, which should be slightly more than the price quoted on the phone or the price printed on your rental voucher. With both tax and airport access fees (meaning money paid to Orlando airport for the right to service clients), your total estimated charge should be about 10% more than the base price you were quoted or that appears on your voucher. If higher — and you're certain you did not order a larger car, gas, or insurance — ask the agent to explain the breakdown.

• Before driving out of the lot, inspect the car. If it has any small dents or problems, tell an attendant. In addition, it should have a full tank of gas. Check the fuel gauge before leaving the parking lot.

HOTEL ROOMS

Like car rental agencies, hotels ask for a credit card imprint as collateral against any charges to your room. While many tour packages prepay the hotel, hotel tax, and gratuities to maids, incidental charges such as long distance phone calls are the responsibility of the guest. If in doubt about which charges are covered and which are not, ask.

One word of warning: don't make long distance phone calls from your hotel room if you wish to save money. While convenient, it's also expensive. Most hotels charge not only for long distance calls but also for local calls. If planning to talk to the folks back home, it's cheaper to use a calling card from a pay phone. Better yet, prearrange a time to have them call you.

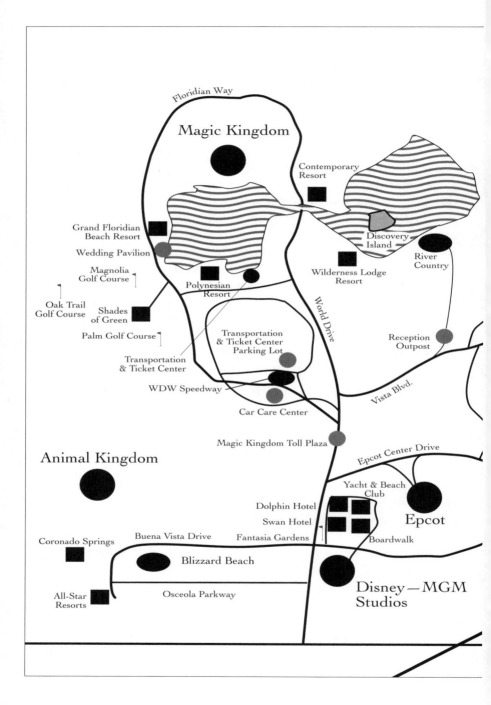

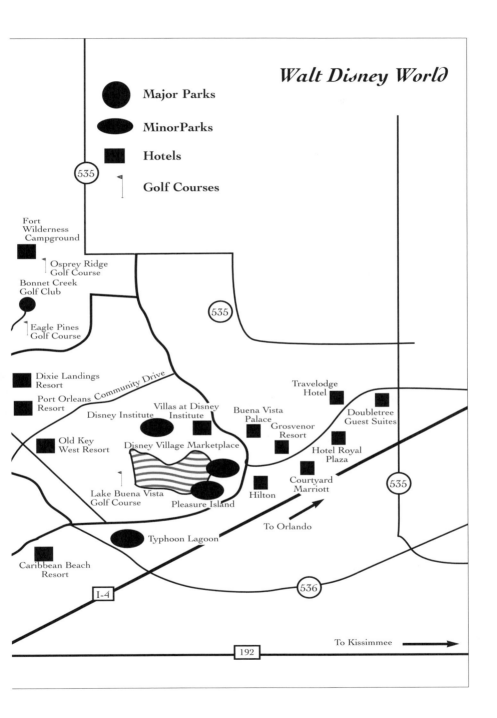

297

INDEX

A

AAA (American Automobile
    Association), 29, 79, 292
accommodations, *see hotels*
admission prices,
    Arabian Nights, 276
    Busch Gardens, 273
    Central Florida Zoo, 276
    Church Street Station, 275
    Citrus Tower, 277
    Cypress Gardens, 257
    discounts, 81-82
    Daytona, USA, 277
    Fantasy of Flight, 277
    Gatorland, 277
    Jungle Adventures, 277
    Jungleland, 277
    Kennedy Space Center, 276
    King Henry's Feast, 278
    Medieval Times, 278
    Ripley's Believe It or Not
        Museum, 278
    Sea World Of Orlando, 261
    Silver Springs, 278
    Splendid China, 262
    Universal Studios, 270
    Walt Disney World,
        Discovery Island, 75
        discounts, 80
        Florida resident, 79
        from outside vendors, 79
        mail order, 79
        military discounts, 78
        Pleasure Island, 75
        suggestions when selecting, 71
        types, 17, 72
        where to buy, 79
        water parks, 75

adult learning programs, 216, 173
Adventureland, 110
Adventurer's Club, 223
air travel, 287
Akershus, Restaurant, 176
Alien Encounter, 130
All-Star Resorts, 15, 50
AMC Theatres, 220
America Gardens Theatre, 167, 172
American Adventure, The, 167
American Film Institute Showcase, 200
AnaComical Theatre, 155
Animation Gallery, 208
Animal Kingdom, 251
Arabian Nights, 276
Ariel's, 229
Artist Point, 229
Art Of Disney, The, 220
Art Of Disney Epcot Gallery, 182
Astro Orbiter, 127
Atlantic Ballroom, 41, 218
ATM,
    Disney-MGM Studios, 190
    Epcot, 148
    Magic Kingdom, 103
attendance information, 2, 21, 95
Aunt Polly's Landing, 113, 139
Au Petit Café, 179
Authentic All Star, 220
AutoTrain, 291

B

Baby Care Center,
    Disney-MGM Studios, 190
    Epcot, 149
    Magic Kingdom, 103
Backlot Express, 207
Backlot Theater, 200

Backlot Tour, 192, 200
Backstage Pass to 101 Dalmatians, 201
Barnstormer, The, 125
Beauty And The Beast Show, 195
beauty salons, 34, 37
Belz Factory Outlet, 65, 248
Biergarten, 167, 177
Big River Grille & Brewing
  Works, 218
Big Thunder Mountain Railroad, 114
biking, 244
Bistro de Paris, 179
Blizzard Beach, 212
Blue Spring State Park, 285
Boardwalk Resort, 41
  entertainment, 218
  restaurants, 231, 234
boating, 242
Boatwright's Dining Hall, 230
Body Wars, 155
Bok Tower Gardens, 284
Bonfamille's Café, 230
Bonnet Creek Golf Club, 238
Boulangerie Pâtisserie, 169, 182
breakfast suggestions, 69, 229
Buena Vista Palace, 59
Busch Gardens, Tampa Bay, 270
bus transportation, 19, 52
Buy The Book, 208

C
cafeteria service, see restaurants
California Grill, 230
cameras and film,
  Disney-MGM Studios, 207
  Epcot, 182
  Magic Kingdom, 141
campfire program, 51
campsites, Fort Wilderness, 53, 282
Canada, 171
Cantina de San Angel, 181
Cape May Café, 230
Cap'n Jack's Oyster Bar, 222

Captain's Tavern, 230
Captain's Tower, The, 220
Caribbean Beach Resort, 45
  restaurants, 230
car, traveling by,
  parking, 16, 101
  rentals, 292
  service and maintenance, 101
Carousel Of Progress, 129
cash machines, see ATM's
Castle Forecourt, 133
Catastrophe Canyon, 201
Celebration, 144, 249
Centorium, 182
Central Florida Zoo, 276
Central Reservations, 28, 31, 85
Character Warehouse, 248
Chef Mickey's, 231
Chefs de France, 179
children, traveling with,
  learning programs, 216
  touring advice, 6, 12
China, 166
Christmas celebrations, 12, 172
Christmas Chalet, 220
Church Street Station, 273
Cinderella's Castle, 138
Cinderella's Golden Carrousel, 123
Circle of Life (Epcot), 160
Citrus Tower, 277
City Hall, 101-104
clothing, suggested, 14
Columbia Harbour House, 139
Comedy Warehouse, 223
Commissary, 207
Concourse Steakhouse, 231
Contemporary Resort, 36
  restaurants, 230, 231
Coral Café, 231
Coral Isle Café, 231
Coral Reef Restaurant, 175
Coronado Springs Resort, 49
Cosmic Ray's Starlight Café, 140

cost-cutting tips, 15, 80-82, 287
costs, *see admission prices*
Country Bear Jamboree, 116
Courtyard by Marriott, 60
Cranium Command, 156
credit cards, 71, 103, 289
crime, 21
Crockett's Tavern, 54
crowds, avoiding, 2, 12
cruise ships, *see Disney Cruise Line*
Crystal Palace, 137
Cypress Gardens, 254

D
Darkroom, The, 207
Daytona USA, 277
day visitors, 9, 73
D.E.E.P. Program, 161
Diamond Horseshoe Revue, 117, 139
dining, *see restaurants*
dinner shows,
    inside WDW, 226-227
    outside WDW, 276-278
Dinosaur Gertie's, 207
disabled visitors,
    in the parks, 86-87
    resorts, handicapped access, 85
    transportation, 86
    wheelchair rental, 88
Discovery Center, 162
Discovery Island, 217
Disney Characters,
    Disney-MGM Studios, 203
    Epcot, 174, 176
    Magic Kingdom, 125, 133
    resorts, 227-235
Disney Cruise Line, 250
Disney dollars, 71
Disney Institute, The, 213-217
    restaurant, 234
    The Villas At, 56
Disney-MGM Studios, 185
    admission prices, 72-78

attractions and rides, 194-202
baby care, 190
best times to visit, 95-96
camera information, 207
comparison to Universal
    Studios, 187
crowd size, 95-96
description, 185
disabled visitor information, 191
early-entry days, 95
first aid, 190
getting oriented, 189
getting to, 188
Guest Relations, 189
Hollywood Boulevard, 189, 202
hours of operation, 95
lockers, 190
lost and found, 190
lounges, 205
map, 186
meals, 97
money information, 190
parades and shows, 202
parking, 188
pets, 190
restaurants, 204-207
same-day reentry, 72
shopping, 207-208
stroller rentals, 190
Sunset Boulevard, 189
Tip Board, 191, 204
touring suggestions, 191-192
visitation guide, 189
wheelchair rentals, 190
Disney's Sports Complex, 237, 247
Disney Store, The, 76,79
Disney Vacation Club, 41, 55
Disney Village Hotel Plaza, 58
Disney Village Marketplace, 219
    getting to, 10
    restaurants/lounges, 221
    stores, 220
    World Of Disney, 221

Disney's West Side, 219
Dixie Landings Resort, 46
  restaurants, 230
Dolphin Resort, 44
  restaurants, 231, 232, 234
Donald's Boat, 125
Donald's Dairy Dip, 222
Doubletree Guest Suites, 60
Downtown Disney, 65, 219
Dumbo The Flying Elephant, 123
D-Zertz, 224

E
Eagle Pines Golf Course, 21, 240
Early Entry, 17, 91
Easter, 12
8Trax, 223
Elderhostels, 66
Electrical Water Pageant, 134
Electric Umbrella Restaurant, 181
ECV's, 88
El Pirata y el Perico, 139
El Río Del Tiempo, 164
Emporium, 141
Enchanted Grove, 140
Enchanted Tiki Room, The, 111
Epcot,
  admission prices, 72-78
  attractions and rides, 152-171
  baby care, 149
  best times to visit, 95-96
  camera information, 182
  crowd size, 95-96
  disabled visitor information, 149
  early-entry days, 95
  first aid, 149
  Future World, 152-162
  getting oriented, 148
  getting to, 146
  Guest Relations, 151
  hours of operation, 95
  IllumiNations, 172
  information, 149
  lockers, 149

lost and found, 149
map, 145
meals, 97
money information, 148
parking, 146
pets, 149
restaurants, 147, 174-182
same-day reentry, 72
shopping, 182-183
shows, 172
stroller rentals, 148
Tip Board, 150
touring suggestions, 149
tours, 173
visitation guide, 148
wheelchair rental, 171
World Showcase, 162-171
ESPN Club, 41, 219
ExtraTERRORestrial Alien
  Encounter, The, 130

F
Fantasy In The Sky Fireworks, 132
Fantasy of Flight, 277
Fantasyland, 120
fast food, 16, 71, 97, 237, 26
  Disney-MGM Studios, 204, 206
  Epcot, 147, 180
  Magic Kingdom, 136, 139
ferry, to Magic Kingdom,
50's Prime Time Café, 205
fireworks,
  Fantasy In The Sky, 132
  IllumiNations, 172
  Sorcery In The Sky, 203
Fireworks Factory, 224
first aid, 88
fishing, 242-243
Flagler's, 232
Florida, 8, 21
  non-Disney attractions, 253-278
  nature parks, 279-285
  resident discounts, 77
flying, 287-290

Flying Fish Café, 231
Food Rocks, 160
Fort Wilderness, 51-54
    activities, 54
    campfire program, 51
    campsites, 53
    restaurant, 234
    transportation, 52
    Wilderness Homes, 54
Fountain View Espresso &
    Bakery, 181
France, 169
Frontierland, 112
Frontierland Shootin' Arcade, 116
Fulton's Crab House, 222
Future World, *see Epcot*

G
Gallery Of Arts And History, 169
Garden Grill Restaurant, 176
Garden Gallery, 231
Garden Grove Café, 232
garden view rooms, 27-28
Gasparilla Grill & Games, 34
Gatorland, 277
Germany, 166
golf, 237-241
    lessons, 240
    miniature, 241
    tournaments, 237
Goofy About Health, 155
Goofy's Grill, 222
Gourmet Pantry, 220
Grand Floridian Café, 232
Grand Floridian Resort, 33
    restaurants, 232, 233, 235
Grand Prix Raceway, 126
Great Movie Ride, The, 196
Great Southern Country Craft
    Co., 220
Greenhouse Tour, 160
Green Thumb Emporium, 160
Grosvenor, 59

Guest Information Board,
    Disney-MGM Studios, 191
    Epcot, 150
    Magic Kingdom, 104
Guest Relations,
    Disney-MGM Studios, 189
    Epcot, 146

H
Hall Of Presidents, The, 118
handicapped, *see disabled visitors*
Harrington Bay Clothiers, 220
Harry P. Leu Gardens, 283
Harry's Safari Bar & Grille, 232
Haunted Mansion, The, 119
hearing impairments, 89
hiking, 282, 284
Hidden Treasures of World
    Showcase, 174
Hilton at LBV, 60
Hollywood and Vine Cafeteria, 206
Hollywood Brown Derby, The, 204
Honey, I Shrunk The Audience, 158
Honey, I Shrunk The Kids Movie
    Set Adventure, 199
honeymoons, 247
Hoop-Dee-Doo Musical Revue, 226
Horizons, 157
horseback riding, 243
hotels, inside WDW,
    advantages/disadvantages, 16
    budget, 50
    check-in/check-out times, 30
    comparisons, 15-18
    cost-cutting, 29
    deposit requirements, 30
    Epcot area, 39
    ID cards, 31
    locations, 9-10
    Magic Kingdom area, 33
    moderately priced, 45
    pet accommodations, 24
    payment methods, 71

rates, 30
reservations, 28
special room requests, 85
hotels outside WDW,
  advantages, 17, 63
  locations, 64-66
  phone calls from room, 295
  questions to ask, 67-69
hours of operation, 12
House of Blues, 221
Hunchback Of Notre Dame Stage
  Show, The, 200
Hyatt Regency Grand Cypress, 17

I
ID Cards, 31
IllumiNations, 172
Image Works, 158
Impressions De France, 170
Indiana Jones Epic Stunt
  Spectacular, 197
Indy 200, 248
Information,
  before you go, 10, 24
  disabled visitors, 84-89
  Disney-MGM Studios, 190
  Epcot, 149
  Magic Kingdom, 104
Innoventions, 161
International Drive hotels, 65
International Gateway, 146, 148
Italy, 167
It's A Small World, 121
It's A Wonderful Shop, 208

J
Japan, 169
Jellyrolls, 219
Jim Henson's MuppetVision 4-D, 199
Journey Into Imagination, 158
Juan & Only's, 232
Judge's Tent, 125
Jungle Adventures, 277

Jungle Cruise, 111
Jungleland, 277

K
Kennedy Space Center, 275
Kimono's, 232
King Henry's Feast, 278
King Stefan's Banquet Hall, 138
Kissimmee, 9, 24, 63-64
Kringla Bakeri og Kafé, 181

L
Lake Buena Vista Hotels, 65
Lake Buena Vista Golf Course, 239
Lake Kissimmee State Park, 284
Land, The, 159
Lario's, 221
Le Cellier Restaurant, 180
Legend Of The Lion King, 122
Liberty Inn, 181
Liberty Square, 117
Liberty Square Riverboat, 118
Liberty Tree Tavern, The, 138
lines, *see queues*
Living Seas, The, 161
Living With The Land, 159
lockers,
  Disney-MGM Studios, 190
  Epcot, 149
  Magic Kingdom, 104
lodging, *see hotels*
L'Originale Alfredo di Roma
  Ristorante, 177
lost and found, 190
Lotus Blossom Café, 181
Lunching Pad, 140

M
Mad Tea Party, 124
Maelstrom, 165
Magic Kingdom,
  admission prices, 72-78
  Adventureland, 110

attractions and rides, 107-131
baby care, 103
best times to visit, 95-96
camera information, 141
Cinderella's Castle, 133, 138
crowd size, 95-96
disabled visitor information, 104
Disney characters, 125, 133
early-entry days, 95
first aid, 103
Fantasyland, 120
Frontierland, 112
getting oriented, 102
getting to, 101
guided tours, 104
hours of operation, 95
information, 104
Liberty Square, 117
lockers, 104
lost and found, 104
Main Street, 108
map, 100
meals, 97
Mickey's Toontown Fair, 124
money information, 103
parades and shows, 131
parking, 101
pets, 104
restaurants, 136-140
same-day reentry, 72
shopping, 140-142
SpectroMagic Parade, 135
stroller rentals, 103
Tip Board, 104
Tomorrowland, 126
touring suggestions, 104-106
WDW 25th Anniversary, 124-125
wheelchair rentals, 103
Magic Kingdom Club, 24, 29, 75
Magic of Disney Animation, The, 195
Magnolia Golf Course, 239
mail, 79
maingate hotels, 9, 64
Main Street Bake Shop, 139

Main Street Cinema, 108
Main Street Transportation, 109
Main Street, USA, 108
Making Of..., The (MGM), 202
Making of Me, The, 155
Mama Melrose's Ristorante Italiano, 206
Mannequins Dance Palace, 222
maps,
    Disney-MGM Studios, 186
    Epcot, 145
    Magic Kingdom, 100
    Walt Disney World, 296
Marrakesh, Restaurant, 178
Matsu No Ma Lounge, 173, 181
Mears Motor Transportation, 291
medical information, 88
Medieval Times, 278
Mexico, 164
Mickey's Country House, 125
Mickey's Toontown Fair, 124
Mickey's Toontown Fair Station, 125
Mickey's Tropical Revue, 227
Mike Fink Keel Boats, 119
military guests, 31, 78
Min & Bill's Dockside Diner, 207
miniature golf, 241
Minnie Mia's Italian Eatery, 222
Minnie's Country House, 125
Missing Links Sausage Co., 224
Mr. Toad's Wild Ride, 124
Mitsukoshi Department Store, 169
Mrs. Pott's Cupboard, 140
money information, 70-81
    Disney Dollars, 71
    Disney-MGM Studios, 190
    Epcot, 148
    Magic Kingdom, 103
Monorail, 10, 18
Monster Sound Show, The, 196
Morocco, 169
movies, 187, 220
Mr. Toad's Wild Ride, 124
MuppetVision 4-D, *see Jim Henson's MuppetVision 4-D*

N
Narcoossee's, 233
Neon Armadillo Music Saloon, 224
Neverland Club, 36
New Year's Eve Party, 222
New York Street, 190
Nickelodeon Studios, 267
nighttime entertainment,
  Boardwalk, 41, 218
  Church Street Station, 273
  dinner shows, 20, 226
  Pleasure Island, 222
Nine Dragons Restaurant, 177
1900 Park Fare, 233
Norway, 164

O
Oak Trail Golf Course, 239
O Canada!, 171
Ocala Information Center, 29, 79
Odyssey Center, 149
off-site hotels,
  descriptions, 64-66
  discounts, 67-69
  types, 63
'Ohana, 233
Old Key West Resort, 55
Olivia's Café, 233
on-site hotels,
  descriptions, 31-61
  discounts, 29
  types, 27-28
Orange Blossom Trail hotels, 66
Orlando area hotels, 67
Orlando International Airport, 79, 290
Oscar's Super Service, 190
Osprey Ride Golf Course, 240

P
package delivery (from parks), 16
package tours, 22
packing suggestions, 14, 25
Palio, 233
Palm Golf Course, 238

parades,
  Disney-MGM Studios, 202
  Magic Kingdom, 131, 135
parasailing, 242
parking,
  costs, 16
  disabled visitors, 89
  Disney-MGM Studios, 188
  Epcot, 146
  Magic Kingdom, 101
  off-site hotels, 68
  trams, 19
passes, *see admission prices*
Pasta Piazza Ristorante, 81
Pecos Bill Café, 131
Peter Pan's Flight, 122
pets, 24, 104
petting zoo, 53
pharmacies, 25
photography, *see cameras and film*
physicians, *see medical information*
Pinocchio Village Haus, 139
Pioneer Hall, 52-54, 218, 227
Pirates Of The Caribbean, 112
Planet Hollywood, 221
planning a vacation,
  admission prices, 71-82
  hours, 96
  information, 10, 24
  locations, 63-67
  package tours, 22
  packing, 14, 25
  reservations, hotel, 27-31
  reservations, restaurants, 20
  senior citizens, 29, 67, 82
  traveling with children, 6, 12
  weather, 14
  weddings and honeymoons, 246
  what to see, , 4
  when to go, 2, 12
  where to stay, 15
Plaza Restaurant, 15
Plaza Ice Cream Parlor, 139
Plaza Pavilion Terrace Dining, 140

Pleasure Island, 222
  admission, 75
  clubs, 223-224
  restaurants, 224
  street party, 222
Polynesian Luau, 227
Polynesian Resort, 35
  restaurants, 227, 231, 233
Portobello Yacht Club, 224
Port Orleans, 48
  restaurants, 230
prescriptions, *see medical information*
Prime Time Café, 205
priority seating, 136
Pure & Simple, 180

Q
queues,
  avoiding, 2, 12
  disabled visitors, 86
  fast food, 97
  Disney-MGM Studios, 191
  Epcot, 151
  Magic Kingdom, 105
  waiting strategies, 93-94

R
Railroad, Walt Disney World, 109
Rainforest Café, 221
rain gear, 14, 141
reentry stamp, 72
Refreshment Outpost, 181
Refreshment Port, 182
rentals,
  bikes, 244
  boats, 242
  cameras, 141, 182, 207
  cars, 292
  electric carts, 88
  fishing gear, 242
  strollers, 88
  wheelchairs, 88
reservations,
  Disney Institute, 217

off-site hotels, 67-69
on-site hotels, 28
restaurants, 20
Resortwear Unlimited, 220
restaurants,
  advice, 97, 237
  character meals, 133, 174, 203
  dinner shows, 226
  Disney-MGM Studios, 204-207
  Disney Village Marketplace, 221
  Epcot, 174-182
  fast food, 97
  healthy food, 136
  Magic Kingdom, 136-140
  Pleasure Island, 224
  priority seating, 136
  resorts, at the, 228-235
  special requests, 228
Ripley's Believe It or Not, 278
River Country, 213
Rivership Romance on the St.
  John's River, 282
Rock 'N' Roll Beach Club, 223
roller coasters, 106, 144, 270
Rose & Crown Pub, 173, 180
Royal Plaza, 60

S
safety, hotel, 17, 66, 68
same-day reentry, 72
San Angel Inn, 176
Sassagoula River, 19, 46
Sci-Fi Dine-In Theater, 205
scuba diving, 161
Sea Base Alpha, 161
Seasonal Passport, 78
Season's Dining Room, 234
Sea World, 257
senior citizens,
  discounts, 22, 62, 78
  Elderhostels, 66
  also see individual attractions
Settlement Trading Post, 53
Shades of Green

restaurants, 231
shopping,
    bargains, 248
    Disney-MGM Studios, 207-208
    Epcot, 182-183
    for necessities, 141
    Magic Kingdom, 140-142
    package delivery, 16
    Village Marketplace, 219-221
Sid Cahuenga's One-Of-A-Kind, 207
sight-impaired guests, 90
Silver Springs, 278
Skyway To Fantasyland, 129
Skyway To Tomorrowland, 121
Sleepy Hollow, 139
Small World, 121
Snow White's Adventures, 123
Sommerfest, 181
Sorcery In The Sky, 203
Soundstage Restaurant, 206
Space Mountain, 128
Spaceship Earth, 154
SpectroMagic Parade, 135
Splash Mountain, 113
Splendid China, 261
Spoodles, 234
sports, 236-244
stamps, 103
Starring Rolls Bakery, 207
Star Tours, 198
steel drum band, 134
storage lockers, *see lockers*
stroller rentals, 88
Studio Catering Company, 207
stunt shows, 197, 265
Sum Chows, 234
Summer Sands, 221
SunTrust Bank, 103, 148, 190
Sunset Boulevard, 189
Sunset Ranch Market, 206
Sunshine Season Food Fair, 181
SuperStar Television, 197
Swan Resort, 43
    restaurants, 232, 233

swimming, 211
Swiss Family Treehouse, 110
Sword in the Stone Ceremony, 134

T
Take Flight, 129
tape players for sight-impaired
    guests, 90
Team Mickey's Athletic Club, 220
telephones,
    for disabled visitors, 85, 89
    costs in hotel rooms, 295
temperature, *see weather*
Tempura Kiku, 179
tennis, 241
Teppanyaki Dining Rooms, 178
Test Track, 157
tickets, *see admission prices*
Timekeeper, The, 130
timeshare resorts, 55, 60
Tinker Bell's flight, 133
Tomorrowland, 126
Tomorrowland Light and Power
    Company, 127
Tomorrowland Transit Authority, 127
Tom Sawyer Island, 115
Tony's Town Square Restaurant, 137
tours, *see guided tours* or *package tours*
touring plans,
    Disney-MGM Studios, 191
    Epcot, 149
    Magic Kingdom, 104-106
    Universal Studios, 263
Toys Fantastic, 220
Toy Story Pizza Planet, 207
trail rides, 243
Trail's End Buffet, 234
train, traveling to Orlando, 291
transportation,
    advice, 287-295
    disabled visitors, 84-87
    Disney system, 18-20
Transportation and Ticket Center,
    18, 101, 146

travel agents, 251, 287
Travelodge, 61
Tri-Circle-D Ranch, 243
Tropical Serenade, 111
Tubbi's, 234
Tune-In Lounge, 205
20,000 Leagues Under the Sea, 121
Twilight Zone Tower Of Terror, 194
2R's Reading And Riting, 220
Typhoon Lagoon, 211

U
United Kingdom, 170
United States (World Showcase), 168
Universal Studios,
    comparison to Disney-MGM, 187
    rides and attractions, 264-268
    touring suggestions, 263
Universe Of Energy,
U.S. 192 (Maingate) Hotels,

V
Value Pass, *see admission prices*
Victoria & Albert's, 235
video camcorder rental, *see cameras
and film*
Villas At The Disney Institute, 56
    restaurants, 234
Voyage Of The Little Mermaid, 196

W
walking, 84
Walt Disney Travel Company, 24
Walt Disney World Guidebook For
    Guests With Disabilities, 87
Walt Disney World/Oldsmobile Golf
    Classic, 237
Walt Disney World Railroad, 109
Water Parks, 210
    Blizzard Beach, 212
    River Country, 213
    Typhoon Lagoon, 211
    Water Mania, 211

Wet 'N Wild, 211
water-skiing, 243
water-ski shows, 254, 258
WDW Information, 10, 29
weather, 14
weddings and honeymoons, 246
Wekiwa Springs State Park, 281
Welcome Center, 29, 79
wheelchair rentals, 84, 88
Whispering Canyon Café, 235
Wilderness Homes, 54
Wilderness Lodge, 38
    restaurants, 229, 235
Wolfgang Puck's Café, 221
Wonders Of China, 166
Wonders Of Life, 155
World-Hopper Pass, *see admission
prices*
World Of Disney, 221
World of Motion, *see Test Track*
World Showcase, *see Epcot*

Y
Yacht Club Galley, 235
Yacht and Beach Club Resort, 39
    restaurants, 229, 230, 235
Yachtsman Steakhouse, 235
Yakitori House, 181

Z
Zoo,
    Animal Kingdom, 251
    Busch Gardens, 270
    Central Florida Zoo, 276
    Discovery Island, 217
    Fort Wilderness, 53
    Silver Springs, 278

The Mature Traveler's Reader Survey

Much of our advice — out of the way escape spots, tricks to make lines go faster, and things-to-avoid — comes directly from readers of this book. After you return from Walt Disney World, please take a minute to answer these short questions. Mail completed surveys to:

Mature Traveler Reader Survey
c/o Mercurial Press
P.O. Box 622616
Oviedo, FL 32762

First, a few facts about you:

1. Age _____   2. ❐ Male   ❐ Female

3. How many times have you visited the Walt Disney World resort? _____

4. If you stayed in a resort, which one? _____

5. On a scale from 1 to 10 (10 being the best), how do you rate your
   room? _____   Your resort? _____

Comments:_____
_____

6. Which parks did you visit (circle all that apply): Magic Kingdom • Epcot Center • Disney-MGM Studios • Universal Studios • Sea World of Orlando • Busch Gardens, Tampa Bay • Cypress Gardens • Splendid China • Church Street Station • Kennedy Space Center • Disney water park • Other water park • Dinner show

7. Which park was your favorite? _____

Why? _____

8. What park was your least favorite? _____

Why? _____

9. Out of all parks visited, list your favorite three attractions:

   1. _____

   2. _____ 3. _____

10. Out of all parks visited, list your least favorite attractions:

   1. _____

   2. _____ 3. _____

11. When looking over past vacations, how did Orlando rate (circle one)?

    a. the best   b. good   c. fair   d. not great   e. the worst

12. Did you buy *The Mature Traveler's Guide*:

    ❒ Before leaving home   ❒ After you arrived

13. What would you like to see covered in future editions?

_____

_____

14. Have you used other guides? _____ On a scale from 1 to 10 (10 being the best), how does this guide compare to others? _____

15. What advice would you offer other mature travelers planning to vacation in the Orlando area? _____

_____

What is a "must-see" attraction?

_____

What should they avoid?

_____

16. Finally, please give us your comments about this guide or your Walt Disney World vacation:

_____

_____

_____

_____

_____